A WEAVER'S GARDEN

A WEAVER'S GARDEN

Growing Plants for
Natural Dyes and Fibers

RITA BUCHANAN

Illustrations by
Steve Buchanan

DOVER PUBLICATIONS, INC.
Mineola, New York

Bibliographical Note

This Dover edition, first published in 1999, is an unabridged republication of *A Weaver's Garden*, by Rita Buchanan, originally published in 1987 by Interweave Press, Inc., Loveland, Colorado. A brief preface to that edition and a section of color photographs have been omitted, some minor corrections have been made, and the "Resources" section has been updated.

Library of Congress Cataloging-in-Publication Data

Buchanan, Rita.
    A weaver's garden : growing plants for natural dyes and fibers / Rita Buchanan ; illustrations by Steve Buchanan. — Dover ed.
      p.   cm.
    Originally published: Loveland, Colo. : Interweave Press, © 1987.
    Includes index.
    ISBN 0-486-40712-8 (pbk.)
    1. Hand weaving—Equipment and supplies. 2. Dye plants. 3. Fiber plants. 4. Gardening. I. Title.
TT848.B83   1999
746.1—dc21   99-39858
                                                           CIP

Manufactured in the United States of America
Dover Publications, Inc., 31 East 2nd Street, Mineola, N.Y. 11501

CONTENTS

INTRODUCTION

This is a book about a particular collection of plants: those that have traditionally been associated with weaving and textiles. It is written for weavers who would like to learn more about the traditions of their craft and the sources of their raw materials, and for gardeners who would like to grow useful and interesting plants. Sometimes one person is both weaver and gardener, or a weaver and gardener might team up to form a partnership!

Each chapter focuses on a different kind of plant product, including fibers, dyes, soaps, fragrances, and tools. The chapter begins with a combination of history and botany, telling the story of where and when people have used each product, and why and how it occurs in plants. You'll learn how cotton fibers grow, what people used for washing before soap was invented, and why indigo blue is a precious and unique dye. Then there are "how-to" sections, with guidelines for using plant products. Would you like to dye your own yarn, or mix an herbal moth repellent? Here are directions to help you. The second half of each chapter is a catalog of the major plants that supply the product, listed alphabetically by common name. There is a description of what each plant looks like as it grows, where it comes from, and how it is used. Horticultural information is given for all the plants in this book that can be grown in gardens or greenhouses in the United States.

The last chapter is about creating a garden of your own. Many of these plants are fast-growing annuals that will mature in a single season. Others are perennials that will last for years. Some are tropical plants that can be raised in greenhouses or as houseplants. Gardeners in different regions can choose one or more plants from each chapter that will do well in their climate. There are weedy plants that thrive on neglect and sensitive plants that must be fussed over. Beginning or experienced gardeners can choose plants that are easy to grow or challenging. Order some seeds and try growing them! Even where it's impractical to grow enough of a certain plant to actually harvest and use the product, it's a lot of fun to grow a single specimen and see what it looks like.

Any subject has its own vocabulary. Terms that weavers use all the time are foreign to gardeners, and words that gardeners say every day sound strange to weavers. I expect that most readers will already be familiar either with weaving or with gardening, but won't know words from the other subject, so there is a complete glossary of terms in the back of the book. I was fortunate to study chemistry in high school and college with teachers who could explain the subject clearly and relate it to everyday life, and so I learned to think of chemistry as a practical approach to understanding materials and processes. Throughout this book I have written about acids and bases, compounds and solutions, atoms and molecules (those words are also in the glossary). I think this is the most accurate way to explain what's really going on when dyes interact with fibers, when greasy clothes are cleaned in soapy water, when clothes moths are deterred by fragrant plants.

The information in this book is drawn from my own experience as a weaver and gardener and from extensive bibliographic research. To make the book easy to read, I have not cited references in the text or in footnotes. My major sources are included in the lists of suggested reading at the end of each chapter. For each subject, I have recommended a selection of books and articles that are interesting and helpful, and that are likely to be available at a good-sized library or bookstore.

In choosing which plants to include in this book, I began with plants that have been significant in our history — crops that were highly valued in Europe and the colonial United States, such as flax and cotton, indigo and madder, lavender, and fuller's teasel. Then I added others that have been just as important, but in different parts of the world — such as jute in India, dyer's knotweed in Japan, and soapbark in South America. Many of these plants have been cultivated in gardens and fields for centuries, but some are simply gathered from natural stands. I emphasized the traditional crops, but included some less familiar plants as well. I omitted plants of restricted occurrence or dubious usefulness, and generally rejected irritating or poisonous plants.

I'll admit right from the start that many of these plants are not commonly available. You can't drive down to your local nursery some fine spring weekend and pick up a six-pack of cotton seedlings along with your tomatoes and marigolds. To plant a weaver's garden requires forethought and planning, so that you can locate sources for the plants you choose to grow. At the end of the chapter about gardening I have listed several mail-order suppliers of seeds and plants, as well as a few networks of gardeners who save special seeds to exchange. Some plants are difficult to obtain even by mail at this point, but perhaps my writing about them will help to change that situation. I can sympathize with gardeners who read about a plant and want to order seeds the same evening and start to grow it as soon as possible! It's frustrating indeed to know about a special plant and not be able to have one of your own. But I have faith that nurserymen and seedsmen respond to the interests of their customers, and that they will offer more of these plants as soon as they sense a demand.

For convenience, I have referred to plants by their common names. Common names can cause plenty of confusion, though. Some names like hemp, indigo, soapweed and reed have been used over and over again to label different plants in different countries. In other cases several different names all refer to the same plant, such as dyer's broom, dyer's greenweed and woadwaxen. Plants usually have different common names in different languages, such as *garance* (French), *robbia* (Italian), *der Krapp* (German), or *madder* (English). But some plants have no common name at all, or at least none in English.

In order to establish the specific identity of each particular plant and sort out one from another, it's necessary to use scientific or Latin names. Following the system originated by the great eighteenth-century botanist Linnaeus, each kind of plant has a unique Latin name, consisting of two words. The first word is the name of the genus; the second word names the species. For most people, the genus is the grouping of plants which is easiest to recognize. For example, we can tell that a plant is a pine tree (genus *Pinus*), a rose bush (genus *Rosa*), or an iris (genus *Iris*); even though we can't tell what kind of pine, rose, or iris the plant is. Each genus of plants has a *generic name*. These names may be derived from classical names for plants, from Greek or Latin words for the properties or uses of plants, from names of people, or from other languages. *Arundo* (giant reedgrass) is an ancient name for reeds, *Saponaria* (soapwort) comes from the Latin word for soap, *Nicotiana* (tobacco) is named for Jean Nicot, who introduced tobacco to France. *Bixa* is a South American vernacular name for annatto. It's common to refer to a group of plants by naming the genus, especially when discussing properties that all the members of the genus have in common.

Within a genus, plants are divided into different species. A genus can contain only one, just a few, dozens, or hundreds of species. A species is the "bottom line" of classification, and the most basic group of organisms; it comprises all those individuals that resemble one another and are able to breed together but unable to breed with members of any other species.[1] Sometimes the details that distinguish one species from another are rather subtle, but

---

1. This definition of a species is useful most of the time, but there are exceptions. Sometimes a species is made up of individuals that resemble each other: most plants of reedgrass *(Phragmites australis)* look just the same. Other species, especially if they have a long history of human use, include individuals of varying appearance: broccoli, cauliflower, cabbage, kale, and brussels sprouts are all in the species *Brassica oleracea.*

other times they are obvious. Specific names are often derived from Greek or Latin and may describe something about the plant, such as *hirsutum* for "hairy" or *odoratum* for "fragrant". By itself, a specific name does not identify a kind of plant, because some specific names have been used over and over again. For example, there are many different kinds of plant called *"So and So" tinctoria* because they are "used by dyers", or *"So and So" sativus* because they are "cultivated". But when it follows the name of a genus, a specific name does indicate one particular kind of plant. Thus, *Indigofera tinctoria* means "the indigo that is used by dyers" and *Dipsacus sativus* means "the teasel that is cultivated".

Similar genera are grouped into families, and a family may include from one to thousands of genera. I have included the family name, in English, at the beginning of the entry for each plant. With practice, you can learn to recognize the characteristics of several different plant families. Sometimes the same useful property shows up repeatedly in plants of a certain family, and it's possible to say that "many plants in the mallow family yield strong stem fibers", or "plants in the mint family tend to be rich with essential oils". More often, however, the plants in a family vary considerably in overall appearance and usefulness.

There are some conventions for using Latin names. They are always written in italics or underlined.[2] The name of the genus is always capitalized, but the name of the species usually begins with a small letter. The first time a certain kind of plant is mentioned, the name is written in full. For example, let's begin with Upland cotton, *Gossypium hirsutum*. In later references to that species, or to other species in the same genus, it's customary to abbreviate the genus with a capital letter, and write *G. hirsutum* or *G. barbadense*. Specific names aren't abbreviated, but sometimes "sp." (singular) or "spp." (plural) is written after the name of a genus in referring to plants that are not precisely identified: *Gossypium* spp. means "unspecified kinds of cotton".

One point can be confusing, and needs discussion. Latin names weren't assigned at the Creation, one for each plant. They've been created by botanists. Working at different times and places, two botanists may reach different conclusions about the identity of a plant and its relation to other plants. People make mistakes, change their minds, and disagree. There are formal, internationally accepted procedures for resolving differences in

---

Where a species includes distinct subgroupings, they are called varieties, cultivars, races or subspecies.

Sometimes members of different species do interbreed and produce hybrid offspring. This is relatively infrequent in nature, but is encouraged by plant breeders. Hybrids sometimes show attributes of both parent species, but often show new traits as well.

2. When a Latin name serves as a common name, it doesn't require italics or a capital. *Iris* is the name of a genus, and iris is a common name.

nomenclature, but it takes a while for these resolutions to be incorporated into gardening books and magazines, nursery catalogs, and other printed information. In the interim, some plants seem to have more than one name. For plants that are described in older books or listed in seed catalogs under different names, I have put the currently preferred name first, and then the synonyms. Where possible, I have used the names given in the authoritative manual of cultivated plants, *Hortus Third*, published in 1976. For plants not listed in *Hortus Third*, I determined current usage by examining the botanical journals.

Many gardeners are reluctant to use Latin names for fear that they will not pronounce them correctly. Take courage! If you can say "asparagus", "chrysanthemum", and "rhododendron", you've already mastered three Latin names. You'll find the names for all the plants in this book in a pronunciation guide at the back, so you can learn to say "kor-ee-OP-sis" *(Coreopsis)*, "gos-SIP-ee-um" *(Gossypium)*, and "DIP-sa-cus" *(Dipsacus)*. Practice in private, then be dauntless and speak with confidence. Some of the best botanists I know use unconventional pronunciations, but it doesn't bother them a bit.

SUGGESTED READINGS

Useful Plants

For more information on how people have used plants as sources of foods, drugs, fibers, dyes and raw materials, read *Plants, Man, and Life* by Edgar Anderson (Berkeley: University of California Press, 1952), *Plants and Civilization* by Herbert Baker (Belmont, California: Wadsorth, 1978), or *Of Plants and Man* by Charles Heiser (Norman: University of Oklahoma Press, 1985). All are written in an engaging style for a general audience. A more formal text is *Economic Botany* by A.F. Hill (2d. ed.; New York: McGraw-Hill, 1952). The quarterly journal of the Society for Economic Botany, *Economic Botany*, contains detailed articles on a variety of useful plants.

The *Dictionary of Economic Plants* by J.C. Uphof (2d. rev. ed.; Wurzburg, Germany: J. Cramer, 1968) lists thousands of useful plants from around the world alphabetically by genus name and mentions the origin and use of each. Many fiber and dye plants are included in *The Commercial Products of India* by Sir George Watt (London: John Murray, 1908). Plants native to eastern North America are included in *Use of Plants for the Past 500 Years* by Charlotte Erichsen-Brown (Aurora, Ontario: Breezy Creeks Press, 1979).

The *Manual of Cultivated Plants* by L.H. Bailey (rev. ed.; New York: Macmillan, 1949) is a systematic treatment of useful plants that can be grown in North America. *Hortus Third* by the staff of the Bailey Hortorium at Cornell University (New York: Macmillan, 1976) is the most up-to-date reference on the taxonomy and nomenclature of cultivated plants, but focuses more on ornamental than on useful plants.

Much detailed information on the chemical compounds obtained from plants and used as dyes, soaps, essential oils and other products is published in chemistry books and journals. All require some background in chemistry. Two of the most useful references are *Plant Biochemistry* edited by James Bonner and Joseph Varner (3d. ed.;

New York: Academic Press, 1976), and *The Organic Constituents of Higher Plants* by Trevor Robinson (5th ed.; North Amherst, Massachusetts: Cordus, 1983).

Finally, for a practical field guide on poisonous plants to avoid, refer to *Poisonous Plants and Mushrooms of North America* by Charles Kingsley Levy and Richard B. Primack (Brattleboro, Vermont: Stephen Greene, 1984).

Textile Crafts

To learn more about the origins and development of spinning and weaving in Western societies, consult *Textiles*, Vol. 4. in *Studies in Ancient Technology*, by E.J. Brill (2d. ed.; Leiden, Netherlands: E.J. Brill, 1964) and relevant chapters in *A History of Technology* (five volumes), edited by Charles Singer (Oxford: Clarendon, 1956). A good survey of textile crafts from different societies is *A History of Textiles* by Kax Wilson (Boulder, Colorado: Westview Press, 1979).

A delightful introduction to the craft of weaving is *Spiders' Games: A Book for Beginning Weavers* by Phyllis Morrison (Seattle: University of Washington Press, 1979). A more comprehensive reference is *The Spinning, Weaving, and Dyeing Book* by Rachel Brown (New York: Alfred Knopf, 1980). A popular text for college-level introductory weaving courses is *Weaving, a Handbook of the Fiber Arts* by Shirley Held (2d. ed.; New York: Holt, Rinehart, and Winston, 1978).

It's worth looking for a library that has bound volumes of the *CIBA Review*, published by the Ciba-Geigy Company from the 1930s to 1960s, which contains fascinating articles on all aspects of the textile crafts. Current periodicals in the textile field present a range of historical, technical, inspirational and practical information. Among these are *Shuttle, Spindle, and Dyepot, Handwoven, Spin·Off, Fiberarts, The Weaver's Journal, Textile Artist's Newsletter* and *Threads*.

PLANT FIBERS FOR SPINNING AND STUFFING

If you associate plant fiber with bran muffins and breakfast cereal, stop now and take a look around. At the very least, you're probably within reach of some cotton fabrics, and you may see coir doormats, jute burlap, sisal twine, ramie-blend sweaters, or fine table linens. Those are just a few common uses of plant fibers.

Handweavers and fiber artists are people who enjoy experimenting with a variety of raw materials, and they continually seek out natural plant fibers. Many appreciate the range of textures available: fluffy or scratchy, yielding or stiff, delicate or sturdy. Plant fiber products bridge the categories of basketry and fabric. They can be coarse or delicate, rigid or flexible, humble or refined.

My personal interest in fiber plants has several facets. I enjoy looking for useful plants as I travel, and raising them at home in my garden to see how they grow and what they look like. Identifying, collecting, and studying fiber plants is part of my work as a botanist. Meanwhile, it's fun to experiment with the fibers, too, and somehow they seem to be more than just raw materials. Gathering, spinning and weaving them is an invitation to feel close to countless unknown women from long ago and far away, to be inspired by their achievements, and to practice the ancient techniques as they did. So working with plant fibers draws different parts of my life together, and at the same time, links me to a rich human tradition.

THE HISTORY AND USES OF PLANT FIBERS

Learning to twist plant fibers into cordage or yarn was among mankind's earliest accomplishments. Archeologists have found bits of fabrics estimated to be ten thousand years old in both the Old and New Worlds; primitive civilizations mastered the arts of spinning and weaving long before they began to refine metals or shape pottery vessels. The history of spinning began when the first spinners rolled strands of fibers between their hands and realized that twisting gave strength to the yarn. Many historians believe that these first yarns were spun from the long fibers of plant stems and that spinning short fibers, like cotton or wool, came later. With the early invention of the spindle and whorl, techniques of handspinning were developed that endure even today in parts of the world. People everywhere have used the fibers from local native plants to make a variety of everyday and ceremonial fabrics: fishnets and bowstrings, thatched roofs and floor mats, sheets and blankets, stuffed cushions, carrying bags and storage sacks, humble garments and elaborate robes, wrappings for babies and shrouds for the dead.

As societies became more complex, the need for certain kinds of fabrics greatly increased. Outfitting boats, for example, required tremendous yard-ages of sailcloth and rope rigging which had to be replaced every few years as they wore out. In post-Renaissance Europe, first the wheel-driven spinning wheel and then mechanical spinning devices were invented to accelerate the spinning process, supply more yarn to be woven, and free human hands for other work. Making cloth had always been so time-consuming and important that spinning and weaving were the first tasks to be mechanized during the Industrial Revolution. Textile production became more and more standard-ized and centralized in the eighteenth and nineteenth centuries. A few fiber crops began to dominate the world market because they had desirable qualities and could be produced in sufficient quantities. Today cotton is truly king, but flax, hemp, jute, sisal, abacá and others have also played important roles.

Until recently, plant fibers were the primary raw materials for clothing and underwear, bedding and towels, carpets and curtains and upholstery, flour and sugar bags, feed sacks, binder twine, tarpaulins and awnings, ropes and belts and hoses, army uniforms and tents, coffee bags and cotton bale covers. Now, many of these products are woven from man-made fibers. Since the 1950s, the replacement of natural fibers with synthetic fibers has been extremely rapid. It results from several factors. As a product, synthetics are sometimes more durable and longer-lasting than natural fibers. Natural fibers are biodegradable and are weakened by decay, but synthetic fibers are quite slow to deteriorate. Fiber plants themselves are an agricultural crop and may not be as valuable as food crops like wheat, corn, peanuts, sugar or bananas. The traditional methods of processing plant fibers have always used hand labor rather than machinery. The manufacturing processes for synthetic fibers are completely automated, so modern factories can produce them much more quickly and cheaply than old-fashioned village workshops could pro-duce natural fibers. Still, synthetics have not completely overtaken the textile world.

THE OCCURRENCE AND PROPERTIES
OF PLANT FIBERS

Botanists have estimated that over two thousand species of plants produce fibers, including at least a thousand kinds of plants in North America alone. Few have reached commercial importance, and some have never been utilized at all, but many have been used locally for one purpose or another. Fibers can be grouped by reference to the plant parts in which they grow. Seed fibers, including cotton and kapok, grow as appendages to seeds or inside seedpods. Most make good stuffing or padding if they can be collected in sufficient quantity, but cotton is the only seed fiber that can be spun into a serviceable yarn. Stem or bast fibers, such as flax, jute, ramie and hemp, form long strands in the inner bark of dicot stems. Also called soft fibers, bast fibers are noted for flexibility, ease of spinning, and durability. Leaf fibers, such as sisal, form parallel bundles that extend lengthwise in the thick leaves of monocots. Leaf fibers are called hard fibers because they are stiffer and more brittle than bast fibers; they are used more for cordage than for woven fabrics. Wood fibers, extracted from trees and coarse plants, are used in papermaking and as a raw material for making rayon. Miscellaneous fibers, mostly from parts of various palm plants, are used to make baskets, hats and brushes.

Individual fiber cells are very thin, usually less than one-thousandth of an inch in diameter. The average length of fiber cells depends on the plant: jute cells are about one-quarter inch long, cotton and flax cells are about one inch long, and ramie cells can be as much as six to twelve inches long. Only cotton is normally handled in the form of single cells. The strands or bundles of fibers that grow in stems and leaves, such as jute or sisal fibers, are usually ten to fifty cells thick in cross section; hundreds or thousands of overlapped cells run lengthwise to make a fiber. Sometimes other fibers are "cottonized", or broken down into individual cells (by a chemical treatment), so that they can be spun on machines designed for cotton, but mostly they are spun in the form that comes from the plant.

In photosynthesis, plants convert carbon dioxide and water into glucose, a simple sugar. Glucose is then converted into a variety of other chemical compounds, including cellulose. Cotton is almost pure cellulose with few impurities; other plant fibers are made of more or less cellulose. Cellulose molecules are very long chains of glucose building blocks joined end to end. The cellulose chains can be loosely arranged or densely packed into a crystalline structure. Parallel bundles of cellulose molecules form tiny fibrils, and as a plant grows, the fibrils are laid down in successive layers to form the cell walls of fiber cells. The patterning of these layers is not random. Each layer of fibrils traces a spiral inside the cell. Thus, plant fibers seem predisposed for spinning. An inherent twist is built into their very structure, and the direction of the twist is constant for any plant species.[1] This twist potential is easily observed: moistened fibers slowly turn in one direction or the other as they dry. Twisted fibers or yarns have diagonal lines that correspond with the crossbars in the letters S or Z. Flax, ramie, milkweed and Indian hemp fibers always show a natural S twist; and hemp, jute, sisal and yucca fibers always show a natural Z twist. Some historians have suggested that the observation of the natural twisting of plant fibers led prehistoric people to the discovery of spinning. Many fiber specialists think that if fibers are spun in the direction of their natural twist, the yarn will be smoother and stronger.

In addition to cellulose, many plant fibers contain pectins and lignins. Pectins, or pectic compounds, are the glue that holds cells together into fiber bundles and binds the different layers of plant stems together. In the kitchen, you might have used pectins to make jam or jelly thicken up. When bast fibers such as flax or jute are retted, bacteria break the pectins down into acetic and butyric acids (these compounds cause the bad odors of the retting process). In the initial stages of decay, the bundles of fibers are loosened from the rest of the stem. That's when the retting process should be stopped. If not, the bacteria will proceed to decompose the pectins that hold the fiber strands together, and the result will be useless loose cells and slime. Pectins also can be removed by boiling the fibers in an alkaline solution; a controlled chemical process now can be substituted for the traditional retting methods.

Lignins are chemical compounds that accumulate between the strands of cellulose in cell walls and give strength and rigidity to plant stems; lignins make stems tough and woody. Lignins are very resistant to decay and decomposition and are not removed by the retting process. Fibers with a high lignin content are stiff and hard and cannot be softened. In stem fibers, the lignin content is low at first but increases after the plants flower and go to seed; overmature flax or jute, for example, is more brittle and rigid than normal. Lignified stem fibers are graded inferior. Strands of leaf fibers normally include some heavily lignified cells, so they are always stiffer than stem fibers, but the percentage of lignin in leaf fiber bundles does not change much over time. Leaves of sisal or abacá, for example, can be harvested when they first expand from the bud or left on the plant for years, with little change in quality.

Stem fibers grow in a layer between the outer skin, or epidermis, of the plant and the woody core of the stem. They are common in both soft-

---

1. Some plants reveal an inherent twist as they grow. Charles Darwin recorded observations on vines, noting that plants of a particular species always twine in the same direction as they climb. Honeysuckle, for example, forms an S twist as it grows, but climbing lima beans make a Z.

stemmed herbaceous plants, like flax, ramie or hemp, and in woody plants, like basswood and cedar trees. Stem fibers are associated with the phloem system, which circulates the plant's sap. (The woody core of a stem is the xylem system, which transports water up from the roots.) Stem fibers run vertically in the stem, but they are not separate parallel bundles. Rather, they are interconnected into a sort of lattice, or net, and form a flexible cylinder that gives support to the stem. The cylinder of stem fibers is as long as the stem is tall, but when separated into thin strands by combing, the processed fibers vary in length.

Leaf fibers grow as distinct strands embedded in the pulp of fleshy or leathery leaves of monocot plants. Deep inside the leaves are fibrovascular bundles which include both fibers, for strength and flexibility, and phloem and xylem elements, for vascular transport. In the outermost tissue, just under the epidermis, are bundles of structural fibers that serve primarily to support and give shape to leaves. In most leaf fiber crops, the structural fibers are more abundant and stronger than the fibers associated with the vascular tissue. Leaf fibers are separate and parallel in the leaf, as tidy as a package of uncooked spaghetti. In processing, they are extracted in a uniform hank. Individual bundles cannot be split into thinner strands.

Any particular type of fiber can vary in fineness, strength, flexibility, color and other properties. The variation within a species can be considerable; as commercial commodities, fibers are graded into several quality categories and priced accordingly. The relative fineness of different fibers, such as jute and sisal, is sometimes compared by using the Tex system. A Tex count is the weight in grams of one thousand meters of yarn. Thicker yarn weighs more and has a higher Tex count than thin yarn. If two different kinds of fiber are spun into yarns as thin as possible, the Tex counts will compare the relative fineness of the fibers themselves. Cotton, line flax and ramie can be spun into much finer yarns than sisal, abacá or coir. Fine fibers are generally more desirable and expensive than coarser fibers.

The quality of leaf fibers is determined primarily by genetic factors, but for stem fibers, growing conditions and processing methods are also influential. For example, soil fertility, moisture supply, light and temperature, and density of spacing affect the quality of flax, and the timing of harvest is important. The temperature and purity of the retting water, the duration of retting, and the care taken in breaking and scutching and hackling also affect flax quality. On a home production scale, there can be difficulties with obtaining seeds for the best varieties or with providing the optimum growing conditions for different kinds of plants. Without the guidance of experience, processing may be inefficient or inferior. But even if the fibers aren't up to top-quality standards, growing and processing fibers yourself can be worthwhile.

COTTON

I remember the first time I saw cotton plants. It was during the winter term of my senior year in college. I was on a botany field trip to Florida for some first-hand experience with tropical plants. We hadn't seen much during the first two days of driving until, somewhere in Georgia, we stopped to stare at a field that was dotted with white puffs. It looked like someone had spilled giant popcorn out of an airplane! We stopped the car and ran over to collect and examine this curious plant, wondering what it could be. Yankees all, we hadn't recognized cotton. The second time I saw cotton, I was in Peace Corps training in the Virgin Islands. Our camp was on a barren, rocky, overgrazed mountainside, but there were some interesting little trees there, with balls of tan fluff on the branches. What could it be? Cotton fooled me again. The third time I saw cotton, I was in Texas. The dirt was black, and the fields were flat. From where I stood to the horizon stretched rows of lush green plants dotted with yellow and pink flowers like hollyhocks. Curious, I asked my hosts about them. Their answer: Cotton, of course. Now, years later, I usually know cotton when I see it.

Botany

The cotton genus *(Gossypium)*, in the mallow family, includes over three dozen species of wild and cultivated plants, native to both the Old and New Worlds. All wild cottons are perennials that grow into shrubs or small trees in tropical regions. Most grow in regions that have distinct wet and dry seasons. They tend to grow new foliage during the wet season and to bear flowers and fruit during the dry season. Some wild cottons don't bear any fibers on their seeds at all, but others do have fuzzy or hairy seeds. Biologists, who are always wondering why organisms have evolved in certain ways, have enjoyed speculating on the adaptive advantage of seed fibers. Some propose that lint provided a means of dispersal for cotton seeds, beginning way back in the Cretaceous period, perhaps as reptiles and birds gathered the seeds to line their nests. Others mention the possibility that lint-covered seeds could float on sea water, and point out that wild cottons commonly grow near shorelines and along coasts.

The process of domesticating cotton began long ago when people first began to gather the lint from wild cotton seeds, perhaps to use as a stuffing or wadding material. In the Old World, spinners were already adept at working with flax and wool before they began to use the short fibers of cotton. The oldest specimens of cotton textiles found by archeologists, at Mohenjo-Daro in the Indus River Valley in Pakistan, were woven about 3000 b.c. In the New World too, it seems that cotton spinning followed the earlier use of stem and

Cotton, *Gossypium hirsutum*

leaf fibers and perhaps alpaca wool. Archeologists working in Peru have found cotton fabrics that date from 2500 B.C. Those specimens were apparently made with fibers from cultivated cottons; the use of fibers gathered from wild cottons may date back much earlier. In the early stages of domestication, selection favored plants with longer seed fibers, fibers easily removed from the seeds, or increased yield of fibers. Most cultivated cotton has white fibers, but some primitive forms (particularly of *G. hirsutum*) have lint colored in shades of rust, tan, gold, brown, pink, gray or green. The naturally colored forms of cotton are relatively rare, but were used to good effect by Peruvian weavers, and are popular among handspinners today.

Four species of cotton have been cultivated as crops. In the Old World, a small tree cotton *(G. arboreum)* and a shrubby cotton *(G. herbaceum)* both produce rather short, coarse fibers, but they occur throughout Africa and Asia and still are used locally in small quantities. The cultivated New World cottons are puzzling species, because they apparently have evolved following hybridization of a cultivated Old World cotton and wild species of New World cotton. How these ancestral species got together, and whether or not humans played a role, has been debated for decades. Perhaps seeds of the Old World species were carried by man across the Pacific Ocean, or perhaps they floated or were carried across the South Atlantic. Anyway, during prehistoric times, the New World cotton species *G. hirsutum* was cultivated in parts of the Caribbean and throughout Central America and Mexico, up into the American Southwest; and the species *G. barbadense* was grown on Caribbean islands and down through South America. At present, *G. barbadense* supplies about eight percent of the annual world cotton crop. Known as Sea Island, Egyptian, or Pima cotton, it has extra-long, silky lint and is considered a luxury fiber. *G. hirsutum*, or Upland cotton, has shorter lint that is nice and fine. There are hundreds of named varieties of Upland cotton. It now provides ninety-two percent of the world cotton crop, which in 1985 added up to seventy-five million bales, at five hundred pounds each.

Upland cotton is an erect, bushy plant reaching five feet tall, with a deep root system and strong stems and branches. It has alternate broad leaves up to six inches wide, usually with three to five lobes. The typically mallow-like flowers emerge between three large, toothed bracts, and open with five yellow petals that later fade to pink. The bolls, or fruits, grow like small, green eggs, opening as they mature to release the expanded seed fibers. Each boll is partitioned into three to five sections, or locules, which bear separate locks of cotton. Cultivated varieties of Upland cotton differ somewhat in size, in form of the mature plant, and in boll characteristics. Some Upland cottons have smooth, black seeds and are easily ginned; others have fuzzy, green seeds and clinging fibers; some are intermediate forms. Upland cottons vary more in lint color than other species of cotton.

Plants of *G. barbadense* look quite similar to plants of Upland cotton. In 1785, this species was introduced from South America to the islands off the coast of South Carolina and Georgia, where it thrived in the maritime climate. Selected for its extremely long and fine fibers, Sea Island cotton commanded premium prices and was an important crop until the early twentieth century, when growers began to suffer total crop failures due to boll weevil infestations. At about this time, in the upper Nile Valley, a cross between Sea Island cotton and another variety of *G. barbadense*, Jumal cotton, was developed into the strain known as Egyptian cotton. Egyptian cotton was then introduced into Arizona, where it acquired the name Pima cotton. All three varieties — Sea Island, Egyptian and Pima cotton — give lower yields than Upland cottons, but their fibers are more valuable.

Wild species of cotton are sensitive to day length, and do not flower unless the photoperiod is less than thirteen or fourteen hours. This poses no problem in the tropics, where day length is short all year round, but does prevent plants from flowering during the long summer days of temperate climates. Tropical varieties planted in northern latitudes will grow vigorously all summer, but will not begin to flower until the short days of fall; and by then, it's too late for the bolls to develop. Introducing cotton as a crop in the colonial United States depended on finding varieties that would begin to flower early enough in the season to produce a harvestable crop before frost. Cotton breeders still are working to create varieties that are less and less sensitive to day length, as it bears quite an impact on where the crop can be grown.

History

In the New World, cotton was used by prehistoric weavers from Peru to Arizona to weave fabrics for clothing, belts, blankets and bags. Some of these fabrics, as we know them from archeological discoveries, were of complex construction; others, for everyday use, were simpler. The cultivation of cotton, associated with the use of the spindle and whorl for spinning and the loom for weaving, had spread throughout the Americas nearly as far as the climate allowed, long before the arrival of European explorers.

In the old World, India was the undisputed headquarters of the cotton industry for centuries. The Egyptians, Greeks and Romans did little more than envy the marvelous cotton fabrics they heard about. Only a little of the Indian cotton was carried in trade, and it was too expensive for any but the wealthiest customers to buy. Marco Polo, writing in 1298 about his travels to India, described ". . . the finest and most beautiful cottons in the world . . . so fine you can hardly feel them in your hand, and the thread when spun is scarcely discernable. . . ." Others described these fabrics as "webs of woven wind", and whetted the European appetite for such luxury. Venice became the center for cotton imports about that time, and Indian fabrics were introduced to the continent.

Of course, cotton can't be grown in most of Europe. The Moors brought cotton into Spain around A.D. 900 and established a cotton center in Barcelona, where it was woven into sailcloth for the Spanish fleet. Later, some cotton was manufactured in Italy, and by the 1400s, northern Europeans were able to get enough cotton fibers and yarns to establish cotton weaving centers in Brussels and Ghent. None of these fabrics competed with the Indian imports in fineness or quality, however; the European weavers made heavy materials called fustians, with linen warps and cotton wefts. Resistance from the European flax and wool producers limited the early acceptance of cotton as a raw material, and high prices limited the availability of imported fabrics.

Then, after 1600, many different factors coincided to change the textile industry. Exploration and discovery, the expansion of shipping routes, the establishment of overseas colonies, the rise of plantation agriculture in the South, the mechanization of spinning and weaving, the immigration of displaced skilled workers, the Civil War: Three centuries of history can be studied in terms of cotton. With Kay's invention of the fly shuttle in 1733, which speeded up the weaving process; Hargreaves' and Arkwright's mechanical spinning devices in 1767 and 1769; Cartwright's patent for a power loom in 1785; and Whitney's invention of the cotton gin in 1793 — the textile industry led the Industrial Revolution, and cotton became king of fibers.

Fiber Development

Long ago, the amazing appearance of cotton was explained by the myth of the "Scythian lamb". Medieval Europeans recited fantastic tales about the mysterious East. One story told of a tree or shrub that grew tiny lambs instead of flowers. Each lamb would bend over on its stalk to browse on the nearby foliage, eat all the leaves within reach, and then wither away. The pure white fleeces of the lambs were "vegetable wool" or cotton bolls.

Cotton fibers are unique, but they grow on seeds, not on little lambs. On the day that the cotton flower is pollinated, little bumps develop on the surface of the tiny seeds. Each bump is a single cell that elongates for two or three weeks, reaching a final length of an inch or more. The cells are all crowded together inside the boll, so they can't grow in a straight line but have to zigzag back and forth, bending like knees. At this stage, each fiber cell is like a thin-walled tube, full of sugar water. Beginning after about three weeks, the cell wall begins to thicken as sugar is converted to cellulose and deposited in layers. Viewed under high-power microscopes, cross sections of mature cotton fibers show concentric layers, like the rings in a tree stump.

Each layer represents a day's deposit of cellulose; it has a dense zone that was produced in daylight and a porous zone that was produced in darkness. During this period, the length, thickness and strength of cotton fibers are greatly influenced by environmental factors, such as temperature and amount of sunlight. About sixty days after flowering, the seeds and fibers are nearly mature and the boll splits open. Exposed to the sun and air, the fibers dry out. As the remainder of the fluid inside the cells evaporates, the fibers collapse into flattened ribbon shapes with frequent twists or convolutions. The dry fibers spread apart from each other and stretch out, and the expanded lock puffs out of the boll. The seeds ripen and enter dormancy, and the cotton is fully mature.

Cottonseeds

Ginning cotton to collect the fibers leaves a by-product: cottonseeds, lots of 'em. Only a small percentage is needed to replant the next year's crop; the rest are extra. For centuries, cottonseeds either were burnt (even though the smoke is nasty and pungent), dumped into streams or rivers, or piled in heaps to rot and stink. This caused enough environmental problems that, even before the days of Environmental Protection Agency regulations, cotton gin owners began looking for something useful to do with cottonseeds. This was a challenge, because the seed coats are dotted with tiny glands that contain a toxic substance, gossypol, that seems to help protect cotton plants from disease. Actually, gossypol may have some medical applications: It is bactericidal, fungicidal and spermicidal—it is used in China as a ninety-nine percent effective male contraceptive. But the gossypol must be removed by solvents in order to use the oil and meal from cottonseeds. After it is pressed from the seeds, filtered, deodorized, and bleached, cottonseed oil is used in salad dressings and mayonnaise, in margarine and shortening, and as a cooking oil, especially in frying vats in fast-food restaurants. Cottonseed oil is now used more than any other vegetable oil. The cottonseed meal is used as a livestock food and as fertilizer. Linters, the little bits of fuzz that stick to the seeds after ginning, are used as a source of cellulose to make paper, rayon, and photographic and X-ray film. Formerly wasted, the by-products of cotton now increase the value of the fiber crop.

Cultivation

If you have five hundred acres in Texas and want to grow a cotton crop, you can find plenty of information on how to go about it. I read one thick book, with chapters on machinery and soil and fertilizers and pest control and diseases and marketing strategy, that even goes so far as to tell you how to recognize the effects of lightning strikes on your fields. Now all that is great information, but it's more than you need to know if you just want to have a little cotton patch in your backyard. So, translated and distilled from volumes of agricultural handbooks, and filtered through my own experience, here is how to grow some Upland cotton.

To begin with, cotton requires a long, hot, sunny growing season; the yield of fibers is very much dependent on the air temperature and the amount of sunlight the plants receive. Unless your frost-free season extends at least 150 to 180 days, with average daily high temperatures in the 80° to 100° F range, the bolls will not mature before fall frosts kill the plants. Northern gardeners can grow cotton, but need to start it indoors in the spring and raise each plant in a large pot that can be set outside in the summer and brought back to a sunny windowsill or greenhouse in the fall. It's worth doing this just to see how the plants grow, but it won't supply you with much cotton to use. If your climate is right, then consider your site. Full sun is essential. It helps to have some plan for watering, in case there are dry spells. Any soil that will do for a flower or vegetable garden will do for cotton. Prepare it for planting by tilling or digging, and adding some manure, compost or fertilizer to promote vigorous growth.

Cotton is raised from seed each year. The seeds germinate quickly in soil warmer than 60° F, but rot away in colder soil. It's best, if possible, to sow cottonseeds directly where the plants are to grow, because the seedlings put forth a vigorous taproot. This primary root can grow down three to five feet before the stem of the plant is a foot tall; a root system like that serves a plant well but resents disturbance. If your season is short and you need an early start, plant the seeds indoors in individual containers (use three-inch peat pots or their equivalent) about four to six weeks before you expect to set the plants out. Then transplant them when the ground has warmed up, but treat the root system with care. Transplanted plants go into shock and look pathetic for a few weeks while the roots are getting reestablished. You'll think they are dying, but don't pull them out. Wait a while, and the stems and leaves will begin to grow again. Space individual cotton plants at least a foot apart, or better yet, two feet apart in every direction. As they grow, cultivate or mulch to control weeds and retain soil moisture.

When the plants are about sixty days old, they will begin to flower. The flowers are yellow on the first day they open, turn pinkish on the second day, and fall off on the third or fourth day. Bumblebees, honeybees and other insects will visit and transfer pollen. Cotton is normally self-pollinating, so even a single flower on a single plant can develop into a boll, but cross-pollination and hybridization occur readily where different kinds of cotton are grown together. This introduces some variation into the crop, which is fine for casual cotton growers. If you want to maintain the purity of a variety or select for certain qualities, though, it's necessary to exclude insects from the flowers and do controlled pollination.

I need to say something about controlling boll weevils and other insect pests, and hardly know what to include. Boll weevils aren't a problem in all areas, but corn earworms may do just as much damage, and dozens of other insects attack cotton, too. Most damage is caused by larvae, immature insects which develop inside the boll and feed on the fiber cells. Remember, the young bolls are quite sugary, full of sweet sap that later will condense as cellulose to make the fibers, so insects are attracted to cotton as a good food source. If you live in cotton country, you are familiar with the sound of spray planes flying low over the fields each week. Commercial growers spray cotton more heavily than any other agricultural crop. State and federal government research stations keep updating their recommendations for cotton pest control, but the problem is never solved. I sympathize with home gardeners who refuse to use strong chemical pesticides, and so far I've been lucky with my little cotton patches. Discuss pest control with the best gardeners in your neighborhood, ask your county extension agent for advice, and do your best to protect your cotton crop.

Because cotton is truly a tropical perennial plant, it will continue to flower indefinitely, even as bolls expand and mature. It's not uncommon to see large plants with flowers and ripe bolls at the same time. If you live in a really warm climate, where cotton is grown as a major crop, you can begin to pick bolls as they ripen and continue until the plants die. If your climate is less favorable for cotton, some crop management will improve your yield. Since it takes at least sixty days after a flower opens for the boll to develop, there isn't enough time for bolls to grow from flowers that open late in the summer. Some short-season varieties, developed for large-scale cotton growers, tend to "cut out" or stop developing flowers after a certain number of bolls have been set. This concentrates the plant's energy on those bolls that are likely to mature. If you have a small enough patch, you can achieve the same effect by selective pruning. Four to six weeks before the average killing frost date, go through and cut off the top and the branch tips of each plant to remove the buds, blooms and young bolls. "Topping" the plants in this way also lets more sunlight through to warm the bolls on the lower branches. As soon as half or more of the bolls have started to open, you can go through again and defoliate the plants. Leave the one leaf that is closest underneath each boll, as it supplies most of the boll's nutrition. Strip off all the other leaves so that increased light and air circulation can help dry out the fibers.

Ideally, cotton bolls develop to full maturity on the plant, and they are dry and fluffy when picked. Machine-picked cotton usually has bits of leaf and stem mixed in with the fibers, but hand-picked cotton is quite clean and pure, with no debris. Naturally ripened, hand-picked cotton is of the highest quality. Under adverse weather conditions, such as extreme drought or early frost, the bolls do not develop well, and the fiber quality is inferior. Usually immature, these fibers are weaker than normal and break into small bits called "neps" during the spinning process, and they don't accept dyes uniformly. Immature cotton has a very bad reputation in the cotton trade. In my experience, it's better than no cotton at all, and it may be all you get in areas where fall frosts come early and the cotton bolls don't have time to mature outdoors. In parts of the American Southwest and parts of China, where the growing season is short, traditional farmers pick the unopened bolls and spread them out in a sunny place or bring them indoors to dry. Later, they open the bolls to pull out the fibers. After frost has killed your cotton plants, go through the patch and pick off all the large bolls. It's no use picking very small or immature bolls, but bolls that are near maturity will yield good fibers if harvested green and dried indoors. When I first read about this, I was skeptical. Then I tried it with about a hundred bolls, and it worked okay. Even next to a hot wood stove, the bolls took weeks to dry, but finally they split open. The fibers didn't expand naturally, but when I pulled on each lock to extract and loosen it, the cotton puffed up like it's supposed to, and I spun it all into a fine yarn.

The yield of cotton per plant is extremely variable, depending on the variety, soil fertility and moisture, crop density, temperatures during the growing season, and other factors. Cotton farmers in the United States harvest an average of about 400 pounds of fiber per acre; this would be equivalent to two or three ounces of fiber per dozen plants. You may get quite a lot more or less than the average yield. It takes a patch at least twenty feet square to yield enough cotton fibers to weave cloth for a blouse.

Processing

A lock of cotton is clean, white and puffy when it expands from the mature boll, but there are lots of seeds embedded in the mass of fibers. Ginning is the process of separating the fibers from the seeds. The simplest kind of cotton gins, roller gins, have been used in India for centuries, and many were made in the United States in the late 1700s and 1800s. They have a pair of wooden rollers, like a washing machine wringer, that can be turned by a hand crank or by water power. As the cotton is fed into the machine, the fibers are pulled back through between the rollers, and the seeds drop free in front. Roller gins are gentle to the fibers, but they work only on smooth-seeded cottons with easily detached seeds. The Hopi and Pima Indians in Arizona sometimes used a simple stick, like a rolling pin, to press the seeds out of their cotton. The Hopi's cotton has fibers that don't adhere tightly to the seeds, and a pile of it can be ginned by just beating it gently with thin sticks or switches until the seeds drop free from the mass of fibers.

The major cotton crop in the early American South was green-seeded Upland cotton. Its short lint stuck tightly to fuzzy seeds, so it couldn't be processed with roller gins. (Black-seeded Upland cotton was a minor crop, grown only for home use in remote rural areas, that yielded much less fiber but had smooth seeds and could be processed in a roller gin.) At first, Upland cotton was tediously hand separated by slaves, but their output was too slow to meet the demands of newly invented cotton spinning machinery. When Eli Whitney invented the hook, or spike gin, in 1793, it was immediately accepted. Whitney's system consisted of toothed disks, like circular saw blades, that rotated inside a box and protruded only through narrow slits on one side. When cotton was fed against the teeth, the fibers were pulled loose and drawn inside the box, and the seeds were left outside. In turn, a set of brushes cleaned the fibers off the teeth of the gin. The design was copied, modified and improved by enthusiastic cotton promoters. With the invention of the hook gin, plantation owners could expect to sell all the cotton they could grow, and the mills could buy all they could spin. Eli's invention and subsequent fortune may have resulted from a flash of inspiration: It is said that his idea of using hooks to draw the cotton lint off the seeds came from watching a cat stretch its claws and reach far into a birdcage.

Small quantities of homegrown cotton can be ginned by hand. Picking the fibers off the seeds by hand is slow but sure. Although it's an easy job to do at odd moments, it can take several hours to separate an ounce of cotton fibers from the seeds. If handled gently and not compressed or wadded up at any point, the fibers are loose and fluffy enough to spin right away. Some cotton spinners use hand cards, with finer and more closely spaced teeth than wool cards, to straighten out and separate the fibers. Although a certain amount of wax coats the cotton fibers and has to be removed before the yarn can be dyed, cotton doesn't have to be washed before it is spun. Ginned cotton can be spun directly into a nice fine yarn on either a hand spindle or a spinning wheel, and the yarn is suitable for knitting or weaving. Check the references for more on handspinning and weaving with cotton, and enjoy using your own crop of fibers.

FLAX

The flax plant *(Linum usitatissimum)*, in the flax family, provides both fibers and seeds. Flax fibers are spun and woven into linen fabric; flaxseeds are better known as linseeds.[2] Cultivated flax is an annual plant, first used by the Egyptians and mentioned frequently in the Bible. Most other species of flax are perennial plants native to either Europe or North America. The Swiss Lake Dwellers spun and wove fibers of a native flax ten thousand years ago; prehistoric Indians in North America also used native flax fibers. Nowadays, several species of perennial flax are raised as ornamentals, because they have lovely clear-colored flowers, but only the annual flax is raised as a crop.

History

Historically, flax has been one of the most important textile fibers. The Egyptians wore linen clothing, slept on linen sheets, diapered their babies with linen, wrapped their mummies in linen, and traveled on boats with linen sails. They wove especially fine and sheer fabrics for pharaohs, priests, and other important people, and coarser fabrics for common folks. Sparkling clean white linen was a symbol of divine light and purity, associated with the goddess Isis. Talmudic and Biblical writings prescribed the proper cultivation of flax and forbade the blending of linen with "impure" wool in mixed fabrics. (Perhaps American colonists didn't know or care about these constraints when they invented linsey-woolsey.) Egyptian linens were exported to other civilizations and carried around the Mediterranean region by Phoenician traders, so the Greeks and Romans didn't grow and spin much of their own flax. Actually, most Greek men wore wool clothing and thought that fine linen fabrics were effeminate and appropriate for homosexuals. The Romans wore some linen clothing, but particularly used linen to make sails for boats.

After the fall of the Roman empire, the flax industry declined until the eighth century, when Charlemagne mandated its reintroduction. Linen garments and domestic textiles (sheets, towels, etc.) were pronounced more sanitary than wool, although sanitation in general was not a strong point of the Middle Ages in Europe. Flanders was the center for the medieval linen industry and the headquarters of the guilds and merchants who dealt with linen goods. But women in nearly every household in northern Europe were occupied with the spinning of flax into linen thread. Improvements in spinning wheel technology, including the development of the flyer and the

---

2. Historically, linen referred to a kind of fabric, not a particular fiber. Table linens and bed linens were usually medium-weight cloth, often in simple plain weave. There were flax linens, hemp linens, nettle linens, and even cotton linens. In modern usage, linen refers to flax products only.

Flax, *Linum usitatissimum*

treadle-driven wheel in the fifteenth and sixteenth centuries, greatly increased the ease and speed of spinning. In the early 1600s, flaxseeds and spinning wheels were carried to Massachusetts and Virginia. Domestic textile production was promoted by early laws requiring that every household had to spin a certain amount of flax yarn (or wool, in some cases) every year or pay a penalty fine. On the American frontier, nearly every family raised a patch of flax for its own use and wove both coarse and fine linen fabrics of all kinds. But in both Europe and the United States, the importance of flax declined very rapidly as mills for spinning cotton sprang up along every waterway in the early 1800s; by the twentieth century, flax wheels everywhere had been put away in attics.

Linseeds

Flaxseeds, or linseeds, are edible and can be eaten in cooked cereals or baked goods, but they also are used medicinally as a laxative. Soaked or boiled in water, they produce a thick, slimy mucilage that weavers use to size linen warps. If ground and pressed, linseeds yield up to thirty-five percent of their weight in linseed oil. The meal left over, known as oilseed cake, is a good food for cattle and poultry. Linseed oil also is edible and was used by eastern European peasants as a substitute for butter and as a home cough remedy. The major applications of linseed oil stem from its tendency to absorb oxygen from the air and dry into a hard varnish. "Boiled" linseed oil has been heated to 300° F, and dries much more rapidly than raw linseed oil. Linseed oil is used as a wood finish, and until the invention of latex paints, most paint formulas were based on linseed oil. Before plastic replacements outdated them, oilcloth and linoleum also were important linseed oil products. Several coats of linseed-oil-based paint were applied to closely woven linen canvas to make oilcloth, used for floor and table coverings, rain gear, and carrying bags. Linseed oil was mixed with rosin and ground cork, pressed onto a burlap backing and rolled to a uniform thickness, baked and dried in huge ovens, and cut into sheets to make linoleum. Tough, smooth, colorful, and easy to clean, linoleum was a housewife's delight when it was invented in 1863, and continued to be a very popular floor covering for most of a century.

Cultivation

Flax has been grown on a small scale by individual families for centuries, and is well-suited for home production. Different varieties of flax are raised for fiber or seed production, and the crops are managed in different ways. Fiber flax is grown at close spacing, so the stems are unbranched and bear straight fibers but few flowers and seeds. Seed flax is grown at much wider spacing, so that the plants branch out and bear numerous flowers and seeds. Of course, the seeds from fiber flax must be collected to plant the next year's crop; the fiber from seed flax isn't thrown away either, but it is used only in coarse fabrics or in papermaking. In growing fiber flax, it's important to start with seeds selected for that purpose. They are sold by a few suppliers, but packaged in small quantities, so you may have to devote a few years to increasing your seed stock before you can grow a patch large enough to yield a reasonable amount of fiber. Families used to plant flax in fields as big as an acre, but it took the labor of several children to help process the crop of fibers. Modern weavers might try a patch fifteen feet square or ten by twenty feet, which would yield enough flax fibers to weave a set of table linens or fabric for a linen blouse or shirt.

Flax grows best in rich, fertile soil that is well-drained. It prefers a climate with uniform rainfall throughout the growing season, but it has been grown successfully in many parts of the world. The patch must not be shaded by nearby trees or tall crops, such as corn. If possible, the ground should be dug and fertilized in the fall, then raked or tilled in the spring to prepare a smooth surface for planting. Flax can be sown a month or so before the average last frost in spring, as soon as the soil can be worked. It is not sown in rows, but is broadcast uniformly over the plot at a rate of about one pound of seeds per two hundred square feet. For good fiber production, the plants need to be very close together: one or two plants per square inch, or two hundred to two hundred fifty plants per square foot. As in sowing grass seed for lawns, it helps to divide the seeds in half, scatter half while walking north and south, and half while walking east and west. Use a rake to draw about one-half inch of soil over the seeds and pat them down firmly. Water lightly if the soil dries out during the week or two before the seedlings emerge. When the little flax plants are a few inches tall, work your way carefully through the patch to pull out any weeds. After the flax grows tall enough to fill in the patch, few weeds appear.

Flax is a graceful plant, with slender stems that sway in the wind and small thin leaves. It's a pretty color of green. About two months after planting, flax begins to bloom. Small flowers with five petals open on sunny mornings and close by noon or on cloudy days. Flowers are abundant for a week or two, then sparse and intermittent as seeds begin to develop and the plants mature. A field of flax in bloom is a lovely sight. The flowers can be white or blue; either color looks like a reflection of the sky. Folklore tells of confused ducks that have landed in flax fields, mistaking the waves of blue blossoms for the surface of a lake. A month or so after full bloom, or about one hundred days after planting, the stems start to turn yellow and the lower leaves begin to drop off. Flowering is past, and seeds are beginning to rattle inside the small round pods. At this point, the flax is ready to harvest.

Processing

Processing flax plants to obtain fine fibers ready for spinning involves a series series of treatments that take time, patience, effort and skill. The reward is twofold: a lovely product and a great sense of achievement. Although most of the process has been mechanized in the last few decades in order to produce flax economically on a commercial scale, the finest quality linens always have been the product of careful hand labor. Flax was processed at home on the farm until the nineteenth century, and in some parts of the country, old flax-working tools are sold at auctions and in antique shops. Many historical museums and living farms have flax tools on display or use them in demonstrations. You can make simple tools yourself or improvise substitutes that achieve the same results.

Flax is harvested by pulling up the plants, since the fibers extend down into the roots. Firmly grasp several stems at the base and tug them up out of the ground, then knock off any loose soil. Combine two or three handfuls into a bundle, taking care to position all the roots together and keep the stems in orderly alignment, then secure the bundle with string ties or rubber bands. Hang the bundles upside down to dry for a week or two inside a shed or barn, or outside on a drying rack or clothesline. During this initial drying, the flax-seeds are maturing inside the round pods. Birds and rodents are fond of flax-seeds and may find yours and eat them up, so watch for signs of predation in case you need to protect your crop of seeds.

When the stems are dry and the pods are brittle, the flax is ready for rippling. A ripple is a coarse-toothed rake that is used to pull the seed pods from the stems. Hold each bundle of flax by the roots and comb the tops through the ripple, letting the pods and seeds drop onto a sheet of plastic or cloth underneath. Lacking a ripple, you can hold the bundles over a cloth or large basin and comb the pods off with a steel dog-grooming comb or an Afro pick. It is very important not to disturb the orderly arrangement of stems during the rippling process. Keep a firm grip on the roots, and always comb in only one direction—from the roots towards the tops. When all the seed pods are stripped off, check and secure the ties on the bundles. Crush or roll the seed pods to release the seeds, and sift or winnow to clean away the chaff. Be sure the seeds are thoroughly dry before bagging them for storage.

The dry bundles of flax stems can be stored indefinitely, or you can proceed right away to the next processing step, which is retting. Only flax enthusiasts use the word "retting"; innocent bystanders would say "rotting". In the retting process, fungus and bacteria decompose the pectin compounds that cement the different layers of the flax stem together and release the strands of fiber from the inner core and the outer skin. Moisture is necessary, and warmth speeds up the rate of decay. Flax can be dew-retted by spreading the bundles on a grassy lawn to absorb the nightly dew; or water-retted by submerging the bundles in a pond, slow-moving stream, or large tank or tub. Dew-retting usually takes three to five weeks and leaves the flax fibers a brownish gray color. Water-retting takes four to twelve days, depending on the water temperature (between 60° and 90° F is acceptable), and leaves the fibers pale yellow. Deciding when the stalks have retted enough is the hardest part of flax processing, since good judgment is based on long experience. Check daily to see if the fibers strip easily from the core and if the outer skin slips away from the fibers. As soon as it is easy to separate the fibers, stop the retting process by rinsing the bundles with clean water and hanging them up to dry.

The retted flax should be dry and crispy for the next steps of breaking and scutching. In breaking, the woody core of the flax stem is broken into crumbs called shives, or boon. The traditional tool for this is a flax-brake, which looks like a large wooden jackknife with a pair of blade-like boards hinged to a grooved base. Each bundle or handful of flax is worked between the jaws of the brake. Repeated blows of the boards chop the core into shives and also loosen the outer skin of the stems, leaving the fibers partially cleaned. After breaking, the flax is further cleaned by scutching, or swingling. For this step, each bundle is held against a sturdy wooden block and scraped with a dull wooden blade to strike off any remaining bits of chaff and straw. Sideswipe the bundles with good firm blows, striking down and away from yourself. Work from the tip to the center of the stem, then turn the bundle and work from the roots toward the center. The steps of breaking and scutching produce a big heap of straw and leave a small strand, or strick, of fibers.

The final processing step is hackling, or hetcheling, the fibers to comb away any short bits, called tow, and split and smooth the long strands, called line. Hackles are mean-looking tools with rows of very sharp pins set into a wooden block and mounted on a stand or base of some kind. Wool combs can do double-duty as flax hackles, but they are expensive. Nails driven through a board are a fair improvisation, and the needle-holders used by flower arrangers are sufficient to comb small bundles. Old-timers had sets of hackles with coarse, medium and fine teeth; they progressed from one to the next to gradually finish cleaning and combing their flax fibers. Hackling takes a light touch, working first the tips of the bundle over the tips of the needles, then drawing more and more of the bundle through deeper and deeper. When thoroughly combed, the line linen will be very smooth and fine, long and uniform. There will be more or less tow, depending on the flax itself and on the experience of the handler; sometimes the tow should be rehackled to sort out any line fibers that got tangled in. After hackling, the stricks of line fibers are twisted into hanks for storage, and the tow is bundled up and saved.

Properties and Use

The chemical composition of flax fibers is similar to that of cotton: Both are very high in cellulose with few impurities. On the average, individual flax cells are about the same size as cotton fibers (0.0008″ in diameter by one inch long), but whereas cotton yarn is spun from individual cotton cells, linen yarn is spun from strands of flax cells. Flax fibers suitable for spinning consist of many overlapping cells joined into bundles (0.002″ to 0.02″ in diameter by twelve to thirty-six inches long). Individual cells that break away from these bundles form lint. (The words lint and linen have a common origin.)

The short tangled strands of flax tow that were pulled out during hackling are usually just carded and spun into coarse yarns for weaving into everyday farm fabrics, like mattress ticking and feed sacks. The long combed strands of line flax are spun into fine yarns and preferred for clothing and household fabrics. Dry-spun flax yarns are somewhat fuzzy, but if the fibers are moistened before or during the spinning process, the loose ends are drawn firmly into place. Handspinners can use saliva or a wet sponge to moisten their fingers as they spin; mechanical spinners run the fibers through a water bath. Wet-spun flax is especially smooth and uniform.

Natural linen usually is a pale gray, green or tan color. As yarn or fabric, it can be bleached to a pure white or dyed with natural or synthetic pigments. Old-fashioned bleaching methods call for sour milk or wood ash solutions and lots of sunbathing on grassy lawns. Alternate soaking and sunning treatments, repeated for weeks, are recommended. Linen also can be mercerized in a lye solution, as cotton is; it makes the yarn or fabric easier to dye and also increases its strength and luster. Cellulose fibers absorb natural dyes less readily than do protein fibers and are harder to color at home, but chemically dyed commercial linen yarns and fabrics are available for the handweaver or tailor in a range of shades.

Linen fabrics wrinkle easily and may be stiff at first, but get softer over time with use. Each washing improves the appearance and texture of the cloth, and pressing clean, damp linen with a hot iron makes the surface very glossy and smooth. Linen absorbs moisture and is cool to the touch; well-worn linen sheets, towels, and clothing feel very comfortable next to your skin. Linen is regaining its popularity after a few decades of stiff competition from synthetic fibers. I heartily recommend it. Check this chapter's references for more information on handspinning and weaving with linen.

FIBER PLANTS TO KNOW AND GROW

In this chapter, I've made a point of including some plants that are a little exotic and hard to come by, hoping that other spinners, weavers and gardeners will become interested in them, too. After reading about a certain plant, people are more likely to look for it as they travel or try to find a source for it. Together, we may rekindle an awareness and appreciation of fiber resources that have been neglected and abandoned, and we'll all benefit from that.

Abacá or Manila Hemp

Banana family. Native to the Philippines and Malaysia, abacá *(Musa textilis)* is a tropical plant closely related and similar to the banana. Although it reaches the height of a small tree, its growth form is quite unlike that of a woody plant. Abacá has a false trunk or stem, six to twelve inches in diameter and ten to twenty feet tall, of tightly overlapping leaf bases. This trunk might be compared to a very large bunch of celery. Glossy leafblades, one foot wide by three to six feet long, spread over the top of the clump and flap like sails in the wind. As many as twenty shoots can arise from a single rootstock during a few years of growth; the large shoots are harvested for fiber, and the small ones may be dug out and replanted to propagate the crop. Abacá grows best in warm, wet, tropical lowlands, and is raised on large plantations in the Philippines and in Central America. Although it is included in some public demonstration gardens in the United States, I don't know of any commercial source for seeds or plants of abacá. Several varieties of edible banana plants are sold through specialty nurseries, but the fibers from these would be weak and inferior.

To harvest abacá, whole trunks are cut off at ground level after about two years of growth. These trunks weigh up to one hundred pounds, because the leaf bases are engorged with water. The older leaves on the outside of the stalk yield the best and strongest fibers and are sorted out from the younger inner leaves that yield softer, weaker fibers. The fibers are concentrated in layers along the edges of each sheathing leaf base and can be stripped off by hand in long ribbons called "tuxies". In traditional hand processing, the tuxies were scraped between a serrated knife and a block of wood before rinsing and drying, but modern abacá production is mechanized; the whole leaf bases are run through crushing and scraping mills. A single trunk yields about a pound of finished fibers.

Abacá fibers are very strong and durable, lightweight and stiff. Although the fibers are very hygroscopic and absorb up to fifty percent of their weight in water, abacá is quite resistant to decay and deterioration and holds up well in outdoor use. Its major contemporary application is as a rope and cordage fiber; most "hemp" rope, especially for marine use, is made from abacá. But individual strands of the fibers can be woven on hand looms into a lustrous cloth. Sinamay fabric, woven from fine abacá, was formerly used for clothing in the Philippines.

Bowstring Hemp

Lily family. The leaves of several species of bowstring hemp (*Sansevieria* spp.), native to Africa, have been used as sources of fiber for making bowstrings and other cordage and for weaving into mats and sacks. These plants all grow clusters of smooth, thick, leathery leaves up to forty-eight inches long, flat or curved in cross section. Thick rootstocks spread along the soil surface and new shoots sprout up among the old until the patch is quite dense. On a more familiar scale, this is the ubiquitous, all-suffering houseplant known as snake plant. Tolerant of low light, dry air and neglect, the snake plant endures conditions that would kill other plants, surviving in bus stations, diners and launderettes. Its appearance in these unfavorable situations gives little hint of the vigor, and even the beauty, of healthy outdoor plantings in the tropics.

Acres of bowstring hemp were planted in Florida during World War II, when it was evaluated as a commercial fiber crop in a series of trials sponsored by the U.S. Department of Agriculture. Several species were compared for ease of propagation and culture, yield, and fiber quality. The tests showed that *Sansevieria* gives a good yield of satisfactory fibers, but its potential was never exploited on a large scale because of high domestic labor costs, the renewed availability of foreign fibers after the war ended, and the development of synthetic fibers.

For home use in Africa, people gather leaves from local wild plants and scrape, rinse and comb until the fibers are loosened from the pulp. Bowstring hemp leaves can be harvested at any time with little variation in fiber quality or quantity. I have experimented with handfuls of leaves from different species of *Sansevieria* grown as indoor plants and obtained fibers that were soft but brittle. However, I handled samples of *Sansevieria* fibers at the U.S. Department of Agriculture archives that were quite flexible and very lustrous.

Coconut and Other Palms

Palm family. The hard brown nut of a coconut (*Cocos nucifera*) grows inside a tough husk as big as a basketball. This husk is the source of a curly, cinnamon-brown fiber called coir. Coir production is a cottage industry in the tropics. Immature coconuts are cut down by agile workers who climb the slender palm trunks barefoot. The nuts are soaked in seawater for several months, then beaten, torn and hackled to release and separate the fibers. The fibers are rather coarse and stiff, and can be used like horsehair for stuffing or spun into cordage. A single husk yields enough fibers to spin about thirty yards of two-ply yarn as thick as a pencil. In India and Sri Lanka, coir still is spun entirely by hand or with very simple spinning wheels. Women and children do most of the processing and spinning as a cottage industry. Coir yarns are woven into durable doormats and attractive, heavy-duty commercial grade carpeting.

Have you ever taken a close look at a coconut palm? Loose fibers crisscross at the base of each giant leaf to form sheets of natural fabric, so the tree trunk appears to be wrapped with coarse burlap. These external fibers hint at the presence of fibers inside the palm. Coconut leaves, much used as roof thatching on tropical shelters, can be processed to make a smooth thread. The leaves are first boiled, then split into upper and lower halves and reduced to thin strips, and boiled again in washing soda solution. After rinsing and drying, the strips are semi-transparent, light, strong, elastic and waterproof. The strips are several feet long, and can be knotted or spun together into a continuous strand for weaving into hats, bags, clothing or slippers. The leaves of the palm-like Panama hat plant *(Carludovica palmata)* are processed in a similar way to make the famous hats (which actually come from Ecuador, not Panama).

If you live where coconuts grow, you probably recognize and know them. The rest of us can see coconut palms only on television or on vacation, because they are unsuited for growing in containers. Although only coconuts yield coir, many other palms have fibrous leaves, including the relatively hardy native palmetto *(Sabal palmetto)* and fan palms *(Washingtonia filifera* and *W. robusta)*, which were used by early Indians in basketry and for cordage. Like palm leaves, the leaves of Southeast Asian screw-pine plants *(Pandanus odoratissimus)* are split and twisted into cordage and sold by crafts suppliers as "sea grass". Doormats and similar products made of sea grass are very durable and, incidentally, are quite fragrant. Finally, flexible and easy-to-tie ribbons of raffia are peeled from young leaflets of raffia *(Raphia* spp.) palms, particularly in Madagascar.

Hemp

Mulberry family. Dozens of fiber plants are known as hemp of one kind or another, but the one and only true hemp is *Cannabis sativa*. Hemp was one of the first plants to be cultivated as a fiber source. Ancient records describe how the emperor Shen Nung, in the twenty-eighth century B.C., taught the people of China to cultivate "ma" for making hempen cloth. "Ma" designated a plant that grew in two forms, male and female. Native to central Asia, hemp was cultivated first for its strong stem fibers, then for its oil-rich seeds, and later for its narcotic leaves and flowers. There are many different varieties of hemp, selected for increased yield of one or another product, or adapted to grow in different climates or latitudes.

The fabric we call canvas gets its name from *kannabis*, the Latin word for hemp. Because of its durability and resistance to rotting, hemp is especially suitable for outdoor use and has been made into sails and rigging for ships and tents for army soldiers. Establishing a domestic hemp industry was a strategic priority in colonial America in order to outfit the armed forces for the Revolutionary War. Thousands of acres again were planted in a war production program during World War II. In the eighteenth and nineteenth centuries, farmers grew fields of hemp for home and local use. Hemp fibers are much like flax and can be woven into similar fabric products. In fact, hemp fabrics were also called linen, or brown linen. Coarse hemp fibers make good strong sacks and bags. The canvas covers on Conestoga wagons were woven from hemp. Fine hemp can be used for bed sheets, tablecloths and clothing.

The farm families that used to raise hemp for its fibers didn't smoke "pot", but nowadays it is illegal to grow hemp in the United States, because the plants are the source of the drug marijuana. Don't plan to grow your own hemp. No local sheriff will believe you if you say that you are raising the plants for fibers, and anyway, I don't know any place you can get seeds for varieties that yield good fibers. I've inquired, because next to flax, hemp is the best fiber crop to grow in northern climates, and I'm really curious about how it would handle. In the 1960s, hemp still was grown on a large scale in Russia and Italy, but its importance probably has declined due to competition from synthetic fibers. It is completely legal to import hemp fibers, but even hemp rope is very rarely available anymore, and finer hemp products may be extinct altogether.

Even though I can't recommend that you try to grow hemp, I can provide information about hemp cultivation. Hemp is an annual crop, and is killed by frost. If seeds are planted in April, the stems are ready to cut by September. For fiber production, hemp is grown at a close spacing of fifteen plants per square foot so the stems grow straight and tall without branching. The ideal fiber hemp stem is one-fifth inch thick by six feet tall. Given plenty of room and rich soil, hemp plants can grow a stem two and a half inches thick by thirty feet tall (that means it grows a foot a week!) and branch out like a Christmas tree. The leaves are palmately compound, with five to eleven slender leaflets. Loose clusters of greenish flowers are borne on separate male and female plants, but the male plants mature and flower almost a month before the female plants do. This presents a problem to hemp growers. Fiber quality is best when the flowers just open and then deteriorates. Overripe or dead plants have harsh, brittle fibers of little value. The best solution is to go through the field and pull up each male plant as it flowers, leaving the female plants to continue growing, but it's hard to walk around among tall plants spaced so close together. Instead, most growers either cut the whole crop when the male plants bloom, and get nice, soft, fine fibers from the immature female plants, or wait and cut the crop when the female plants bloom, and get coarse, stiff fibers from the old male plants. After cutting, the stems are bundled and dried for a few days until the leaves fall off, then retted on the ground, with moisture from dew, rain or snow, or water-retted in streams or ponds. After retting has loosened the fibers from the stems, the stalks are cracked into chunks by breaking, the fibers are scraped clean by scutching, and then the fibers are combed through metal-toothed hackles. Hemp fibers are handled the same as flax, and the same tools can be used for either.

Indian Hemp

Dogbane family. Indian hemp *(Apocynum cannabinum)* and the similar species spreading dogbane *(A. androsaemifolium)* are perennial herbs native to North America. Indian hemp branches less, is more erect, grows up to six feet tall, and has upright greenish white flowers. Dogbane is bushier and grows less than three feet tall, and has drooping pale pink flowers. Both have smooth opposite leaves, tough stems, and milky sap. Indian hemp and dogbane grow in sun or shade, moist or dry soil, warm or cold climates, across the United States. They occur as roadside weeds, in vacant lots, or in farmer's fields; and are occasionally offered as ornamentals because of their graceful silhouette, fragrant flowers, and bright fall color. They can be propagated easily by seed or root division. Indian hemp and dogbane are both attractive and useful, but because they are vigorous and potentially weedy, use an edging or barrier to contain the roots and limit their spread, and remove the spent flowers after blooming to prevent seed formation.

Indian hemp fibers were used by prehistoric Indians to make cords, fishing nets, bags, mats, belts, sandals and garments. The fibers are creamy pale or cinnamon colored, fine, long, and strong. They resist weathering and decay. A knotted net drawstring bag made of Indian hemp fibers was found in Danger Cave, Utah; archeologists estimate it to be seven thousand years old. Early European colonists in eastern North America were impressed with the properties of Indian hemp and compared the fibers favorably to both flax and cotton. The Europeans usually did not undertake growing and using Indian hemp themselves, because they were able to obtain it by trading with local Indians. The botanist Peter Kalm wrote of colonists in Delaware who bought Indian hemp ropes at a price of fourteen yards for a piece of bread. Other settlers acquired Indian hemp storage sacks, carrying bags, and mats through similar trade.

Indian hemp fibers can be gathered and processed anytime after the leaves drop off in the fall. I have read that the fibers are supposed to be at their best when the seed pods are developing. Stems cut at this stage could be retted and cleaned like flax or true hemp. I find it unpleasant to handle the plants while the sticky, milky sap is still present in the stems, so I gather Indian hemp in fall or winter, when the stems have dried out. It seems to me that the fibers are still soft and easy to spin. If the stems have weathered naturally, just soak them for a few hours, then peel off long strips of fibers and rub off the flaky outer bark by hand. The goal is to separate the fibers into fine clean strands. Prepared fibers can be spun by hand, or on a spindle or spinning wheel.

Jute

Basswood family. About forty species of jute grow in Africa and Asia, but round-pod jute *(Corchorus capsularis)* and long-pod jute *(C. olitorius)* are by far the most important. Round-pod or "white" jute has a round seed pod, grows wild in China, and can grow in fields that are flooded by monsoon rains. Long-pod or "tossa" jute has a slender pointed pod, grows wild in Africa and central Asia, and does not tolerate waterlogged soil. In commerce, jute fibers come from either of these plants. Jute has been used in India for centuries but was not exported until a system for spinning and weaving jute by machine was invented in Dundee, Scotland, in the 1880s. Then jute products were marketed quite widely and soon replaced their hemp or flax equivalents. Burlap fabric woven of jute is made into grain bags, coffee sacks, cotton bale covers, sand bags, carpet backing, upholstery webbing, and many other humble textiles. Jute is used where cheapness is more important than durability or strength.

Jute is an annual crop that grows best in very fertile soil and hot humid weather. Most jute is raised in the Bengal region of India and Bangladesh, where summer temperatures are in the 80° to 90° F range and as much as sixty to seventy-five inches of rain falls during the growing season from March to September. The plants grow quickly from tiny seeds, and are thinned to a spacing of five to eight plants per square foot. At that density, the stems grow straight without branching, and the stalks get as thick as a finger and eight to twelve feet tall. The plants are a light green color and have alternate leaves with toothed margins. The stems are ready to cut after about four months, when most of the lower leaves have dropped off and the small, pale yellow flowers are starting to open.

It takes a large labor force to harvest and process a crop of jute, which can yield four times as much fiber per acre as a crop of flax. In the jute fields around Calcutta, a working population of a thousand people per acre is employed. The fields may be flooded when the crop is harvested, and men have to wade into the water to cut the stalks off at ground level. The stems are tied into bundles, stacked and layered into big rafts, weighted with clods of soil, and submerged in shallow ponds to ret until the bark and fibers slip easily from the woody core. Retting takes two or three weeks if the water is warm (75° to 80° F). Then the workers stand waist deep in slimy, foul pools or in the Ganges River and work all day separating the fibers from the stems and cleaning them in the water. It's a hard job and the pay is poor. The cleaned fibers are spread on bushes to dry, packed into bales, and sent off to the spinning mills. The characteristic smell of jute twine and burlap doesn't come from the fiber itself or even the polluted water of the retting pools; instead, it comes from the oil that is applied to the fibers to make them easier to handle during spinning and weaving.

There have been some attempts to raise jute as a crop in Louisiana and other southern states, and the plants grew well. But there was a shortage of labor willing to process the fibers, and experiments with processing jute by machine yielded very inferior fibers. Jute is too particular about soil and climate to do well in most regions of the United States. I don't know of any source of seeds, so it is an unlikely candidate for home gardening.

Jute fibers are silky and lustrous, with a nice golden brown color, and fine jute has a soft texture. But jute has many disadvantages as a textile fiber. Although it takes dyes readily, it quickly fades again. It deteriorates quickly, especially if exposed to water or sunlight. Jute fibers contain much less cellulose and more lignin and pectin than other commonly used plant fibers. The chemical compounds that constitute lignin and pectin are not too stable, and as they react with oxygen the whole fiber strand comes unglued. Individual cells of jute are very short, much shorter than flax or ramie fibers, for example, so when the strand breaks apart it just shreds into lint. As garden twine, jute breaks down in a single season. As burlap backing for carpets or rugs, it may last a few decades, but it is not the stuff of heirlooms. Still, jute is so inexpensive that it may be useful for student projects or temporary constructions.[3]

---

3. In a recent mail-order catalog, I noticed a men's sport coat tailored from jute fabric. The accompanying description read, "Once used only for rope, jute is now an ultra-soft, wrinkle-resistant fabric. . . . It's true that jute in its cruder form is used for making burlap sacks, but this fine imported fabric bears no relation to its predecessor. . . ." Perhaps jute will make a comeback as a luxury fiber! It might be just the thing for high-fashion garments where the fabric has to last only until the item goes out of style.

Kapok

Bombax family. Kapok or silk-cotton *(Ceiba pentandra)* is collected from the fruits or seed pods of a giant tropical tree native to Central America. The kapok tree grows to one hundred feet tall, with a buttressed trunk up to ten feet in diameter and wide-spreading branches armed with fierce thorns. The tree loses its leaves for several months during the tropical dry season, revealing first the previous season's mature pods and later, a new flush of showy flowers. Kapok trees cast light shade over a large area; often a single tree shelters the central plaza of a Mexican village. Closely related and similar to kapok are pochote *(C. aesculifolia* and *C. acuminata)* and silk-floss *(Chorisia speciosa)* trees; these also yield pods full of fibers. These trees are all tender to frost and can be raised outdoors only in extreme southern Florida or California. Although seed catalogs sometimes suggest planting them as greenhouse trees or houseplants, they soon outgrow their containers and are unlikely to flower or bear fruit indoors.

Commercially, most kapok has been produced on large plantations in Java, although the floss is used for stuffing and padding in other tropical countries too. The mature fruits are leathery pods, five to ten inches long, that split open to release the mass of silky hairs that surrounds the many small seeds. In nature, the silk puffs out and blows away when the pods open on the tree. To harvest kapok, boys with long pole knives cut unopened pods down from the limbs and spread them under roofs to dry. The floss is later separated from the seeds and is ready to use.

Kapok fibers are individual cells about one inch long, made of nearly pure cellulose with a coating of waterproof wax. Because air is enclosed in the large cavity of each thin-walled fiber, kapok has great buoyancy and is ideal for filling life preservers. A kapok-stuffed life vest will support over fifteen times its own weight and stay afloat for years. Kapok is a good insulating material and has been used to stuff outerwear, sleeping bags and quilts. It also makes lush bed pillows, because the slippery fibers adjust right under your head and don't wad up or fight back like some stuffings do. Kapok stuffing deteriorates eventually with heavy use, as the hollow fibers pop and collapse, but in the meantime, it's very desirable. Kapok fibers are too smooth and slippery to spin into yarn, but the fibers of silk floss do cling together enough to be spun and woven by hand and are said to make fabrics "almost indistinguishable from silk."

Kenaf and Its Relatives

Mallow family. Kenaf *(Hibiscus cannabinus)* and its relatives roselle *(H. sabdariffa)*, aramina or cadillo *(Urena lobata)*, and China jute *(Abutilon theophrasti)* are all annual plants whose stem fibers are similar to jute. None is produced or processed on a large scale, but all have been used to some extent for cordage and coarse fabrics. In addition to these four, a great many other plants in the mallow family yield stem fibers of variable quality, including okra *(H. esculentus)* and cotton plants *(Gossypium spp.)*, but these other plants have never been utilized to any extent.

Kenaf grows eight to ten feet tall, with a strong main stem, several branches, variably heart-shaped or lobed leaves, and an overall prickly texture. It grows from seed to maturity in about four months, and needs temperatures in the 60° to 80° F range and well-drained soil with plenty of rain or irrigation water. Kenaf is sensitive to day length and begins to flower when daylight lasts less than twelve to thirteen hours. For the best and softest fibers, the stems are harvested before the yellow hollyhock-like flowers begin to develop. Ribbons of fibers can be stripped off the woody stems immediately after they are cut, or the stems can be retted for ten or more days in warm water until the fibers slip off readily. Washing, scraping and combing to clean the fibers increase the quality of the product. Kenaf fibers are more durable than jute, but are somewhat stiff, brittle and coarse. They are mostly used in Africa to make sacks and mats.

Roselle is similar to kenaf in appearance and growth, but it is smooth instead of prickly and has an enlarged, fleshy red calyx under its yellow petals. Different varieties have been developed to improve the quality of either the fibers or the calyx, which has an appealing tart flavor. It's a popular ingredient for fresh beverages in the Caribbean and herbal tea products in the United States. Roselle fibers are softer and more silky than kenaf, but the plants do not mature as quickly, and it is more difficult to strip roselle fibers away from the woody core of the stem. Like kenaf, roselle is sensitive to day length, and even six-inch-tall seedlings begin to flower if grown with less than thirteen hours of light a day. Kenaf and roselle would grow well in many parts of the United States. Interested spinners and weavers could experiment with extracting and using the fibers, but it is hard to obtain any seeds, particularly of good varieties.

Aramina is a weed that grows throughout most of the tropics and in parts of Florida. It is a hairy plant of variable size that looks like other mallows, with alternate branches, simple leaves, and pink to lavender hollyhock-like flowers. Aramina fibers are processed like kenaf and can be spun on machinery designed for jute. Although used locally in parts of Africa and Asia, aramina is used on a large scale only in Brazil, where it is woven into coffee sacks.

China jute is a native of China and India that was introduced into the United States as a potential fiber crop. It never achieved commercial success as a crop, but did become a widespread weed. China jute, also named velvet-leaf for its velvety heart-shaped leaves, is especially troublesome as a weed in corn and soybean fields in the Midwest, but grows on vacant lots and in gardens and fields across the country. Because of its weedy nature, China jute seeds are not sold, but any farmer would welcome you to collect it from the edges of his fields. I once gathered dozens of straight, unbranched eight- to ten-foot-tall China jute plants from a single patch at the edge of a cornfield, and I'm sure the farmer would have liked me to continue around the whole field. The stems can be retted for ten to fourteen days and then stripped, or the fiber and bark can be peeled off the freshly cut stems and then soaked. Either way, to complete the processing, the fibers need to be scraped and combed, rinsed and dried. China jute fibers are coarse but flexible and strong. In China, they have been used primarily in making rugs.

Milkweeds

Milkweed family. Several dozen species of milkweeds *(Asclepias)* grow as perennial wildflowers in North and South America. When broken or bruised, milkweed plants ooze a white latex or "milk" that contains potent compounds (the genus is named for Asclepius, the Greek god of medicine and healing). Some of the more widespread and familiar species are common milkweed *(A. syriaca)*, swamp milkweed *(A. incarnata)*, showy milkweed *(A. speciosa)*, and butterfly weed *(A. tuberosa)*. Milkweeds, particularly the common milkweed and swamp milkweed, are potential sources of two fiber types: a strong bast fiber from the stems, and a silky floss from the seed pods. Milkweed fibers were used by prehistoric Indians for spinning and weaving fine fabrics, and the floss was used for stuffing and padding. More than any other native fiber plant, milkweed has been studied as a potential crop for commercial processing. Reports of U.S. Department of Agriculture studies in the 1890s and 1940s claimed that milkweed showed more promise than any other indigenous bast fiber plant, with estimated yields as high as hemp crops, and quality as good as flax. Farmers and manufacturers were not convinced by these reports, and milkweed never earned a place in the fiber market.

For that matter, garden writers haven't shown too much enthusiasm for milkweeds either. They favor only the popular orange-flowered butterfly weed and dismiss the others as "coarse weeds". I disagree! Common milkweed has deliciously fragrant flowers and sculpturesque dried pods; swamp milkweed bears its delicate pink flowers for a full ten-week season; and both are hardy, trouble-free ornamentals that attract butterflies, especially the monarch butterfly, to your garden. Milkweeds grow in any ordinary soil with full sun. They can be propagated by sowing fresh seed in the fall for germination the following spring, or by dividing and transplanting a section of roots. In nature, swamp milkweed grows in moist areas near streams and rivers, but in cultivation it doesn't require special treatment. It grows to five

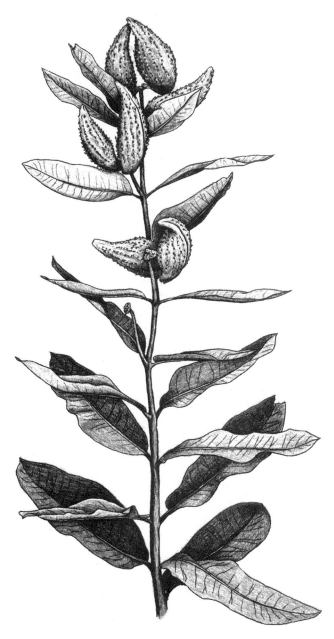

Milkweed, *Asclepias syriaca*

feet tall and forms a bushy clump with several branched stems. Common milkweed sends up unbranched stems three to four feet tall. It spreads by underground runners, and over a period of decades a single plant can expand to form a patch fifty feet in diameter. But I don't think you need to fear that your garden will be overtaken by milkweed—use a strip of metal edging to contain it if you wish.

The floss from milkweed pods is light, waterproof, and buoyant like kapok, so it has been used to stuff life preservers. It takes over eight hundred pods to yield a pound of floss, but three and one-half pounds of floss will keep a hundred and fifty pound man afloat for seventy-two hours. In a massive collection drive for the war effort in 1943, citizens around Petosky, Michigan, went out and collected over one hundred thousand pounds of milkweed fluff for the Navy to use in "Mae Wests", inflatable life jackets worn by fliers. The silky floss also is very good for stuffing pillows and mattresses, according to the reports of early settlers who substituted milkweed floss for expensive down.

Spinning the floss into yarn is quite a challenge, because the silky fibers are very fine and smooth. Gather the pods just as they are about to open naturally. Check a patch of plants daily and wait until the first few pods have opened, then choose yours. Open each pod along its suture, gently strip off the flat seeds, loosen up the mass of fibers, and spin them right away. For a day or so, you can spin the floss into a fine yarn, but after the fibers dry out, they become too brittle and slippery to use. The yarn will look silky and nice, but it has little strength.[4] Milkweed floss can be carded with other fibers, though, and adds warmth and luster to the blend.

The stem or bast fibers of milkweed are much easier to handle. Gather dead stalks in the winter after decay has removed the outer skin, and you can strip off strands of fibers as long as the stems are tall. These fibers are white, gray or brown, depending on how much the stems have weathered. They are strong but soft and flexible, and can be spun, knotted or braided for use in weaving, twining and basketry.

Nettles

Nettle family. Stinging nettle *(Urtica dioica)* is a perennial weed that grows in moist places, along roadsides, and in vacant lots throughout the United States and Europe. It has unbranched stems up to six feet tall and opposite, heart-

---

4. I am fascinated by reports dated to 1862 of a Miss Margaret Gerrish in Salem, Massachusetts, who is said to have spun milkweed floss into beautiful skeins of thread dyed many colors, and to have woven and knitted that yarn into purses, bags and socks. She must have had considerably more patience and skill than I do.

shaped leaves with toothed edges. Loose clusters of minute greenish flowers droop from the leaf axils. Nettle plants are covered with tiny hairs that penetrate your skin and inject chemicals that cause painful burning and itching. (It could be worse—there are tropical nettles whose sting can be fatal!) Related and similar plants are the wood nettle (*Laportea canadensis*) and the stingless nettle (*Boehmeria cylindrica*).

All of these nettles are sources of fibers. North American Indians used the fibers from the wood nettle and stingless nettle to spin cordage and make fishnets. In Europe, nettle fibers have been used since the Bronze Age to weave sails for boats and mesh fabrics for sifting flour and filtering honey. Fibers from wild nettle plants were used as substitutes for fibers from the cultivated crops hemp and flax. The poet Thomas Campbell wrote in the early 1800s, "I have slept in Nettle-sheets, and I have dined off a Nettle-table-cloth . . . the stalks of the old Nettle are as good as flax for making cloth. I have heard my mother say, that she thought nettle cloth more durable than any other linen." In Campbell's days, nettles had quite a few advocates, and experiments with nettle cultivation and use were conducted in Europe, Russia, Japan, Canada, and the United States. Some enthusiasts claimed that nettles would replace flax, but this never happened. Only during the hardships of World War I in Germany were nettle fibers used on a large scale. At that time, cultivated fibers were so scarce that the Germans collected over two thousand tons of wild nettles, and used the fibers to weave fabric for military uniforms. During peacetime, nettles were abandoned again.

In German, nettle yarn is "Nesselgarn", and nettle cloth is "Nesseltuch". I have read that the fabric can be bleached to a pure white, with a rich, glossy appearance and smooth texture. I also have read that nettle fibers can be woven into a velvet fabric even smoother and finer than cotton or silk velvet. This may be true, but the fact remains that nettles are irritating and unfriendly plants, and I won't have them on my property. Once I did pull up to a roadside patch of nettles, growing in what must have been particularly rich, moist soil, that had straight stems nearly eight feet tall. I rolled down my sleeves, pulled on a pair of gloves, got the pruning shears out of the glove compartment, and stepped out to harvest a bundle of stems. When the first stem I cut brushed against my face, I got back in my truck and drove away. So much for nettles, if you ask me.

If anyone else wants to try nettle fibers, here are three methods for separating the fibers from the stems. The first is to cut green stems and peel off the outer layer of fibers and skin right away (within an hour or two of cutting), and then ret the strips of fiber. The second is to cut and ret whole stems until the fibers strip off easily. Either way you begin, finish by scraping, rinsing, combing, and drying the fibers. The third method, used by North American Indians for wood nettles and stingless nettles, is to leave the dead stalks outdoors to decay until winter, then peel the fibers from the dry stem and flake off the remnants of outer skin.

New Zealand Flax

Lily family. New Zealand flax (*Phormium tenax*) really is from New Zealand, but it isn't flax at all. It is a vigorous and attractive plant, grown for fiber in New Zealand and for ornament in California, Oregon and Florida. Stalks of red or yellow flowers reach above the huge clumps of foliage, which may have red, purple, bronze or yellow stripes on a green background. Individual leaves are tough but fortunately not spiny, and grow up to twelve feet long by five inches wide. New Zealand flax grows readily from seed or division and is recommended for landscaping in mild climates. The plants are tolerant of a variety of soils and exposures, but suffer in temperatures below 25° F or above 90° F, and grow best where the temperature is nearly constant at about 65° F. Dwarf varieties are available for container growing in colder regions and make attractive greenhouse or indoor plants.

In New Zealand, most leaves are gathered from wild plants. Few farmers have been willing to invest in New Zealand flax as a crop because it develops too slowly. There is an initial delay of five or six years after setting out the plants before the first crop can be cut, and subsequent harvests are made at four- to six-year intervals. Most of the New Zealand flax that is processed gets woven into cloth to package bales of wool, which is a much more valuable and profitable fiber for New Zealand farmers to produce.

New Zealand flax leaves can be cut at any time. The fibers are extracted by crushing and scraping the leaves, then they are washed and spread to dry. Normally a lustrous white, they may become stained by the pigment of colored leaves during extraction. Strands of cleaned fibers are several feet long. The fibers are softer and more flexible than most other leaf fibers, but they are also weaker and deteriorate more quickly when wet. The Maoris of New Zealand used the fibers to weave fine fabrics. Some contemporary New Zealand spinners have experimented with processing and spinning the fibers. In the United States, basket makers enjoy working with the leaves of New Zealand flax.

Piña

Pineapple family. The leaves of the pineapple plant (*Ananas comosus*) yield fibers that are woven into a fine fabric called piña cloth in the Philippines. Pineapple plants are native to Latin America, but the tasty sweet fruit was so popular with Spanish and Portuguese explorers that pineapples were introduced into other tropical regions by the 1600s. Pineapples are now a major crop in Hawaii. The plants need warmth but tolerate a poor, dry sandy soil.

They are started by planting the crown of leaves, which grows atop the fruit, or by separating suckers off the main plant. The plants form a rosette of stiff leaves three feet long, with spiny tips and prickly margins. When the plants are about two years old, leaves are gathered by cutting them off at the base with a long sharp knife or machete. Fiber preparation does not require retting. The fresh leaves are scraped to remove the pulp and split into very thin strips, then rinsed, dried and combed. The shiny white fibers are very fine, soft and flexible. Piña cloth resembles fine linen and is quite durable in spite of its delicate appearance.

It's fun to grow a pineapple plant, starting with a fresh fruit from the supermarket. Grasp the leafy top firmly and twist until it comes off. Strip off several of the lower leaves to expose the thick stem, then let it sit on the counter for a few days to dry and seal at the base. Stick the stem down into a pot of coarse potting soil with plenty of sand added, and place the pot in a warm location. After several weeks, new roots will grow to establish the plant. It will grow best with plenty of sun and heat, and can grow several new leaves a year until it forms a large rosette. It is difficult to produce pineapple fruits on the windowsill or in the greenhouse, but a dozen or more leaves will yield a sample of piña fiber to experiment with.

Ramie

Nettle family. Fibers from the stems of ramie *(Boehmeria nivea* var. *nivea)* and the similar plant rhea *(B. nivea* var. *tenacissima)* have been used in China and Southeast Asia since prehistoric times. References in early Sanskrit literature mention ramie plants, fibers and fabrics. Some historians think that the Egyptians used ramie also, although their sources do not distinguish clearly between ramie and its close relative, the common nettle. Ramie was introduced into European textile mills in the 1850s. Then for over a century, it was acknowledged as a fiber crop with great potential, only if it could be processed efficiently. Finally in the 1980s, improvements in processing technology and a renewed interest in natural fibers for high fashion clothing have combined to bring ramie into wider use and recognition.

Ramie is a perennial plant with a spreading root system. Ramie plants look quite a lot like nettles but lack the prickles. From spring to fall, ramie puts up stems that grow about a half-inch thick and three to six feet tall with few branches. Its crinkly-textured leaves may be heart-shaped or have irregular lobes. As the stems reach their maximum height, small greenish flowers form in clusters at the leaf axils; the pollen-bearing male (staminate) flowers are lower on the stem and open first, and the seed-producing female (ovulate) flowers are above and open later. The stems are ready to harvest when the female flowers begin to open. At this point, the stem color fades from green to yellow, and the leaves are ready to drop off. Traditional Chinese farmers

Ramie, *Boehmeria nivea*

go through their fields each week and hand cut single stems as they mature. Modern growers use a cutting machine and harvest the whole crop at once when most stems are ready.

Processing the cut stems of ramie presents a particular challenge, because the fibers are held together by gummy resins. These resins are not decomposed by the kinds of bacteria that act on the pectin compounds which bind the fibers of flax, jute, hemp, and other bast fibers. So the retting process, which usually serves to release and separate fibers from stems, is not effective for ramie. There are two alternative methods: an ancient hand technique, and a modern mechanical/chemical technique. Either way, the processing should begin within a few hours of cutting the stems, before the gum starts to harden and set. The Chinese handle one stem at a time and first peel all the fibers and bark off the stem in narrow strips. Then they scrape each strip with a dull blade, from butt to tip and back again from tip to butt, to remove the outer skin. Washed and dried, these strips turn into stiff yellowish or greenish ribbons called "China grass", and they can be woven into coarse fabrics for work clothes. China grass has not been degummed, but if it is repeatedly washed, boiled in wood ash solution, and dried in the sun, it eventually gets softer, cleaner and whiter. The traditional Oriental approach to using ramie fibers was to weave China grass ribbons into fabric and sew it up, then continue the degumming process over the lifetime of the garment. Years of washing and wearing could transform a shirt from outerwear to underwear as the ramie softened up.

China grass is more of a curiosity than a useful commodity to modern weavers, but pure degummed ramie fibers are now available as a result of advances in processing technology. Crops of ramie stems are run through mechanical strippers that peel off the fibers and bark. The fibers are degummed chemically, by soaking in acidic and then basic solutions, or by a controlled fermentation using a particular strain of bacteria. Ramie processed in this way is said to be "cottonized" and shares many properties with cotton. Cottonized ramie has been broken down to single cells, which are very fine in diameter but as much as six to twelve inches long. Ramie fibers are by far the longest cells in the plant kingdom. The fibers are stronger than cotton or flax, smooth, and lustrous. They absorb and release moisture rapidly and make comfortable summer clothing. Ramie fibers don't shrink or swell when wet and are easy to launder. Ramie wrinkles less than linen, dyes as well as cotton, and combines well with other fibers in blended yarns or fabrics. Handspinners can purchase combed ramie and spin it into fine, smooth, strong yarns. Knitters and weavers can choose from a variety of ramie and ramie-blend yarns.

Ramie grows best in very fertile, sandy loam soil, and needs plenty of composted manure or fertilizer to sustain repeated harvest. Full sun and frequent rain or watering are necessary. Ramie is rarely propagated by seed, but plants are available from some herb nurseries. Buy one or two plants to start with and increase your stock by division. In early spring or early fall, dig up plants that are two or three years old, cut the thick roots into sections about six inches long, and replant the pieces of roots two inches deep and twenty inches apart. Leave the plants to grow for the first year. Then they can be harvested two or three times annually for several years, until the soil is depleted and the patch needs to be divided and renewed.

Ramie is not completely hardy, but it is not as tender as sometimes reported. Although the shoots are killed back by the first fall frost, ramie actually grows better in Washington, D.C., where it has a winter resting period, than in Puerto Rico, where it grows year-round. Even in climates where the ground freezes down four to six inches, ramie can overwinter successfully if the roots are protected by a thick mulch and the soil is well drained and not waterlogged. In the spring, new shoots will grow up. In colder climates, ramie needs to be brought inside for the winter. Carefully dig up large sections of roots after the first frost, and bury them in tubs of moist sand. Store in a cool dark place until spring and then replant. A cellar, cold frame, unheated greenhouse or garage will do for storage if the temperature stays between 20° and 60° F. Plants that are carried back and forth in this way can be harvested only once a year.

Sisal and Other Agaves

Agave family. The agaves are conspicuous plants in arid regions of the southwestern United States, Mexico, and Central America. The strong fibers extracted from their leaves have been used since prehistoric times. Sisal (*Agave sisalana*), a fierce-looking plant with leaves like fleshy daggers, was used by the Aztecs and is now widely cultivated in the tropics as a source of long, strong fibers. Henequen (*A. fourcroydes*) and cantala (*A. cantala*) are similar to sisal, but istle (*A. lecheguilla*) is a smaller plant that yields shorter, stiffer fibers. Related plants, used by Indians but not commercially, are beargrass (*Nolina* spp.) and sotol (*Dasylirion* spp.). In general, agaves are sturdy plants native to rugged terrain. They form rosettes of stout, often spiny, leaves, and are sometimes called "century" plants for their habit of growing many years (but not a whole century) before flowering and dying. When agaves do flower, it happens quickly. A stalk that looks like a giant spear of asparagus emerges from the center of the rosette and reaches a height of ten to twenty feet in as little as a week. The flowers open and mature, then some agaves bear seeds. Others reproduce by means of little bulbs or live plantlets that develop from the flowers instead of seeds. These little plants drop off the old stalk ready to root and grow. Agaves grow wild and are used in land-

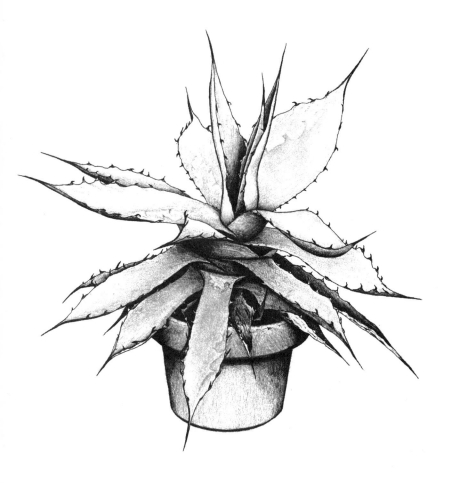

Agave, *Agave americana*

scaping in the Southwest, where the climate is dry and winter temperatures don't drop much below 20° F. Several species are sold as ornamentals for greenhouses or houseplants. All appreciate a summer vacation on the patio and then go dormant for the winter indoors. Unless overwatered, agaves are nearly indestructible, but more than once I have discarded perfectly healthy agave plants in angry response to being poked by the leaf spines.

Besides fibers, several species of agaves supply food and drink. I have eaten the pulp from roasted agave leaf bases in Mexico and would compare it with oversweetened pumpkin pie filling. A sweet and nourishing sap collects in the cavity left when the emerging flower stalk is cut out of an agave plant. Called aguamiel (Spanish for honey-water), it can be drunk fresh, or fermented into the beverages mescal and tequila. In rural Mexico, the rootstocks and leaf pulp of some agaves, particularly istle, are used as soap plants for shampoo, laundry and dishwashing.

In the twentieth century, sisal has been the primary source of fibers for baler-twine, henequen and cantala are minor cordage fibers, and istle is mostly used to make brush bristles. Loose sisal fibers are sometimes available for handspinners, and sisal twines and ropes are familiar to fiber artists. Sisal products are sometimes dyed, but the color often fades quickly. Centuries ago, fibers from the different species of agaves were much more widely used. Prehistoric Indians spun fine cordage and made nets, bags, and articles of clothing from agave fibers. The strong spine from the tip of an agave leaf, extracted with a length of fiber attached, served as a primitive needle and thread. The needle could even be rethreaded by splicing a new length of spun fibers onto the initial strand.

Agave fibers vary in fineness, according to the species, and in length, depending on the length of the leaves. Each leaf contains two fiber types: strong strands of fibers formed close to the surface, and weak ribbons of interior fibers. As many as two to four thousand strands of strong fibers can be extracted from a single agave leaf, but the weak fibers are mostly removed in processing. The length, strength, and number of fibers in a leaf are determined by the time the leaf unfolds from the central bud. Fiber properties do not change much as the leaf ages, but older leaves have a more dense pulp that is harder to remove from the fibers.

Commercially, sisal and henequen are raised on giant plantations. Each plant bears two hundred or more leaves over a lifetime of seven to ten years, yielding a total of seven pounds of clean fiber. A single leaf can be six inches wide and five feet long. Workers go through the fields several times a year, cutting a few leaves at a time from each plant. The leaves are heavy, so they are loaded on burros and carried to a central processing mill, where they are crushed between rollers, scraped, and rinsed. Bundles of clean, wet fibers are hung on lines to dry, then baled for export. On a small scale, agave leaves can be processed by hand. The yield of fibers is high, but it takes some muscle power to extract them. Young or old leaves, cut from the plant, must be scraped with a dull knife until all the skin and pulp are worked away from the fibers. Indians and Mexicans used to soften the leaves by pounding them with a rounded stone or a block of wood before beginning to scrape. I cheat and soak the leaves in warm water for a week or more. This stains the fibers, but does help soften the pulp. A small supply of agave fibers is enough to make a bag, stitch a basket, or add texture to a wall hanging.

Spanish Moss

Pineapple family. Spanish moss *(Tillandsia usneoides)* is a familiar sight in the hot moist regions of the southeastern states. Draping from live or dead trees, particularly live oaks and cypresses, or even from telephone and power wires, it hangs in tapered swags and sways in the wind, a graceful symbol of the South. From a distance, it looks like a grayish green foam or mist, but seen up close, it has long and thread-like stems and leaves. The flowers are tiny and insignificant. Spanish moss is an epiphyte, not a parasite. It grows perched on the limbs of other plants but absorbs water and nutrients directly from the air. It will grow indefinitely in a greenhouse as long as it is watered occasionally and the atmosphere is humid.

From the turn of the century through the 1950s, Spanish moss was an important stuffing material, used to pad upholstered furniture and automobile seat cushions. Collectors gathered moss by pulling it down from the trees or picking it up from the ground after storms blew it down. The green moss was cured and ginned in large quantities. For curing, the moss was piled about six feet deep in piles twenty feet wide by one hundred feet long. Thoroughly watered and trampled upon, it was left to compost for several weeks in the heat of summer. The pile settled considerably as the greenish covering on the leaves and stems rotted away, leaving just the dark brownish-black inner fibers. After curing, the moss was dried, then rolled through a gin and shaken over a screen to loosen and remove any remaining particles of skin or bark. About ten pounds of dry, clean black moss could be extracted from one hundred pounds of raw green moss. Although the black fibers can be spun into a coarse hairy rope or cord, they have had no application in textiles other than as stuffing.

Sunn Hemp and Other Legumes

Legume family. Sunn hemp *(Crotalaria juncea)* has been cultivated as a fiber crop in India and Asia for centuries. It is grown as cattle fodder in some of our southern states but not as a fiber crop here. It grows from seed to maturity in four to five months, preferring hot rainy weather. The slender stalks reach up to twelve feet tall, with rather sparse foliage and bright yellow flowers. Harvested and processed like jute or kenaf, the fibers are used in Asia to spin cordage and weave sacks. Exported fibers are used primarily in the manufacture of tissue paper and cigarette paper, not for textile products.

Two perennial shrubs in the legume family, the Spanish broom *(Spartium junceum)* and dyer's broom *(Genista tinctoria)*, contain stem fibers that have been used from time to time in parts of Europe for spinning cordage and weaving coarse cloth. These plants are better known as sources of yellow dye (chapter 2).

A North American legume that is cited as a fiber source is the Colorado river hemp *(Sesbania exaltata,* syn. *S. macrocarpa)*. Growing five to ten feet tall in a single season, it is an annual weed of the rich river bottoms along the Colorado River, particularly in Arizona. It has smooth stems, long, feathery, compound leaves, pea-like yellow flowers, and slender pods. The strong stem fibers were used by prehistoric Indians for fishnets and fishing lines.

Another legume that provides a useful stem fiber is kudzu *(Pueraria lobata)*. Kudzu is a vigorous perennial vine, native to Japan and used there as a fiber source. It has a huge tuberous root system, sends out runners with three-lobed leaves wider than a handspan, and has fragrant purple flowers in clusters like hyacinths. Although it grows quickly each summer, kudzu is killed back by winter frosts. It was introduced to the United States as a fodder crop and a ground cover for erosion control, but grew too exuberantly in the long, hot summers of our southern states. It has spread out of control, smothering everything it covers. Southerners will be skeptical to hear that kudzu is good for anything, and will warn you never to let it get started on your property. I agree: don't grow kudzu, but take a trip to the South and gather all you want.

Japanese spinners cut the stems, pencil thick and up to fifteen feet long, in mid- to late summer. They strip off the leaves, coil up the stems so they will fit in a large kettle, and boil the coils for half an hour or more to loosen the bark. After an overnight soaking in cool stream water, the soaked kudzu stems are buried in a pile of fresh grass or straw clippings to compost for a few days at about 100° F, until the bark and fibers strip off easily. Then long strands of fibers are peeled off and washed. Split into narrow strips and knotted end to end, kudzu fibers were woven into a linen-like fabric for work clothes in Japan.

I cut sections of stems eight to ten feet long and coil them in groups of a dozen or so. I cover the coils with water in a large kettle and boil them for an hour, then set the pot aside for a few days. The water gets frothy and foul as the stems ferment, but after they have been rinsed and cleaned the fibers smell like nice fresh hay. Each coil of stems yields a thin "ponytail" of fiber strands. Translucent and lustrous as plastic wrap, kudzu fibers make attractive products. Try using strands of kudzu as weft on a cotton or linen warp to make placemats, table runners, and bags or purses that are smooth and pliant, flexible and lightweight.

Yuccas

Lily family. Yuccas are large, impressive plants with tough, leathery sword-like leaves and towering stalks of white cup-shaped flowers. Although they are most abundant in the arid Southwest and on into Mexico, yuccas also grow in dry sandy spots throughout the East and Midwest. There are about forty species of yuccas. All have fibers in the leaves, and many serve as soap plants also (chapter 3). Yuccas are conspicuous wherever they grow, and are recognized and called by many common names. Spanish bayonet *(Yucca aloifolia)*, growing across the southern United States, has stiff leaves two and a half feet long on a simple or branched trunk ten to fifteen feet high. The flowers are nearly four inches wide and make a very showy cluster. Amole, datil, or banana yucca *(Y. baccata)*, native to the Southwest, grows in single rosettes or clumps, with thick two-foot-long leaves and a dense mass of white flowers on a stubby stalk. Soaptree yucca *(Y. elata)*, found from western Texas to Arizona, grows four-foot-long leaves on a single or branched trunk up to twenty feet high, with huge tall spikes of flowers in midsummer. Silkgrass or Adam's needle *(Y. filamentosa* and *Y. flaccida)* are hardy species native to the Southeast and growing as far north as Massachusetts and Michigan. Both grow stemless clumps of flexible, slender leaves two to three feet long, with loose fibers peeling from the leaf edges, and flower in late June. Beargrass or small soapweed *(Y. glauca)* has stiff narrow leaves, a half-inch wide by about two feet long and thready on the margins. Its flowers are smaller than those of other yuccas but still quite distinctive in midsummer. The small soapweed yucca is quite hardy and grows throughout the Midwest and up into the Dakotas. All yuccas are easily propagated by dividing young plants or offsets from an existing clump, but seedlings take many years to develop. Yuccas prefer well-drained soil and full sun and are carefree garden plants that last for decades, flowering each year and gradually spreading to form a patch.

Yucca leaves, and fibers derived from them, were some of the first plant materials used by early man in North America. Long before early hunters and gatherers settled down to building villages or raising crops, they already were making baskets, fishnets, carrying bags, sandals and mats from yucca and other native plant fibers. In the Southwest, yucca leaves are still used to make round trays and baskets. The fibers from yucca leaves compare favorably with other leaf fibers, and there have been various attempts to harvest and produce them as substitutes for sisal and abacá. Silk grass yucca was introduced to Germany in the 1920s in hopes of developing a hard fiber industry there, but it grew slowly in that climate and labor costs for harvest and processing were very high. During World War II, researchers studied the possibility of harvesting fibers from existing wild populations of yucca in the Southwest, but as the war ended the effort was abandoned.

Yucca fibers vary in length and fineness depending on the species, but in general they are softer and more flexible than sisal or agave fibers. The fibers can be extracted from young or old yucca leaves, gathered in any season by cutting them from the plant with shears or a long knife. As many as thirty to fifty leaves a year can be cut from healthy plants in cultivation, by continually removing the older outside leaves and allowing the center to keep growing. If you harvest from wild plants, take as little as you need and harvest from a large stand only. Fresh leaves can be alternately pounded and scraped with wooden mallets and blades until the soft pulp is removed and only the fibers remain. This works best with young leaves. Older leaves may be softened before scraping by boiling in a wood ash solution for a day or two or by retting for a week or more in a stream or a pail of water. Retting is not a traditional technique for processing leaf fibers, but I think it reduces the time needed for scraping. Indians used to extract leaf fibers by chewing, spitting, and scraping with their teeth, but I find that method quite unpleasant. It is important to do a thorough job of removing and rinsing away the pulp, or the fibers will be stiff when they dry. With prolonged maceration and plenty of rubbing, however, yucca fibers can be made quite soft. Hand-processed yucca fibers can be spun into fine yarns for use in weaving, braiding or twining.

SUGGESTED READINGS

Fiber Plants

For detailed information on fiber cells and how fibers develop in plant stems and leaves, refer to *Practical Plant Anatomy* by Adriance Foster (Princeton: Van Nostrand Reinhold, 1949), and *The Structure of Economic Plants* by Herman Hayward (New York: Macmillan, 1938).

The identification of plant fibers in woven fabrics is quite a challenging assignment, usually left to trained specialists. A method for distinguishing the major commercial fibers is presented in *Identification of Vegetable Fibers* by Dorothy Catling and John Grayson (London: Chapman and Hall, 1983). Many minor fibers as well are included in *Textile Fibers: Their Physical, Microscopical, and Chemical Properties* by J.M. Matthews (5th ed.; New York: John Wiley, 1947). An introductory article is "Fiber Identification in Ethnological Textile Artifacts" by Erika Schaffer (*Studies in Conservation* 26 [1981]: 119-29).

The early development of spinning and the role of plant fibers are discussed in "The Significance and Technical Analysis of Ancient Textiles as Historical Documents" by René Batigne and Louisa Bellinger *(American Philosophical Society Proceedings* 98, no. 6 [1953]: 670-80), and in "Plant Fibers and Civilization – Cotton, A Case in Point" by C. Earle Smith *(Economic Botany* 19 [1965]: 71-82). Other aspects of the development of spinning are discussed in the references on textile tools.

The use of fibers from native North American plants by prehistoric Indians is described in "The Preparation of Fibers and Dyes," in *Prehistoric Textiles of the Southwest* by Kate Peck Kent (Santa Fe, New Mexico: School of American Research, 1983), and "Fiber Plants of the North American Aborigines" by A.C. Whitford *(Journal of the New York Botanic Garden* 44 [1943]: 25-34). *Aboriginal American Indian Basketry* by Otis Tufton Mason (reprint of the original 1904 edition; Salt Lake City: Peregrine Smith, 1976) contains photographs and descriptions of an assortment of rigid and flexible baskets and textiles made from plant materials. *A Report on the Uncultivated Bast Fibers of the United States* by Charles Richards Dodge (Fiber Investigations Report No. 6; Washington: U.S. Department of Agriculture, 1894) discusses native plants as potential fiber crops.

The history of flax is reviewed in "The History of Flax Cultivation" and "The Cultivation and Preparation of Flax" by G. Schaefer *(CIBA Review* 49 [1945]: 1762-96). A very attractive book on flax production and use in colonial days is *All Sorts of Good Sufficient Cloth: Linen Making in New England 1640-1860* by Martha Coons (N. Andover, Massachusetts: Merrimack Valley Textile Museum, 1980). Practical information on growing, processing and spinning flax has been published in several sources; for examples see "Flax-Fiber Production" by Brittain B. Robinson (U.S.D.A. Farmer's Bulletin No. 1728; Washington: U.S. Department of Agriculture, 1940), and "Flax Processing" and "The Weaving of Linen" by Mary A. Chase *(Weaver's Journal* No. 26 [Fall 1982]: 5-11 and 18-22). *Handspinning Flax* by Olive and Harry Linder (Phoenix, Arizona: Bizarre Butterfly, 1986) covers all aspects of spinning flax into yarn. Directions for weaving fine linen fabrics are given in *Linen Heirlooms* by Constance Dann Gallagher (Newton, Massachusetts: Charles T. Branford, 1968).

An interesting account of the historical role of cotton is given in *Cotton: The Plant That Would Be King* by Bertha S. Dodge (Austin: University of Texas, 1984). For complete information on growing cotton as a crop, refer to *Cotton* by H.B. Brown and J.O. Ware (3d. ed.; New York: McGraw-Hill, 1958), and *Cotton* edited by R.J. Kohel and C.F. Lewis (Madison, Wisconsin: American Society of Agronomy, 1984). For more on spinning and weaving with cotton, see *Handspinning Cotton* by Olive and Harry Linder (Phoenix, Arizona: Cotton Squares, 1977), and look through the textile magazines for information and inspiration on using cotton fibers and yarns.

Comprehensive works on the cultivation and utilization of fiber crops include "Hard Fibers" by W. Bally and F. Tosler *(CIBA Review* 99 [1953]: 3538-72), "Vegetable Fibres" in *The Botany of Tropical Crops* by Leslie S. Cobley, revised by W.M. Steele (New York: Longman, 1977), and *Fiber Production in the Western Hemisphere* by L.H. Dewey (U.S.D.A. Misc. Pub. No. 518; Washington: U.S. Department of Agriculture, 1943). Major books on the subject are *Fiber Crops* by James H. Dempsey (Gainesville: University of Florida, 1975), *Vegetable Fibres: Botany, Cultivation, and Utilization* by R.H. Kirby (New York: Interscience, 1963), and *Long Vegetable Fibers* by Ludwig Weindling (New York: Columbia University, 1947).

There are numerous research publications on specific crops; for example, "Jute I" and "Jute II" by B.C. Kundu *(Economic Botany* 10 [1956]: 103-33 and 203-40), "Hemp" by Brittain B. Robinson (U.S.D.A. Farmer's Bulletin No. 1935; Washington: U.S. Department of Agriculture, 1943), and "Ramie Fiber Production" by Brittain B. Robinson (U.S.D.A. Circular No. 585; Washington: U.S. Department of Agriculture, December 1940). Although hard to come by, the series of *Fiber Investigations Reports* Nos. 1-215 published by the U.S. Department of Agriculture (Washington: U.S.

Department of Agriculture, 1892-1958) contains information on many of the major and minor fiber crops. Of particular value is *A Descriptive Catalogue of Useful Fiber Plants of the World* by Charles Richards Dodge (Fiber Investigations Report No. 9; Washington: U.S. Department of Agriculture, 1897): this report describes hundreds of different plants used as fiber sources.

DYES FROM PLANTS

The truth is, I'm a real slugabed—always the last person in the house to roll out, lazy and reluctant. No matter how much I enjoy my activities in the day-time and evening, in the morning, nothing calls me from my pillow, nothing makes me eager to get up. That's how I've always been, with one exception. One summer I lived in Colorado, up in the mountains next to a river. I had my spinning wheel, and I made a little fireplace outdoors. Every day I spun a skein of wool yarn and gathered a different kind of flowers or leaves to try. Each evening I lit a fire and cooked up a dyebath, added the yarn, and went to bed. The yarn simmered until the fire went out and then cooled off over-night. And that summer I hopped out of bed first thing in the morning to see each new color of yarn. That's the lure of dyeing, the fascination of making colors, and I'm hooked on it.

Using dyes from plants is an ancient craft, rich in history and tradition. Of course it's outdated today by modern industry and chemical technology. Everybody knows you can buy colored yarn and don't have to make it your-self. But to a dyer, that's beside the point. Dyeing is fun, it's full of surprises, it's a little like magic. And the colors—the reds and golds and blues and browns—are all so lovely. Learn to use dyes, and you too will wake up to color!

A BRIEF HISTORY OF NATURAL DYEING

The Origins of Dyeing

The use of colorants dates back thousands of years in all societies around the globe. Even before people began to spin yarn and weave cloth, they applied colored earth, plant saps and juices directly to their skin. We often hear about the Picts, ancient Britons who dyed their bodies blue with woad to frighten their enemies in battle, but there are many other examples of plant pigments used as cosmetics and paints. Women in the Mediterranean region applied alkanet as rouge and lipstick and used chamomile and henna to dye their hair. Indians in South America prepared a paste of annato seeds for painting their bodies; tribes in North America squeezed the red saps from different plants they called puccoons and drew decorative patterns on their skin. In Europe, people rubbed walnut hulls on their faces to darken them as a disguise when they traveled in unfriendly territory.

Applying dyes to fibers and fabrics is more complex than simply using plants to stain the skin, but throughout history, people have developed systems of dyeing. Certainly there was transfer of materials and ideas between cultures from time to time, but it would be wrong to think that the art of dyeing was invented or discovered in any one place and spread from there. Instead, the development of dyeing processes and skills was interwoven with other cultural advances, proceeding at different rates and by various means in each separate society.

Perhaps the first step in the history of dyeing was the identification of potential dye plants. Our major dye plants, along with our staple foodstuffs and a vast dispensary of medicinal plants, were all recognized thousands of years ago. Most modern people, who shop for food and drugs in supermarkets and buy their clothes already colored, are relatively unaware of the plants in their neighborhoods. If they think about them at all, they feel bewildered by all the different kinds of grasses, herbs, bushes and trees, and can't imagine how anyone could ever tell one from another. Earlier generations of people spent most of their time outdoors and explored their environment very thoroughly. By trial and error, they learned which plants were nourishing and which were poisonous, which contained fibers, which provided dyes, which were narcotic. Sooner or later, they found all the good stuff. For example, five unrelated plants (coffee, tea, cocoa, kola nut and yerba maté) that grow in different parts of the world provide the stimulant caffeine. These were discovered long ago, and modern man hasn't been able to add a single new caffeine source to the list. Likewise, the blue pigment indigo is invisibly present in several completely different kinds of plants, but ancient dyers found these varied sources and learned to extract indigo and use it as a dye. Perhaps modern dyers are naïve and vain when they talk of discovering dye plants; as written in Ecclesiastes, "What has been is what will be, and what has been done is what will be done. . . ."

In tracing the origins of dyeing, various dyeing methods and processes seem to have developed along with other activities of increasing technological sophistication. Simmering plants to make a dyebath was like cooking food in boiling water. Both required waterproof, heat-resistant vessels, such as ceramic or metal pots; more primitive containers such as gourds and baskets would not suffice. Techniques for fermenting berries and fruits to develop and extract the pigment may have developed alongside the discovery of fermenting fruit and grain to make wine and beer. The Egyptians' use of alum minerals as mordants could be related to their use of natron salts in laundering clothes. The value of tannin-rich barks in tanning and coloring hides for leather almost certainly led to their use in dyeing fibers; in particular, scholars consider that tanning sheepskins preceded dyeing wool in the Middle East. The important point, I think, is that the different processes of extracting colors from plants and fixing them onto fibers have much in common with other everyday activities, and that as primitive cultures discovered new technologies, one point of progress would overlap another.

Colors often play roles more important than mere decoration or ornament; they serve as cultural symbols. Different colors may be associated with cosmic and religious forces, with status and class, and with illness and health. Some beliefs and superstitions about color persist: Brides wear white and widows wear black, baby boys wear blue and baby girls wear pink, Halloween colors are orange and black, etc. But much of our use of color is a matter of personal preference or following fashion. In societies more governed by tradition, rules for using specific colors were (and in some places still are) much more strict. Choice dyes from rare sources were reserved for the garments of kings or priests; more common colors were available for ordinary folks. Some colors of clothing were believed to protect the wearer from earthly pests and diseases, or from supernatural forces. The particulars varied with different cultures, but many societies have attached strong significance to colors. Along with this, the dyeing process was directed by ritual. Primitive dyeing techniques often were very elaborate, as the goods to be dyed were alternately treated and dried over a period of weeks or months. Yarns or fabrics were soaked in, dipped in and coated with a variety of different substances. Some of this was necessary to fix the colors in the absence of metallic mordants, and some to achieve good color saturation. But much was a matter of the dyer's concern about doing things the "right" way, guided by tradition and belief.

Dyeing as a Professional Craft

Dyeing was well established as a skilled craft among the ancient civilizations that surrounded the Mediterranean. The Phoenicians, Egyptians, Greeks and Romans all loved beautiful colors and strove to attain pure, clear shades for their woolen garments. The Greek physician Dioscorides and the Roman naturalist Pliny the Elder, both writing in the first century, described sources of dyes and dyeing techniques known in those days. They mentioned several of the dye plants listed in this chapter, including indigo and woad for blue, alkanet and madder for red, weld and saffron for yellow, and oak bark and walnut hulls for golds and browns. In those cultures, although surely some people dyed their own yarns and clothing at home, most dyeing was done in special workshops, equipped with big vats, sinks and drying racks.

To the east, dyers from the Caucasus to Persia developed techniques for imparting beautiful, vivid colors to wool and silk yarns for weaving their elaborately figured knotted rugs. Seen in museums today, many of these textiles from central Asia are still distinctly colorful; they must have been even more remarkable when they were made hundreds of years ago. Dyers in India and southeast Asia not only mastered the art of producing bright colors on cotton (no mean feat in itself), but also developed techniques for printing colors on woven fabric and making designs with resist dyeing.

By the Middle Ages, dyers in Europe were well organized into professional guilds, with prolonged training periods for apprentices and high standards for master dyers. Remember that, in general, the textile industry in those days was based on division of labor; processes such as spinning, weaving and dyeing were done by different workers. Guilds in different regions often specialized in the use of one or another dyestuff or the dyeing of specific fibers. There was considerable rivalry and jealousy between guilds, and dyers frequently attempted to infiltrate each others' workshops and steal trade secrets. In particular, European dyers coveted the knowledge of how to derive Turkey-red dye from madder, a complex process that was practiced only in the East. Meanwhile, merchants and traders were busy importing exotic dyestuffs and brightly colored yarns and fabrics. These choice imports were simultaneously coveted by the public and condemned by the guildsmen who, then as now, complained of unfair foreign competition. For example, woad growers in England bitterly resisted the importation of indigo, which they called "the devil's dye", because it threatened their monopoly on the production of blue dye. Guilds lobbied the government for protective legislation, but once introduced, the importation of foreign goods could not be suppressed.

In the cities and more populated regions of the colonial United States, dyeing was again the business of trained craftsmen, many of whom had learned their skills in European workshops and were dependent on imported dyestuffs. Many books of dye recipes were written and published in both Europe and the United States during the 1700s and early 1800s. By contrast with modern dye books, which usually give recipes for dyeing one pound or less of fibers at a time, these old sources gave directions for mixing vats of dyestuffs and handling long bolts of fabric. During this time, spinning and weaving were becoming increasingly mechanized, so more and more cloth was being produced. Commercial dye workshops had to handle large quantities and produce consistent results. Of course, there were plenty of pioneer women on the frontier who gathered native plants and dyed their own home-spun yardage, but more and more, anyone who could afford to purchased finished fabric.

The Advent of Synthetic Dyes

By the nineteenth century, dyers had an increasing knowledge of chemistry and began to experiment with different mordants and dyebath additives. Where dyeing had been governed previously by tradition and ritual, by this time some of the processes had been analyzed. New techniques and compounds were patented and new formulas proposed, as science and industry eyed each other as partners. Cloth was getting cheaper, woven by machine instead of by hand, but dyes and the dyeing process were still expensive. Some inventors began to experiment with mineral dyes as alternatives to dyes from plants. They developed the chrome yellow and Prussian blue dyes for cotton.

At the same time, chemists were beginning to isolate and purify organic compounds and to identify their component elements and molecular structures. Knowing the structure of a natural compound was the first step toward recreating it synthetically in the laboratory. We now take synthetics for granted, but two hundred years ago it was inconceivable that man could duplicate God's work. In 1828, when the German chemist Friederich Wohler obtained urea from a reaction between inorganic substances, he opened up a whole new arena—the science of synthetic organic chemistry, with the prospect of producing inexpensive synthetic substitutes for costly natural products, or creating abundant supplies of naturally rare substances.

As a chemistry student in 1856, eighteen-year-old William Perkin was investigating the structure of quinone, an anti-malarial drug derived from the bark of tropical American *Cinchona* trees. Using the hydrocarbons in coal tar as a source of raw materials, Perkin was exploring different pathways for synthesizing quinone when he observed that one of his products made a vivid purple solution. Curious, he tested it as a dye on silk and had his results confirmed by a major dye house. Perkin was in business within a year, manufacturing the first synthetic aniline dye, which he called mauve. Perkin dyed silk first, and then, with tannic acid as a mordant, cotton. His business boomed as mauve became *the* fashion color of the era. Even Queen Victoria wore a mauve dress.

Other chemists, especially in Germany, quickly began to study the structures of natural pigments and tried to duplicate them. A process for synthesizing alizarin, the red pigment in madder roots, was patented in 1869. The blue of indigo was described in 1880, and synthetic indigo was marketed after 1897. Within a few decades after the discovery of synthetic dyes, the market for natural dyestuffs collapsed, never to recover. Although the first synthetic dyes tended to run, or bleed, into wash water and to fade in the sun, they were bright, inexpensive and very fashionable. Aside from a temporary setback during World War I, when the German dye houses were shut down, the synthetic dye industry has made steady progress to the present day. But the use of natural dyes continues in remote areas and among crafts enthusiasts.

PLANTS AS SOURCES OF PIGMENTS

Pigments in Nature

Flowers, leaves, stems and bark, seeds and fruits, and wood assume their characteristic colors because they contain naturally colored compounds called pigments. Biochemists have identified thousands of different pigments produced by plants. Why are there so many? What do they do for the plants? These questions are largely unanswered, although it's known that some pigments play important roles. Chlorophyll captures energy from sunlight in the process of photosynthesis. The bright colors of flowers are important in attracting insects and hummingbirds as pollinators. Conspicuously colored fruits attract birds and other animals that eat the pulp and disperse the seeds. Certain pigments may help to protect plants from bacterial or fungal infections. But the biological significance of most pigments is a mystery.

The diversity and abundance of these colored compounds is quite remarkable, considering that the majority of plant pigments are made up of varying combinations of only three elements: carbon, hydrogen and oxygen. A few, notably, indigo, contain nitrogen; chlorophyll is unique in containing magnesium. But nearly all the different colors of flowers and leaves, and all the dyes from plants, are synthesized by plants from just two raw materials, carbon dioxide and water. By contrast, the pigments of the mineral world — gemstones, metals, rocks and colored earth — include dozens of different chemical elements. The medieval alchemists were familiar with many of the inorganic pigments, but only in the last century have modern chemists isolated and described the structure of pigments from plants. If you have any training in chemistry, it's fascinating to study the molecular diagrams of dye compounds and to relate their properties as dyestuffs to their composition and structure.

Plants are not the only source of natural dye pigments. Several minerals can be used as pigments. In some ancient cultures exotic stones, such as bright green malachite and blue lapis lazuli, were ground into fine powder, mixed with oil, and used as paints. European and early American dyers used an iron compound called Prussian blue as a blue dye, and, in dilute solutions, as laundry blueing. Chrome yellow and copper penny blue were other mineral dyes commonly used in the 1800s. Basket makers in different cultures around the world learned that mud, clay and water from springs and swamps containing dissolved iron would darken or dye reeds, stems, leaves and plant fibers.

Far more important than mineral pigments, though, were the dyes derived from humble shellfish and insects. The shellfish the dyers used were marine snails of the genera *Murex* and *Purpura* that lived in the warm coastal water of the Mediterranean and along both coasts of Central America. The ancient Phoenicians — master sailors, traders and dyers — left behind mountains of shells as they exploited populations of these mollusks to make the famous dye Tyrian purple, or royal purple, which actually produced a range of colors from red to blue, including violet. Dyers in the state of Oaxaca, Mexico, still use shellfish to dye cotton yarn purple. Men go out along the coast at low tide to collect and "milk" the snails, which secrete a few drops of fluid when irritated. This fluid is meant to repel natural predators; human dyers aren't deterred by it, but do comment on its strong odor. Applied directly to the yarn, the fluid is clear at first, but develops its colors when exposed to air and sun for a few hours. Shellfish dye is very fast; once set, the color lasts indefinitely. But because the snails yield so little, the dye has always been expensive and valuable.

The use of certain insects as dyes is equally valuable (or equally disgusting, if you are squeamish). In different parts of the world, four kinds of scale insects have been used to make bright, fast red dyes. In each case, the insects are tediously collected from the branches or leaves of the plants they feed on. The insect bodies are usually dried in the sun, then ground, soaked, and simmered in a mildly acidic solution to make the dyebath, and used with alum or other mordants. Kermes insects feed on leaves of the evergreen kermes oak *(Quercus coccifera)* and the holm oak *(Q. ilex)* in the Mediterranean countries. St. John's blood insects parasitize the roots of a particular weed *(Scleranthus perennis)* in northern Europe. Lac insects, that feed on a variety of host plants in Southeast Asia, secrete a sticky resin that is used to make shellac, and also contain a red dye. But most important of all the insects are cochineal insects that feed on the succulent pads of the prickly pear cactus *(Opuntia* spp.) throughout Mexico, Central America, and parts of South America. After the Spaniards discovered New World Indians using cochineal in 1518 and carried some back to Europe, this dye quickly replaced the other red dyes from insect sources. Cochineal always has been expensive, though. In arid regions where prickly pear is the dominant vegetation and cochineal insects are abundant, as much as two hundred pounds of dried insects can be collected from an acre each year. But since it takes seventy thousand insect bodies to make a pound, you can imagine how many women and children are needed to collect enough cochineal to harvest an acre's crop. I tried it once and pooped out before I'd collected a tablespoonful.

Finally, many lichens give good dyes. Lichens are such unique organisms, combining fungal and algal partners into a single symbiotic relationship, that we can consider them here. They grow very slowly on rocks, bare soil, or tree trunks, in hot or cold, wet or dry climates. Lichens are soft when moist and crisp when dry, and come in many forms: flat crusts, erect clusters, drooping strands, ear-like flaps. Several kinds of lichens give yellows, golds and browns when simmered in a dyepot. Some also impart a pleasant fragrance to dyed wool. The famous Harris tweeds from Scotland were dyed and scented with a lichen called crottal. Other lichens contain pigments called orchils; treated with ammonia and oxygen, these develop into rich red, magenta and purple dyes.

Pigments as Dyes

Not all pigments serve as dyes. Some pigments will not dissolve in water, for example, and so it's difficult to mix them into a dyebath. Some dissolve well and make a brightly colored solution but have no affinity for fibers. Others dissolve easily in the dyebath and are readily taken up by the fibers, but after dyeing they promptly fade away to leave just a dull stain. Some lose their color when they react with oxygen in the air, especially in the presence of sunlight. Some are decomposed by heat and alkalinity, so they can't be washed in hot soapy water. So, although there are lots of colored substances in plants, there are only a few dozen dye pigments of lasting value to weavers.

These useful dyes are usually grouped into three categories: direct, mordant and vat. Simple, direct, or substantive dyes are those that react directly with fibers. These direct dyes normally aren't very fast to light and washing and often fade away until just a grayish beige or tan stain is left on the fibers. Berry juices, barberry roots and bark, safflower petals, annatto seeds, and walnut hulls all act as direct dyes on both plant and animal fibers. The fastness of direct dyes can sometimes be improved by using a mordant, a compound which helps to fix dyes to fibers. Adjective, or mordant-assisted dyes are always used in combination with a mordant; otherwise, they won't stick to the fibers. Mordant dyes have satisfactory to excellent fastness and give a good range of bright, clear colors. Most dyes from plants, whether from flowers, leaves, wood or roots, are mordant dyes. Many work much better for dyeing wool and silk than cotton or flax, because the mordants themselves react more with animal fibers than with plant fibers. Vat dyes do not react chemically with either animal or plant fibers but are merely deposited on the surfaces of the fibers. Preparing and applying vat dyes requires special procedures, but they are particularly fast and work equally well on animal and plant fibers. The indigo pigment is the only vat dye derived from plants.

Some of the important dyes have been found only in one or two species of plants. Bixin is found only in annatto seeds, for example, and curcumin comes from the rhizomes of only four species of turmeric. Other dyes are more widely distributed, often occurring in completely unrelated plant species. The yellow compound quercitin, for example, is produced in black oak bark, grape leaves, red rose petals, and onion skins! The famous blue pigment, indigo, occurs in several species of indigo (*Indigofera* spp.) plants, in woad (*Isatis tinctoria*), in dyer's knotweed (*Polygonum tinctorium*) and in many other plants.

Plant parts, such as leaves, always contain a mixture of pigments, a combination of natural compounds. Dyes from plants are not pure and refined but are blends of different colored substances. This impurity, I think, is what gives plant-dyed fibers such an appealing richness and subtlety of shade. It also explains why plant-dyed colors "all go together". One color will dominate, but it contains hints of other colors. Plant-dyed yarns are rarely described as pure colors – red, yellow or blue – but rather as modified hues – reddish brown, greenish yellow or purplish blue. Plants that do give rather pure dyes, such as the clear yellow from weld, are exceptional.

Dye Plants

The chemical "know-how" to produce a certain pigment, the part(s) of a plant in which the pigment will be most concentrated, and the average or maximum yield of that pigment are under genetic control. Particular species of plants are justly reknowned as dye plants, and sometimes superior varieties have been selected within the species. Closely related plants sometimes produce some of the same pigments, but often one species gives a much higher yield. Dyers often try wild bedstraws as substitutes for madder, for example, since all contain alizarin and related compounds in their roots. Once you've tried and compared them, though, you'll understand why madder is a famous dye plant and bedstraws are not; madder gives greater concentrations of a better red.

Aside from genetics, other factors influence the outcome of any given harvest of plant material. The amount of dye pigment usually varies with growing conditions, including soil fertility, moisture supply, temperature, and day length. Different parts of the same plant will contain different amounts of pigments, and the pigment content varies at different stages in the plant's life cycle. As examples: madder plants grown in rich, slightly alkaline soil give more red dye; indigo plants grown in cool weather, especially with cool nights, give much less blue dye; pokeweed leaves and stems have insignificant pigment content; woad leaves harvested when the plant is in bloom have lost most of their potential to give blue. The specifics of what, when, where and how to use different dye plants have been passed on through generations of dyers by word of mouth, but much of that traditional knowledge has been lost today.

In the 1970s, when dyeing with plants enjoyed a rebirth of popularity in the United States, new dyers had few references to study and few authorities to consult. As a result, a generation of enthusiastic and inventive dyers developed many new approaches and rediscovered some old ones and they tried all the plants they could gather. I did that for years, sampling the flora of several different states. It was fun and educational, and I made lots of colors. But now I'm less voracious about trying all kinds of plants; instead, I stick with a handful of reliable favorites. Although I still enjoy trying new plants to see what dyes they give, I've gained more and more respect for good old madder, woad, indigo, weld, walnuts, and the other traditional dyes.

A Warning about Poisonous Plants

I think that authors of dye books have done a good job over the years in advising dyers to take precautions when handling mordant chemicals. It's very important, especially if there are young children about. Here's another important point: Many commonly recommended dye plants are poisonous.

Here's a good example. Bloodroot *(Sanguinaria canadensis)* is a native wildflower with a swollen rhizome full of bright red sap. Indians used it as a body paint, and since colonial days, dyers have tried to capture that pigment on textiles. Actually, I've never gotten more than a rusty red or a dull orange from bloodroot, but that isn't the problem. The bright-colored sap is nature's way of saying "Keep Away". It is quite toxic if ingested, causing vomiting, dizziness, nerve damage, and even death. No dyer is going to eat bloodroot; it tastes awful, anyway. Originally, I didn't worry about these things. Then I dyed some wool fleece with bloodroot, rinsed it carefully, and let it dry. Days later I began to card it for spinning. Within seconds, my nose and throat were inflamed, my face got red, and my head felt like it was going to burst. I stumbled into the next room and got out my book on poisonous plants and read, "Bloodroot sap is a potent irritant of the moist membranes. . . . [it] causes almost immediate irritation." I had inhaled bits of dried sap that came off the fibers in the carding process! I was miserable for hours. If it happened to me, it could happen to you.

Bloodroot is just one of several plants to beware of. Many books recommend these plant materials for dyeing: lily of the valley leaves *(Convallaria majalis)*, rhododendron and azalea leaves, privet hedge trimmings *(Ligustrum vulgare)*, yellow flag iris rhizomes *(Iris pseudacorus)*, and larkspur or delphinium flowers (*Delphinium* spp.). These are all poisonous if taken internally. I'll admit that I've collected and used them all anyway; but it turns out that none are remarkable dye plants. So I advise you not to mess with them. Why take chances?

USING PLANTS TO DYE FIBERS AND FABRICS

Making a Dyebath from Plants

The first step in dyeing, after gathering the plant material, is to get the color out of the plants and into a pan of water. Some of the plants in this chapter require special procedures, but in general, it's a simple matter.

• Shred fresh, soft plant parts, such as flowers and leaves, into a pan, cover with water, and simmer for a half hour to an hour, until the water is colored and the tissues look bleached out. If the flowers or leaves have been dried, soak for several hours or overnight and then simmer in the same water.

• Press down on juicy fruits or berries to break the skins, then cover with water and add a little vinegar. Soak a few days at room temperature for best results, or heat to 150° F for a half hour.

• Chop or grind hard material, such as roots, bark or nut hulls, into chips. The smaller the chips, the better the dye flows. I use an old Waring blender to grind a handful of chips at a time into a fine meal. A hand-cranked flour mill or meat grinder works well, too. Set aside a special tool for this job, though; *don't* use your regular kitchen appliances. After grinding, soak the chips or meal for a few days, then heat and simmer for an hour or more.

Some dyers add the fibers at the same time they simmer the plant material, a method called "simultaneous" dyeing. In simultaneous dyeing, either the plants or the fibers should be protected in a net bag so they don't get stuck together. I usually prefer to make a dyebath and filter it through a mesh strainer, then add the fibers to the filtered liquid. There's only so much pigment to be extracted, and once it appears that I've gotten most of it out of the plant and into the dyebath, I throw the plant material away.

Dyebath Concentration

Dyebaths can be weak or strong, depending on different factors. Dry dyestuffs are more concentrated than fresh material, so an ounce of dried weld will give more color to a gallon of water than an ounce of fresh weld will. In the same way, an ounce of weld gathered during a spell of dry weather will give more pigment than an ounce of weld gathered after rains have swollen the plant cells with watery sap. Picked at the same time, an ounce of weld gives more pigment than an ounce of marigold flowers, because weld plants, in general, produce more pigment than marigold plants do. These factors have to do with how much pigment you can get out of the plant, and thus how much pigment there is to color the fibers. Some of the best dye plants are rich in pigment; a few handfuls of chopped madder root will give a rich color to a whole pot of water. Other plants aren't much good for dyeing; even if you cram as much material as possible into a pot and barely cover it with water, the color will be pale.

There's a relationship between the amount of dyestuff, the amount of fiber, and the intensity of the colors you get. An ounce of walnut hulls, for example, will give a strong dark brown to an ounce of wool, but only a medium brownish tan to four ounces of wool. And this holds true whether the walnut hulls are simmered in just a little water or in a whole panful of water. It doesn't hurt to use plenty of water when preparing a dyebath; that one ounce of wool can swim freely in a big pan. But no matter if you have water to cover four ounces of wool all at once, if you have only a dozen nut hulls' worth of pigment in that water, the wool won't get much color. If you want to dye a lot of wool at once, and to get a good rich color, you need to start out with plenty of dyestuff. Knowing exactly how much dyestuff to use is partly a matter of following recipes and partly a matter of experience. If the first batch of fibers dyes to a good dark color, you can enter second, third, and successive lots of fibers and get progressively paler shades. This gives a lovely sequence of coordinated colors ranging from vivid to pastel.[1]

Although mixtures of pigments occur naturally in plants, mixing different plants in the dyepot, or mixing different dyebaths together, usually produces a muddy effect and gives brownish or tan colors. A better way to obtain secondary colors is to superimpose layers of color on the fibers, or "top" dye. Yarn can be dyed green, for example, by first dyeing it yellow, rinsing and drying it, then dipping it in blue dye. Sequential dyeing, or top dyeing, will give the best results if each separate dyebath is a clear, pure color.

Dyebath pH

A dyebath is affected by properties of the water itself. Pure distilled water is neutral, but many substances react with water to form solutions that are acidic or basic (alkaline). The degree of acidity or alkalinity is measured on a

---

1. In theory, it's possible to "exhaust" a dyebath and transfer all the dissolved pigment from the water to the fibers. In practice, though, you reach a point where there's only a wee bit of pigment left. It's enough that the water still shows color, but it gives only a weak pastel shade on the fibers.

scale called the pH scale, which goes from 0 (extremely strong acid), to 7 (pure water), to 14 (extremely strong alkaline). Rain water, well water and tap water are rarely pure; they are affected by the presence of dissolved gasses, mineral salts and impurities. In many parts of the country, rain water is quite acidic, with a pH as low as 3.5. In other parts of the country, water from shallow reservoirs over limestone rock is quite alkaline, with a pH as high as 10. (The calcium, magnesium and iron dissolved in "hard" water can affect dye colors and also cause spotting or unevenness on the fibers.) Pure neutral water is by far the best for dyeing, but any water with a pH between 5.5 and 8.5 will not alter the dye results too much. You can have a sample of your water tested by your local water board to see if it is neutral, acidic or basic. I recommend purchasing a roll of special pH test paper from a pharmacist or dye supplier (it's inexpensive and goes a long way). To use it, you tear off an inch or so and dip one end into the dyebath water. The paper changes color as soon as it gets wet. Then you compare it with a chart on the side of the dispenser to find the pH value.

Controlling the pH of a dyebath is important to a dyer, because it affects the colors that will be produced. Some plant pigments dissolve much better in acidic than basic solutions, and vice versa. Some pigments change color in different solutions. Traditionally, dyers have added various substances to dyebath solutions to obtain the best results with particular plants. Most of these additives act by affecting the pH of the dyebath. As alkaline additives, dyers have used stale urine and dung (ammonia), wood and plant ashes (potassium carbonates), lye or caustic soda (sodium hydroxide), washing soda (sodium carbonate), and lime or chalk (calcium carbonate). For acid additives, they have used vinegar, sour wine, and fermented fruit juices (acetic acid), sour milk (lactic acid), cream of tartar and tartaric acid from wine casks, rhubarb and sorrel leaves (oxalic acid), and tree leaves and bark containing tannins (tannic acid). Sometimes fibers were soaked or treated in vats of these substances before or after dyeing as well, to improve the color or the fastness of different dyes.

Modern dyers will find it easy to use household chemicals as dyebath additives, but these vary considerably in strength and in the quantity needed to have an affect on the dyebath. To make a gallon of water more acidic, add a cup of vinegar, one-half cup of lemon juice, a tablespoon of cream of tartar, or a tablespoon of citric acid crystals. To make a gallon of water more alkaline, add one-half cup of ground chalk or limestone, one tablespoon of household ammonia, one tablespoon of baking soda, or one teaspoon of washing soda. Start with less, add more gradually, and test as you go. Avoid extremes. Common salt and Glauber's salts (sodium sulfate) don't affect pH, but can be added to a dyebath as "leveling agents" to make the fiber take dye evenly. Finally, remember that fibers should be rinsed and washed in solu-

tions compatible with those they were dyed in, or the colors may be changed
or destroyed. Soap is alkaline; while it is fine for alkaline-dyed fibers, if you
use it on acid-dyed fibers, you will risk a color shift.

Mordants

Most plant dyes give better results if used in combination with a mordant.
The word mordant is derived from the French word *mordre*, to bite, because
early dyers realized that a mordant enables the dye to get a better bite on the
fibers. Mordants increase the uptake of dye on the fibers, giving brighter,
deeper colors; they increase the dye's fastness to light and washing; and they
can increase the range of colors which can be obtained from a single dye
plant. Around the world, "primitive" dyers used a variety of natural substances to achieve the effect of mordanting, but the ancient Egyptians are
credited with having discovered the value of mineral compounds as mordants. Pliny the Elder described their accomplishment this way: "In Egypt
they dye clothing in a remarkable way. The white material is treated not with
the colors, but with chemicals which absorb the colors. This done, the
materials appear unchanged, but when immersed in a cauldron of boiling dye
and immediately removed, they are colored. It is remarkable that though the
dye in the cauldron is of one color only, the materials when taken out are of
various colors according to the quality of the chemicals applied, and it cannot
afterwards be washed out."

Positively charged metallic ions are the active ingredients in mordanting
wool and other animal fibers. These ions bond with the protein molecules of
the fibers and also combine with the dyestuff. The metals can come from the
dye vessel itself, or metallic salts can be dissolved in water to make mordant
solutions. These are the mordants most popular among contemporary dyers:
• Aluminum. For an aluminum mordant, use potassium aluminum sulfate,
$KAl(SO_4)_2 \cdot 12H_2O$, commonly called alum. (There are other compounds that
are also called alum, but they are less desirable as mordants.) Alum is a white
powder that is safe to handle and easy to use. It produces bright shades and
gives relatively good light-fastness. In excess, alum makes wool feel sticky, so
measure carefully. Using aluminum pans for dyeing has some effect on the
brightness of colors, but does not contribute as much to dye fastness as using
powdered alum. A few plants are sources of aluminum and can be used as
natural mordants; these include club mosses (*Lycopodium* spp.), leaves of the
sweetleaf tree *(Symplocos tinctoria)* and its tropical relatives, and tea leaves.[2]

---

2. Alum is a very astringent substance that has a long history of medicinal uses. Early
American colonists found wild plants whose roots had alum-like properties useful for
stopping bleeding and treating sores. They called them "alum root". Two wild plants
commonly known as alum root are *Geranium maculatum* and *Heuchera americana;*

These plants contain only two to four percent aluminum by dry weight, so large quantities are needed to produce much of a mordanting effect.

• Iron. For an iron mordant, use ferrous sulfate, $FeSO_4$, a greenish powder that dissolves to make a rusty-colored solution. You can also simmer the dyebath in a cast-iron pan, or make rusty water by soaking some nails or steel wool. As a mordant, iron gives dull or dark colors that are good and fast, but if used in excess it weakens wool fibers and causes yarns and fabrics to wear out prematurely.

• Copper. For a copper mordant, use copper sulfate, $CuSO_4$, beautiful blue crystals that dissolve in water to make a bright, clear colution. Copper sulfate is used widely to kill algae and scum in ponds and lakes, but it also is toxic to humans and should be handled with care. As a mordant, copper darkens colors and often gives a greenish cast. It gives good light-fastness and is less hard on fibers than iron. If you can afford a solid copper dye pot, this is a good way to use copper as a mordant.

• Tin. For a tin mordant, use stannous chloride, $SnCl_2$, a white powder that dissolves into a clear solution. It brightens the dye colors, sometimes giving a startlingly "unnatural" effect. Tin gives good fastness, but can make wool feel very brittle and rough. I find it best to use alum as the primary mordant and add just a pinch of tin, for brightness without brittleness. Always rinse tin-mordanted wool thoroughly. Stannous chloride, the form of tin used as a mordant, is mildly poisonous; in particular, it reacts with human skin to give off a nasty smell.

• Chromium or chrome. For a chrome mordant, use potassium dichromate, $K_2Cr_2O_7$, bright orange crystals that make an orange solution. This solution is unstable if exposed to light, so keep a lid on the pot and use chrome-mordanted fibers promptly. Chrome in any form is a toxic metal, so treat this mordant with respect and caution. Chrome is by far the most widely used mordant in industrial dyeing processes, because it gives good bright colors that are very fast, and because it gives a particularly soft texture to the wool.

Aside from metals and metallic salts, tannins and tannic acids are frequently referred to as mordants. Tannins are present in many kinds of tree bark and other plant parts. Especially rich sources are the stems and leaves of sumac (*Rhus* spp.), taproots of dock (*Rumex* spp.), bark of hemlock trees (*Tsuga canjdensis*), bark and leaf galls from oak trees (*Quercus* spp.), and bark of willows (*Salix* spp.). Dried sumac leaves can contain as much as thirty-five percent tannic acids by dry weight. Purified tannic acid is a fluffy beige powder. Tannin-rich materials can be used to give drab colors to wool,

---

both are herbaceous perennials found in deciduous forests. Alum roots don't really contain alum or aluminum in any measurable quantities. Instead, they are rich in tannins, which have similar astringent properties. Any usefulness that alum roots have as natural mordants depends on their tannin content, not their aluminum content.

which tend to darken over time from tan to brown. Nearly all recipes for obtaining black dyes from plants depend on a particular reaction between tannins and iron compounds.[3] Tannins also are used in combination with other mordants on wool, and in combination with alum to mordant plant fibers. Tannins are quite safe to use, although if handled without gloves they will dry and discolor your skin. That is, they'll "Tan your hide"!

Equipment, Safety and Records

Little special equipment is needed to begin dyeing, and most of it is readily available and inexpensive. These items are useful:

• A large kettle or dyepot, preferably big enough to hold several gallons of water. Enameled steel or stainless steel pots work best because they do not react with the dyes or mordants. Some dyers use institutional-size tin cans, aluminum, copper, or cast-iron pans, realizing that the different metals affect the dye colors. Plastic pails work fine for soaking and rinsing and are good containers for dyebaths that don't have to be simmered. Using lids on the pots helps reduce evaporation and contain odors.

• Wood or metal rods for stirring the dyebath and handling the fibers.

• Scales for weighing out quantities of fibers, and scales or measuring spoons for measuring mordants.

• A mesh strainer for separating plant material from the dyebath. Old nylon stockings are useful too, for holding plant material or fibers.

• A thermometer for measuring the temperature of the dyebath.

• pH test paper for measuring the acidity or alkalinity of the dyebath.

Using plants to dye fibers and yarns can be a little messy. In mild weather it's nice to work outdoors, if you have a water source and a camp stove or fireplace for heating the dyepots. But I've always done most of my dyeing in my kitchen. Aside from a few puddles on the floor and stains on the counters, this practice has worked pretty well. I often have a dyepot simmering while I'm reading, writing, or working on other projects at home, and it's convenient to be able to check it frequently. It's important to have good ventilation, though — open a window or use the vent on your stove.

Follow reasonable safety precautions. Decide which pans, measuring spoons and other equipment you will use for your dyeing, mark them with indelible labels, and *don't* use the same equipment for cooking. Choose a safe location out of harm's way for storing your equipment, and be especially

---

3. The reaction of tannins with iron compounds was used by primitive dyers to color basketry materials and plant fibers. The plant parts, rich in tannins, were buried in deposits of iron-rich earth and left for several weeks. When retrieved, they were dyed with a fast, dark color.

careful to store your mordant chemicals in sealed, labeled containers that are out of reach of children. Wear rubber gloves to handle the plant materials and fibers. For disposal, plant wastes can be composted or put in the trash. Most liquid wastes can be put down the drain and will not harm septic or municipal sewage systems. Even the copper, tin and chrome salts used as mordants shouldn't cause problems if they have been properly measured and applied; the mordant is supposed to stick to the fibers, not stay in the water. If you do a *lot* of dyeing and are concerned about safe disposal, contact your local water department or pollution control board.

It's hard, in the excitement of watching colors happen, but try to keep good records. Go to an office supply store and get a bunch of those little white labels on strings and use them to mark different dye lots. Get a notebook, too, and write down which mordants, additives and plant materials you used. Take note of anything you did that produced an interesting or unusual effect, or anything that went wrong. Press specimens of the plants you use and put them in your notebook, noting when and where you collected them. Keep samples of the different colors you get with different dye lots and different fibers. Having records is no guarantee that you will get exactly the same results again. But it does preserve the information about how you did it once, and if you're like me, your memory just won't hold all those details. It's especially useful, from one year to the next, to refer back to see what you've tried before and how it turned out.

Handling and Dyeing Different Fiber Products

Fibers can be dyed loose, as spun yarn, or as knitted or woven fabrics. Traditionally, wool fleece was dyed before it was spun, or "dyed in the wool". Silk, cotton or other fibers also can be dyed before spinning. Some dyers feel that the color penetrates better into a mass of loose fibers than into tightly twisted yarns. Dyeing the fibers first also provides opportunities to blend different colors when spinning the yarn. But there are two disadvantages to dyeing loose fibers. First, loose fibers take up more room in a dyepot. Although you can dye a whole pound of wool yarn in four gallons of water, the same dyebath seems crowded with just four ounces of wool fleece. The fleece is puffier, the yarn more compact. Second, even if you do allow plenty of room for the fibers to float around and are careful about not agitating them, loose fibers can get terribly tangled up in a dyebath. Short fibers clump into dense wads, and long fibers entwine and snarl. Both of these problems, the puffiness and the tangling, are partially remedied by enclosing the fibers in nylon stockings or netting. The dyed liquid can move in and out through the mesh, but the fibers are kept in order.

On the other hand, dyeing woven fabric or even finished garments is a possibility. This is "piece" dyeing. I have a friend who weaves lengths of cloth, sews up several different blouses or skirts, and then dyes each garment a different color when she is done. You can do this with fabric or with sewn or knitted garments, if they weigh less than a pound or so, and will fit into your dyepot. To dye piece goods evenly, you must lift, turn, readjust, and stir them frequently. Keep rearranging the material so that all parts are exposed to the dye, and don't leave the fabric to soak in the dyepot. If left in one position for too long, blotches of darker and lighter colors will develop. Remember that different natural fibers do not absorb dyes in the same way, and that synthetic fibers usually do not absorb plant dyes at all. For uniform results, dye only those fabrics or goods that are all the same fiber — for example, pure wool, cotton or silk.

For many dyers, the easiest and most reliable approach is to dye yarn, which can be either purchased or handspun. Yarn is easier to handle than loose fibers or finished goods. Make it into skeins, putting only one to four ounces of yarn in a skein. Tie the two ends together, leaving a tail that you'll be able to find later. Use short pieces of cotton string to make figure-eight "security ties" at three or four places around the skeins. These ties are important; they prevent tangling in the dyepot. Leave them loose enough, though, for dye to penetrate the yarn fully.

Dyeing Wool. Wool is the most popular fiber among home dyers. Most books about using dyes from plants are oriented towards dyeing wool. Check the references at the end of this chapter for more information — you'll find a fascinating variety of approaches to the subject.

• Wool dyes readily, because the fibers are made up from protein molecules in a way that provides plenty of active sites that can interact with other kinds of substances. This makes it easy to achieve good color saturation and produce rich or dark shades.

• Wool must be cleaned of all dirt and grease before dyeing. Raw fleece, or yarn spun "in the grease", in particular, must be scoured (see chapter 4) and well-rinsed. Clean wool should be soaked in plain water for half an hour or so before mordanting or dyeing, in order to relax and expand the fibers.

• It doesn't hurt wool to simmer it, or even to boil it a little, but it does hurt it to go abruptly from cold to hot water or vice versa. Heat a dyepot slowly, allowing a half hour or more for it to reach simmering temperature. After dyeing, you can leave the wool in the dyebath to cool off gradually, or remove it to successively cooler rinse waters. Rapid temperature changes can damage the texture of the fibers, weaken them, and cause matting.

• Wool dissolves into shreds in strong alkaline solutions. Be careful about adding lye soap, ammonia or washing soda to wool dyebaths! If the pH is higher than 9.0 to 9.5, the wool will be weakened and damaged. On the other hand, acid dye solutions work very well on wool, as it tolerates exposure to acids as strong as pH 3.0 to 3.5. It's a good precaution to monitor the acidity/alkalinity of dyebaths by using pH test paper.

There are many ways to proceed with mordanting wool. It can be done before, during or after the dyeing; mordants can be used singly or combined; acids, bases, salts, and other dyebath additives can be used in combination with metallic mordants. All of this provides plenty of room for experimentation, and you'll want to read more about it in other sources. Here are basic guidelines for premordanting wool:

• Use a big dyepot and allow at least four gallons of water per pound of wool.

• For one pound of wool, measure one of the following mordanting choices: four tablespoons of alum plus four teaspoons of cream of tartar; or one tablespoon of chrome; or two tablespoons of copper; or two tablespoons of iron; or two teaspoons of tin.

• Dissolve the measured amount of mordant in a cup of boiling water (add chemical to water, and not the reverse), add it to the pot full of warm water, and stir well.

• Add the wetted wool, heat slowly to a simmer, and simmer for an hour. Set the pot off the heat and let it cool for several hours until it is lukewarm. Remove the wool and rinse well, then dye the wool immediately or dry it to store for future use.

Dyeing Silk.

Silk fibers absorb dye eagerly. Naturally dyed silk can be delightfully brilliant and lustrous. All of the dyes that work well on wool will also work on silk. There are just a few precautions to observe in handling silk.

• The silk must be thoroughly clean before you begin, and raw silk must be degummed. Purchased yarns and fabrics are usually clean and ready to dye, but handspun yarns and handwoven fabrics should be washed to remove any dust or oils. To relax and prepare the fibers, soak the silk in tepid water for an hour or so before beginning the dyeing process.

• Use plenty of water in a large kettle — at least four gallons per pound of silk. Don't wad a lot of fibers into a small vessel, or the dyeing will be uneven. Silk fibers seem to expand when wet, and this makes it all the more important to provide enough room. While dyeing, stir or turn the fibers (gently!) to be sure all portions are evenly exposed.

• Allow plenty of time for heating and cooling the dyebath solution. Hasty temperature changes are shocking to the fibers. Putting cold silk into a hot dyebath, or taking it out of a hot dyebath into cold rinse water, or even exposing it to cool air temperatures, sets wrinkles into place, and you don't want that! Start by putting the silk into tepid water, and heat it to a simmer over a period of an hour or more. After simmering, leave the fibers in the dyebath to cool naturally, even if this takes all day or overnight. Then rinse again in tepid water.

• Simmering at 180° F is hot enough to mordant and dye silk. Bubbly, boiling water is too hot and causes damage. The silk loses its luster, yarns get irreversibly tangled, and fabrics get incurable wrinkles. Note that several dyes, including annatto, indigo, madder and safflower, can be applied at temperatures much lower than boiling.

• Be careful about alkalinity. Strong bases dissolve silk. Do not soak or simmer silk in a solution with pH higher than 9.0 to 9.5. As for wool, acids are okay. A vinegar rinse usually improves the luster and feel of silk.

• Silk is mordanted like wool, but smaller quantities of mordant chemicals are required. Allow three tablespoons of alum and three teaspoons of cream of tartar; or two teaspoons of chrome; or four teaspoons of copper; or one and one-half teaspoons of tin per pound of silk fibers. Iron is not usually recommended for silk, as it can damage the fine fibers.

Dyeing Cotton, Flax, Ramie, and Other Plant Fibers. Cotton, flax, ramie and other plant fibers are composed mostly of cellulose, which is a compound that is quite chemically inert. Cellulose molecules are pretty much all tied up with themselves and have few sites available for interaction with other kinds of molecules, such as pigments. Manufacturers of modern synthetic dyes for cotton have found ways of getting cellulose molecules to open up and interact, so we now have plenty of brightly colored cotton clothing and household fabrics. But traditionally, and for the dyer who uses dyes from plants, dyeing cotton and other plant fibers has been much more challenging than dyeing wool and other animal fibers.

• Before dyeing, the plant fibers must be both very clean and very wet. Raw cotton and flax, for example, should be simmered for an hour in soapy water with one tablespoon of washing soda added per gallon of water. The soap removes any waxes, oils or residues from the surfaces of the fibers. The washing soda strengthens the fibers and makes them more receptive to the dye pigments. Plant fibers float on the surface when you first put them in water and aren't thoroughly wet until they sink of their own accord to the bottom. When wet, they are ready to dye.

• Some dyestuffs will dye plant fibers directly, without mordants. These include the indigo pigment, from indigo, dyer's knotweed, and woad; the yellow and red pigments from safflower; and the orange pigment from annatto. The following will all dye plant fibers directly to some extent, but may fade badly with light and washing: the Hopi dye sunflower, maize, and beans; pokeberry and other berries; weld; and walnut hulls.

• Don't be in a hurry when dyeing plant fibers. It doesn't hurt them a bit to soak for hours, or even days, in a dyebath. Allow plenty of time for the dye to penetrate.

• Regarding pH, plant fibers are the opposite of animal fibers. Alkaline solutions do not harm plant fibers, but strongly acidic solutions can weaken flax, jute, and other stem fibers. Gentle boiling for an hour or so does not hurt plant fibers. Rapid temperature changes are okay, too.

Plant fibers can be mordanted as animal fibers are, with salts of tin, chrome, iron, and copper. But because these salts do not react much with cellulose, the effect may be disappointing. Usually, the best results are obtained by mordanting with a combination of alum and tannic acid. A three-step process is recommended for cotton, flax, ramie, or other plant fibers. To mordant one pound of plant fibers, make up two solutions:

• Mix one-half cup of alum and two tablespoons of washing soda with four gallons of water in one pan.

• Make four gallons of tannic acid solution by simmering several ounces of sumac leaves or other natural sources of tannins. Or add two tablespoons of tannic acid powder to four gallons of water.

Put the fibers in the alum solution, heat and simmer for an hour, then set aside to cool for several hours. Rinse the fibers, put them in the tannic acid solution, heat and simmer for an hour, then let them cool for several hours. Rinse again and put the fibers back into the alum solution. Soak without heating for several hours, then take the wet fibers and proceed with dyeing. This isn't as much trouble as it sounds, and it gives good results.

DYE PLANTS TO KNOW AND GROW

There are so many potential dye plants that I had to leave out many more than I could put in this collection. It was hard to choose, but I tried to include dye plants of historic significance, plants that are interesting to grow, and/or plants that are reliable to use. A few fit all three requirements!

Alkanet

Borage family. Alkanet (*Anchusa tinctoria* or *Alkanna tinctoria*) is a perennial herb native to southern Europe whose root bark yields a reddish dye. Alkanet and alkanna are English forms of the Spanish name alcanna, which is derived from the Arabic "al hinna", which likens alkanet to henna.[4] This

---

4. Henna (*Lawsonia inermis*) is a shrub native to dry hillsides in the Middle East. Since biblical days, it has been planted in ornamental hedges. Henna bushes have small

ancient comparison between alkanet and henna was based on their uses and properties as dyes and cosmetics; their pigments are similar in chemical structure, although the plants themselves are totally unrelated. The red pigment from alkanet, alkannin, was used by the Egyptians and Greeks to make "red" wine, to color oil and butter, to stain wood, and especially as a lip stain and rouge. The generic name *Anchusa* comes from the Greek word for face paint, or skin paint, referring to its use as a cosmetic. Historical records refer to alkanet as a dyestuff for wool as well, used in Europe and the colonial United States.

I'm partial to red, so I started looking around for alkanet seeds or plants a few years ago, thinking I'd grow myself a good, big supply. Well, that's harder than it sounds. In the first place, when I compared references, I discovered there is considerable confusion on the identity and properties of alkanet. This is characteristic of borage family plants; it's easy to lump them together as a group of sprawling perennial herbs with hairy, grayish leaves and one-sided clusters of flowers in clear forget-me-not blue and other colors. They all look alike, although some horticultural varieties have more and bigger flowers. On the basis of its aboveground parts, true alkanet, *A. tinctoria*, is just one species out of many, nothing noteworthy about it.

Having red roots, however, is a different story. Several authors have suggested that the roots of any species in the genus *Anchusa* will provide a red dye. Even though I'm usually skeptical of comments like that, I could never find a source for seeds or plants of the true alkanet (*A. tinctoria*), so I've tried raising *A. officinalis* and *A. azurea* instead. After growing the plants and digging them up, my skepticism was confirmed. Nothing red at first sight, no red after soaking in various solutions, apparently no red at all. Shucks. Now, it may be that soil, climate, or other environmental factors are involved, but my guess is that having red roots is a genetic trait. And this is an important point. A plant species that is "closely related to" another is not "the same as" the other. They may be similar in many ways, but different in the very one that matters.

Well, what if you turn to a dye supplier and purchase alkanet roots imported from Europe? The red pigment, alkannin, is difficult to extract. It will dissolve in alcohol, such as rubbing alcohol, and then you can dilute that with water. Or it will dissolve in alkaline solutions, made by adding a tea-

---

clusters of white, pinkish or yellowish flowers, like crape myrtles. These flowers have a delicious fragrance and were a favorite of the prophet Muhammad. Henna leaves were perhaps the first form of fingernail polish and hair dye, and were also used as a skin paint. No mordant is needed; dried, powdered leaves are mixed with water and spread on the hands or head until the desired amount of color has been absorbed. Henna-dyed hair is a rather startling shade of reddish orange and quite shiny. Henna is a substantive dye that will give yellows and oranges on unmordanted wools and silks.

spoon of ammonia or washing soda to a gallon of water, but this changes the red to a bluish shade. Add alum-mordanted wool and heat the dyebath to about 150° F — do not boil — for an hour. This will give lavender and purple shades. Soak the dyed wool in a vinegar-water solution to obtain more of a red color. Alkanet dyes fade with light and washing.

Annatto

Bixa family. Also called arnatto, roucou, urucu and achiote, annatto *(Bixa orellana)* is a large shrub or small tree native to Central and South America. Annatto usually grows ten to fifteen feet tall, but can reach thirty feet. It has large, heart-shaped leaves with a papery texture and clusters of rosy pink flowers about two inches across. Following the flowers, bunches of bright scarlet or maroon pods develop, the size of peach pits and covered with bristles or soft spines. When ripe, these burr-like pods open to reveal three or four dozen small seeds with red, sticky pulp. This pulp is the source of a reddish orange dye. Annatto is an attractive tree, planted in hedges and door-yards throughout the tropics. It grows quickly, beginning to bear within five years. A mature tree can produce a five-hundred-pound crop of pods a year. Annatto can be grown in a container, set outside in the summer, and wintered in a greenhouse or indoors. It is normally propagated by seeds, which germinate in two or three weeks in warm soil.

Annatto attracted the attention of early explorers when they found some Indians in South America using it as a body paint. Talk about *red* men! No doubt it produced quite a striking effect. Seeds were sent back to Europe throughout the 1700s and 1800s. As a textile dye, annatto came in second behind another New World dye discovery, cochineal, and never caught up with madder or brazilwood either. However, because annatto is nontoxic and is readily absorbed into fats and oils, it is quite desirable as a food coloring. It is used to color butter, margarine and cheese in the United States and as a special flavoring and coloring ingredient in Mexican and Central American cuisine. The seeds are sold under the name achiote in many Latin grocery stores and markets.

Annatto seeds are the size of match heads. They have a waxy texture and are rather fragrant. Native Americans, who used them to make body paint, went to a lot of trouble to get the seeds out and make a paste of the pulp. Fortunately, all that work isn't necessary for modern dyers. Expect an ounce of seeds to dye two or three ounces of alum-mordanted wool or silk to a bright reddish orange. To use, cover the seeds with water and simmer for half an hour or more at about 150° F. Add the fibers and simmer with the seeds for another hour, then leave to cool overnight. Remove and rinse the fibers. The color is relatively fast to light and washing. Annatto also dyes cotton; the bright orange immediately fades to a medium shade but seems to stabilize there.

Chamomile and Some Other Composites

Composite family. Several common herbs, garden flowers and wild flowers in the composite family can be used as dye sources. In most cases, the flowers are used to produce yellow or gold shades on wool, but sometimes the whole plant can be used to make greenish golds. Some of the same pigments are present, in varying proportions, in several of these plants. Most are reliable sources of dyes, regardless of the soil or growing season, but large quantities of plant material may be needed to achieve good color saturation on the fibers.

Dyer's chamomile, or golden marguerite *(Anthemis tinctoria*, preferably *A. tinctoria* var. *kelwayi)*, is a bushy, herbaceous perennial but can be raised as an annual since it grows quickly from seed to flower in the first season. It has ferny dissected foliage that is pleasantly or pungently fragrant, depending on your taste. The foliage is prone to wilt during even moderately hot and dry weather and invariably provokes the question, "What's wrong with this plant?" The daisy-like, yellow flowers produce yellows, golds and tans on mordanted wool, but large quantities are required. Use at least a quart of fresh blooms per ounce of wool to get intense shades. Other chamomiles also can be used for dyeing, including the herb chamomile *(A. nobilis)*, which is used to make a soothing hot tea, and the fetid chamomile, stinkweed, or dog fennel *(A. cotula)*, which is quite weedy.

Tansy *(Tanacetum vulgare)*, discussed in chapter 4, gives shades of yellow and yellow-green. Both leaves and flowers can be used, fresh or dried, with alum or other mordants. A simmering dyebath of tansy is quite strong-scented, so work where there is plenty of ventilation and fresh air. Goldenrod *(Solidago* spp.) is a native North American perennial wildflower that also gives good yellows and greenish yellows on wool. Goldenrod is often included in wildflower gardens and provides a good show of bloom in the fall. Contrary to folklore, goldenrod pollen does not cause hay fever. Gather tansy or goldenrod flowers just as they open for the clearest yellow dyes, or use the whole plants throughout the summer for mustard and olive shades.

Other garden flowers that give yellow, gold and orange dyes include marigolds *(Tagetes* spp.), dahlias *(Dahlia* spp.), and zinnias *(Zinnia* spp.). These are all popular for flower beds and are easily raised from seed or purchased plants. Pick off the flowers as they pass their prime, cover with water in the dye kettle, and simmer for half an hour or so. The simmered flowers look quite bleached after the pigments have dissolved into the dyebath. Using different colors of flowers doesn't seem to make much difference in the dyeing, but different mordants do have quite an effect. Chrome and tin give especially vivid shades. The composite flower dyes work much better on wool than on plant fibers.

Coreopsis and Cosmos: More Composites

Composite family. Several species of annual and perennial plants native to sunny, dry sites in North America bear long-stemmed, golden yellow to rusty orange or reddish flower heads that are rich in dye. Although the native wildflowers can be harvested in some areas, the plants are easy to grow and welcome in any garden. One of the best annual dye plants, available from many seed catalogs, is the dyer's coreopsis (*Calliopsis tinctoria*, also sold as *Coreopsis tinctoria*, although taxonomists prefer to distinguish the annual species of *Calliopsis* from the perennial species of *Coreopsis*). Just as good for dyeing are two garden varieties of cosmos (*Cosmos sulphureus*), "Diablo" and "Sunny Red".

Either coreopsis or cosmos can be started indoors a few weeks before last frost for transplanting, or sown directly where they are to grow. Transplant or thin to a spacing of six inches or so once seedlings are a few inches high. Any ordinary garden soil will do, but the plants need full sun to flower freely. They are quite tolerant of heat and drought but also grow well in cool moist weather. The young plants grow quickly with dull-colored, thin stringy leaves that look quite weedy. At eight to twelve weeks, though, the plants blaze into bloom and from July through fall each plant bears hundreds of flowers. Everyone who visits your garden during the blooming season will ask what kind of plants they are and will want to have some seeds. Gather a few ripe seed heads each year to share and to save for your next crop. Both coreopsis and cosmos self-seed regularly, and you can keep a patch going for years in the same location with little maintenance.

To collect flowers for dyeing, cut or snap off the flower heads, either at full bloom or just as the petals begin to fade. Even if you pick the plants completely bare, more flowers will open in a few days; in fact, the duration and amount of blooming is increased by harvesting the flowers before they begin to set seed. The flowers can be used fresh for dyeing, dried on a rack or in a paper bag, or stuffed into a plastic bag and frozen for storage. Soak and simmer the flowers to make a dyebath. Chalcones, the most important class of pigments in these flowers, are sensitive to pH and change from yellowish color in acid solution to reddish color in alkaline or basic solution. Adding a teaspoon of ammonia or a pinch of washing soda to the dyebath will bring out the red color quite visibly. A concentrated dyebath made from coreopsis or cosmos flowers will give a good reddish orange on chrome-mordanted wool, or yellows and golds with alum or tin mordants. Two dozen plants pro-

Coreopsis, *Calliopsis tinctoria*

duce enough flowers in a season to dye a pound of wool or silk. Coreopsis and cosmos give disappointing results on cotton, flax, and other plant fibers.

Dyer's Broom

Legume family. Dyer's broom *(Genista tinctoria)* also is called dyer's greenwood, woadwaxen or woodwaxen. It is a perennial shrub native to Eurasia, widespread in Britain, and established in parts of New England and the eastern United States. Branching near the ground, it produces erect green stems up to three feet tall, rather sparsely furnished with slender leaflets about one inch long. The stems and even the leaflets are more or less evergreen in mild climates. From midsummer to fall, dense spikes of bright yellow, pea-like flowers tip each branch, giving a bright and cheerful effect. Dyer's broom is one of many species of *Genista*, and the related genera *Cytisus* and *Spartium*, that are called "broom". In general, these are hardy, tough long-lasting shrubs with lots of stems, occasional thorns, meager foliage, and profuse, often fragrant flowers. Broom plants were used to make brooms in England and Europe and are mentioned frequently in heraldry, folk medicine and folklore. Scotch broom *(Cytisus scoparius)* is often used like dyer's broom to make a yellow dye.

Dyer's broom grows best in dry sandy soil and requires full sun. It is hardy in all regions of the United States except the northern Great Plains. Once established, it thrives if left in the same spot but doesn't transplant well. It grows well as a foundation planting along the south wall of a house, or on a south-facing bank. Ordinary dyer's broom and special varieties, with dwarf growth habit and with double flowers, are available from nurseries, or they can be started from seed. The little seeds are very hard-shelled, so to prepare them for sowing, you must either file them with sandpaper or soak them overnight in warm water. After such treatment, they germinate in two to three weeks. Sow them in the garden where they are to grow or start them in pots. The plants grow slowly at first and may only reach six inches in height the first year. But they should flower the second summer and can be harvested for years after that. In my experience, they are immune to insects and diseases but very attractive to rabbits.

For dyeing, gather stems when the plants are in bloom. The plants will grow and flower over a longer season if you keep pruning them, so don't hesitate to harvest often. Stems can be dried for future use; colonial American dyers imported barrels of dried, powdered dyer's broom. Allow about a gallon of chopped stems for four ounces of wool or other fibers. Simmer the stems for an hour and strain off the dyebath for use. Dyer's broom contains the same yellow pigment as weld (luteolin) which gives a yellow that is clear and extremely fast. It is especially nice on wool and silk and also dyes cotton

Dyer's broom, *Genista tinctoria*

and linen. The names dyer's greenwood and woadwaxen have to do with the use of dyer's broom in sequence with woad to obtain a good green; dyed first yellow and then blue, or vice versa, wool and other fibers end up a nice green.

Dye Woods and Barks

The wood and bark from several different tropical and temperate trees can be used as dye sources. Some of these dyestuffs can be purchased from dye suppliers, and others can be collected from prunings or from felled trees. Historically, the dye woods were considered to be rich sources of pigment that were relatively inexpensive, easy to process and store, and convenient to use.

Brazilwood is the name for a wood which produces a red dye; it can be obtained from several tropical trees in the legume family. By 1250 or so, Europeans were familiar with a form of brazilwood *(Caesalpinia sappan)* used as a red dye in India and Malaya. They called the wood and the dye "bresil" or "brasil", comparing the color to glowing coals. When explorers discovered forests of similar trees *(C. echinata)* in the New World in the early 1500s, they named the region Brazil. *C. sappan,* called sappan, grows to only twenty feet tall and has showy clusters of brightly colored, fragrant flowers. *C. echinata,* called brazilwood, grows to one hundred feet tall and is sawn into lumber called pernambuco. Both trees have mimosa-like compound leaves. Young plants, raised from seed, can be kept in containers for a few years as indoor or greenhouse trees. Chips of brazilwood are available from dye suppliers. They should be soaked overnight and then simmered to produce a dye for cotton or wool. Various mordants give different shades of red, of good but not excellent fastness.

Cutch is an extract made from the wood of an acacia *(Acacia catechu),* a small, thorny leguminous tree native to India and Burma. When the trees are cut, the bark is stripped off and the wood is chopped up and put in great cauldrons of water to boil. The sap dissolves into the solution, and the extract becomes concentrated as the water evaporates. When cool, the cutch extract solidifies and hardens into a brown mass, not unlike very dark amber. Cutch dissolves readily in warm water. As a dye, cutch produces very fast shades of brown, drab and tan on cotton or wool, mordanted with copper. Khaki cloth is cotton dyed with cutch. The wood, bark and pods of many other species of acacias are also rich in tannins and have been used as dyes in Africa, Australia, and other countries where they grow.

Fustic is a yellow wood that produces a range of yellow, gold and greenish dyes. Fustic has been used since the Middle Ages. The name was first applied to the wood of the European smoke tree *(Cotinus coggygria),* a relative of sumacs, with feathery masses of flowers that look like puffs of smoke. With the discovery of the New World, other woods called fustic were introduced to dyers. One was the American smoke tree *(C. obovatus)* native to mountainous regions in the southern states. Smoke trees grow only ten to fifteen tall and make very nice ornamental shrubs. They are hardy throughout the United States; many nurseries sell them. For some curious reason, wood from the European and American smoke trees has been called "young" fustic. Meanwhile, "old" fustic refers to wood from either of two tropical trees in the mulberry family *(Morus tinctoria* or *Chlorophora tinctoria)*, which are harvested from forests in the West Indies. Fustic wood is bright yellow when fresh, but darkens to a gold color after it has been exposed to air. It is cut or ground into chips for use in dyeing. Old fustic can be purchased from dye suppliers; new fustic can be obtained by pruning the twigs from smoke trees planted as ornamentals. In practice, the woods from these different trees can be used interchangeably; all contain similar pigments. They have been widely used on wool and cotton, with various mordants to achieve different shades. Fustic dyes are not fast to light, and may either fade or darken over time, so the net effect is unpredictable.

Logwood *(Haemotoxylum campechianum)* is a small, thorny leguminous tree native to Central America. It grows quickly from seed; the trees can be cut down and harvested after ten years. Rather than having a single cylindrical trunk, a logwood tree looks like a bundle of sticks that have fused and grown together. The trunks are cut into ten-foot-long sections for export. The reddish-colored heartwood is cut or chopped into small chips for use in dyeing. The best colors are obtained from damp logwood sawdust that has fermented for a few weeks. Chips of wood should be soaked for a few days at least. Haematein, the pigment in logwood, dissolves better in an alkaline solution, so add a little ammonia or washing soda to the water. After fermenting or soaking, the wood should be simmered at 150° F for a half hour to produce the dye liquor. Logwood can be used on wool or silk which has been mordanted before or during the dyeing, and on premordanted plant fibers. It produces a range of blues and purples, and, with an iron mordant, a good gray or black. The fastness of logwood is quite dependent on its reaction with mordants, and is best with chrome and iron; its colors are rather short-lived on plant fibers mordanted with alum and tannins.

Osage orange *(Maclura pomifera)* is also known as hedge apple, horse apple, and bois d'arc (French for bow wood, for its use by the Osage Indians in making bows). It is a medium-size, thorny tree in the mulberry family, native to Oklahoma and Texas but planted in hedgerows as a natural fence throughout the eastern states. It's easy to locate osage oranges in the fall, when chartreuse, grapefruit-size fruits litter the ground under the trees. The wood of the tree is so hard and dense that it dulls tool edges, but it is a remarkable bright orange color that darkens with age to a rich copper tone.

Chips, shavings or sawdust, soaked and simmered, produce yellow, gold and orange shades on premordanted wool, silk and cotton.

Quercitron is the inner bark, not the wood, of the black oak or yellow-bark oak *(Quercus velutina,* formerly called *Q. tinctoria).*[5] Black oak is a common tree on upland soils in the eastern United States. It grows to sixty feet or taller and has deeply lobed leaves that turn bright red in fall. Black oak trees are difficult to transplant, so they are not commonly found in nurseries, but they grow readily from acorns and do make attractive landscape specimens. The inner bark of the black oak is a bright yellow-orange color and can be used fresh or dried to produce yellow dyes. It is a rich source of dye pigment, equal to ten times its weight in weld or four times its weight in fustic. The bark was used as a dyestuff by American colonists. It was introduced to British and European dyers in 1785 by the famous dyer Edward Bancroft. Bancroft and other dyers patented methods for extracting the pure yellow pigment, quercitin, from the raw bark, quercitron. Quercitron is used with alum and other mordants on wool and cotton, alone, or in sequence with other dyes, such as madder or indigo.

Oak bark is rich in tannins, which give a tan dye (the words tannin and tan both derive from old European names for oaks) that darkens with time and exposure. Barks from hemlock, alder, redwood, apple, cherry, maple, willow and other trees also contain tannins and pigments. Collect bark from pruned-off limbs or felled trees. Chip and soak these barks for several days before simmering, and they will yield rosy tan, beige and brown dyes.

Hopi Dye Seed Crops

The Hopi Indians in Arizona have traditionally dyed basketry materials and cotton or wool yarns with dyes made from the seeds of special crops. These include a dye sunflower *(Helianthus annuus),* a dye bean *(Phaseolus vulgaris),* and a dye corn or maize *(Zea mays).* In each case, the dry, ripe seeds (technically fruits, in the cases of sunflower and maize) were soaked or simmered to produce a range of red, purple and blue dyes. Colton's book *Hopi Dyes,* based on field work done in the 1930s and 1940s, discusses these dye plants at great length. The Hopis selected and maintained these special varieties for generations, but in recent years life has changed on the reservation. Few dyers still grow and use these crops, and they may be near extinction. The seeds are hard to come by. I've chosen to call attention to them, as they are unique and significant dye plants. If modern dyers take an interest, perhaps seeds will be made available to the public.[6]

---

5. There is a *Quercus nigra,* but it is the water oak, a different tree.
6. In 1979 and 1980, when I was doing the research for my master's degree, I grew large

Hopi dye sunflowers look like regular garden sunflowers, but have hints of purple color on their stems and on the disk flowers in the center of each head. The ray flowers are yellow, as usual. The center head may be five inches or so in diameter, and the side heads on all the branches will be somewhat smaller. The plants grow to six feet or taller. Sunflowers are easy to grow in any sunny spot with average garden soil. Sown direct where they are to grow, they will flower within sixty to ninety days. Once the yellow ray flowers wilt and begin to drop off, fasten a large paper bag over each head to prevent birds and squirrels from feasting on them. Different varieties of sunflowers cross readily as they are visited by pollinating insects, so to prevent hybridization between dye sunflowers and regular sunflowers, they should be planted in separate fields or gardens at least a quarter mile apart. Even with this precaution, it is wise to save only the best-colored seeds for replanting the next crop. Note: What we call sunflower "seeds" are really single-seeded dry fruits, or "achenes". The pigmentation of dye sunflowers is in the hull of the fruit; the actual seeds are grayish green like ordinary sunflower seeds.

Perhaps other kinds of dry beans with very dark seeds are worth trying as a dye source, but the Hopis recognize a particular blue-black bean as their dye bean. Women in southern Mexico and Guatemala have used a small black bean to dye their rebozos, or shawls. Dye beans, like other common beans grown for drying, need a rather long growing season with not too much rain towards the end. It usually takes ninety days or more for beans to mature fully and dry on the vines. Grow beans in a row in the garden, in full sun. You can pick individual pods as they dry out, or pull and thresh the whole vines, depending on the quantity you're faced with. A fifteen-foot row of bean plants may yield between one and four quarts of dry beans. Bean plants are self-pollinating, so there's little crossing between varieties, and it's okay to grow different kinds of beans in the same garden. In dye beans, the pigmentation is in the seed coat, or "testa"; the cotyledons inside the bean are the normal creamy white color.

Like many people, I used to think there were four kinds of corn: sweet corn, popcorn, field corn, and Indian corn. Indian corn, to me, was any kind of corn with colored kernels. Well, it's not that simple. Any particular tribe is likely to have selected several different varieties, distinguished by the hardness of the kernels, kernel color, earliness or lateness of bearing, flavor, sweetness or starchiness, plant vigor, tolerance of cold and drought, and many other attributes. There are zillions of kinds of Indian corn and each kind is recognized and valued by the people who depend on it. Hopi dye corn

crops of Hopi blue flour corn, which at that time was a very little-known plant. In the years since I wrote my thesis, Hopi blue flour corn has been written up in several major newspapers, in *National Geographic*, and other magazines, and has been featured on PBS-TV shows. You just never know when a crop is going to rise from obscurity to fame! So maybe these dye seed crops are next in line.

is a variety with purple-colored husks and cobs, and dark, almost black, kernels. The Hopis are not the only group to have used corn for dyeing; George Washington reported that Indians in New England used a dark-kerneled corn for dyeing in the late 1700s; the noted corn authority Paul Weatherwax recorded the use of dye corns in Peru in the 1950s.

Corn kernels have an inner, starchy endosperm, which can be white or yellow, capped with a layer of dense outer cells that may be colorless, yellow, brown, blue or red. The color of these cells, in what is called the aleurone layer, is what we see in most colored corn. But most colored corn is useless for dyeing. Corn kernels are enclosed in a parchment-like hull called the pericarp, which is usually transparent, but can be colored. Only if the pericarp is richly pigmented can corn kernels be used as a dye source; plants that produce dark-colored pericarps nearly always have colored cobs and husks, too. These can also be used in dyeing.

I won't tell you how to grow corn; if you haven't done it before, surely you know someone who has. But in trying to grow and maintain a unique variety of corn, there are two important things you should know. First, you should plant at least fifty or more seeds, chosen from different ears, to have a patch big enough for good pollination. And plant the seeds in a block of several rows, not a single long row. Second, to maintain the purity of a variety, it must be separated from other kinds of corn by at least a quarter mile (better yet, even further), or you must plant varieties that release their pollen at different times during the season. Fresh corn silk accepts any pollen that drifts by, just like a dog in heat draws all the mutts in the neighborhood. So if you ever get a chance to grow special dye corn, take steps to isolate it.

For use, dye sunflowers, beans or corn are put in a pan with cold water, brought to a boil, then simmered only until the hulls or seed coats split. This takes about twenty minutes to a half hour. As soon as the starchy insides of the seeds are exposed, strain off the liquid for a dyebath. (Add fresh water to the drained seeds and go ahead cooking them so you can eat them.) Add alum-mordanted wool or alum/tannic acid-mordanted cotton to the dyebath, heat to between 120° and 150° F. for an hour or two, and leave the fibers to soak overnight before rinsing. I have had better results with using the dye seeds to color cotton, flax, basketry materials and other plant fiber products than to color wool; the dye seems better suited to cellulose than protein fibers. The pigments in these seeds are compounds called anthocyanins. They change color at different pH levels, turning more red in acidic and more blue in basic solutions. Anthocyanins are likely to fade in bright light or if washed in hot soapy water, but their fastness is improved by mordanting. Colton devotes several pages in *Hopi Dyes* to her observations on using these seeds, and I recommend her work to other curious dyers.

Madder

Madder family. Madder *(Rubia tinctorum,* is a herbaceous perennial native to the Mediterranean region, the Middle East, and Asia Minor. Its fleshy roots are unique as a dyestuff; they are a concentrated source of a good red dye. Each spring new shoots grow out from the roots. The four-sided stems climb weakly or merely sprawl on the ground, reaching up to six or eight feet in length in a season's growth. Narrow pointed leaves about two inches long grow in whorls of four to eight every few inches along the stems. Both leaves and stems are somewhat prickly. Tiny greenish yellow star flowers develop in clusters at the tips of the stems in midsummer, but they do not reliably set fruit. When produced, the fruits are firm, spherical berries less than a quarter inch in diameter which turn black when they are mature and contain one or two seeds.

Holland was the major madder-producing region in medieval Europe, but a lot was also grown and used in the East. Both areas exported large quantities of madder to dyers around Europe and Britain, who used it with an alum mordant to dye wool red. The famous red coats of British soldiers were dyed with madder, and civilians wore red clothes too. But the acme of madder usage was Turkey red dyeing. Developed in India and transmitted through Turkey and eventually to France, Turkey red dyeing was a complex system of fixing a particularly brilliant red on cotton yarns and fabrics. Turkey red dyeing involved treating the cotton with a series of different substances to improve the absorption and retention of the dye, and purifying the madder itself to isolate the clear red pigment and remove the dull brown component. Alternately soaked and dried over a period of several weeks, the yarn or cloth was treated with rancid oils, washing soda, cow or sheep dung, gallnuts or sumac, alum, ox blood, potash, and incidentally, madder.

Turkey red was imbued with ritual and full of magical and mystical overtones, especially in the East.[7] Perhaps the notorious complexity and secrecy of the process was a marketing ploy to enhance the value of the product! Fabrics dyed with Turkey red were desirable and expensive, and the Eastern dyers maintained a monopoly on their production for centuries.

---

7. I have some questions about those fellows who did Turkey red dyeing. One ingredient that's often mentioned as part of the process is the seeds of Syrian rue *(Peganum harmala)*, a shrubby plant native to the Middle Eastern region where the dyeing was done. These seeds may or may not contain much red pigment, but they have been notorious since biblical days as a narcotic that induces a sense of gaiety and euphoria and releases inhibitions. You'd expect the Turkey red dyers to nibble a Syrian rue seed now and then, to relieve the boredom of smearing cloth with sheep dung and ox blood. But eating the seeds could undermine the rules about keeping the secrets of how the dyeing process was carried out! People under the influence of the drug tend to talk freely; the Germans in World War II used an extract from Syrian rue seeds as a "truth serum" to loosen the tongues of political prisoners.

Madder, *Rubia tinctorum*

Attempts in France to simulate the process met with failure until the 1700s, when immigrant Greek workers revealed the trade secrets. The French later introduced variations of Turkey red dyeing that improved the brilliance and fastness of the color. They simplified the process and reduced the cost. In the 1800s, printed bandannas, gingham tablecloths, and other machine-woven cotton goods dyed with madder were relatively inexpensive and very popular in Europe and North America.

The red pigment in madder roots is called alizarin; also present are smaller quantities of yellow and brown pigments. Alizarin is related in chemical structure to the red pigments in the insect dyes kermes and cochineal and to the litmus pigments from certain lichens. The German chemist Heinrich Caro patented a method for producing synthetic alizarin on June 25, 1869; on June 26, 1869, William Perkin (of "mauve" fame) independently patented his method. Caro sold Perkin the rights of production, and within years madder crops were abandoned.

A century has passed, and now some of us want to grow madder again. Madder prefers full sun and well-drained soil. It is hardy to cold and immune to pests and diseases. It grows readily from seeds, but they are rarely available. Several nurseries do sell madder plants, propagated by division. If you buy one or two to start with, you can multiply your own stock. Work up a circle of soil at least a yard wide and put a single madder plant in the center, or, if you have the space, prepare a madder bed. A patch five feet by eight feet will hold a dozen plants. Prepare the bed by digging at least twelve to eighteen inches deep, and add generous quantities of compost, manure, lime and potash. Madder roots produce much more alizarin pigment if the plants are grown in fertile, well-limed soil. The plants will be growing there for three years, so go the extra mile and do a really thorough job of soil preparation. You might want to edge the bed with boards or blocks, to hold the fluffed-up soil in position.

Set plants eighteen to twenty-four inches apart and keep the bed weeded. When the madder tops get a foot tall, pull them down to the ground and draw a little soil over the middle of the stems so that they will form new roots. Madder tops are floppy and tend to sprawl over the ground naturally, and you want to encourage this spreading. Several times a season for the first, second and third years, keep covering sections of the stems with soil. This will make a solid bed full of plants and roots. In spring of the third year, pull out a few plants to start a new bed in fresh soil. That fall, use a digging fork and work through the soil to harvest all the madder roots. You'll recognize them as soon as you turn up the first forkful; they're thick as straws, and bright red. A dozen plants can provide at least six pounds of fresh roots, which shrink down to two or three pounds of dried roots. Madder stems and leaves, best gathered in the fall or winter, can also be used for dyeing. In addition to alizarin, the tops contain purpurin pigments that add desirable brilliance and luster to the dyed goods. The tops can be used as livestock fodder, but cows and goats that feed on madder give red milk and orange butter!

It's important to do a thorough job of washing fresh madder roots — this not only removes the loose soil but also flushes away some of the yellow and brown pigments which would otherwise dull the red dye. If you want to use the fresh roots right away, chop them into tiny bits, mash them with a mortar and pestle, or use a blender to grind them into paste. To store them for future use, spread the clean roots on a screen to dry; when they are crisp and brittle, put them away in jars or bags. Historically, madder roots were dug, washed, and dried outdoors or in sheds, then ground into fine powder and stored in casks. Aging and fermenting were considered to improve the quality and increase the intensity of the red dye, but if the powder absorbed too much moisture it would spoil. Today, most purchased and homegrown madder is stored as dry roots. Recipes for using madder begin with the instruction, "Crush the roots to a fine powder". Crush, indeed. You might as well try to crush a handful of pencils. Try snapping the dry roots into short lengths and milling them in a blender. Crushing dry roots is a much harder job than grinding fresh roots, but the more finely the madder is prepared, the more dye is released.

Different batches of roots vary in strength, but usually about eight ounces of fresh or dried madder root will dye a pound of fibers. Old recipes for using madder call for a dyebath of hard water, but you get the same effect by adding some lime or chalk dust. Or you can add a tablespoon of baking soda per gallon of water. The point is that the pigment alizarin dissolves better in alkaline solutions. Soak the ground roots in water overnight or all day long. After soaking, heat the dyebath very slowly to between 140° and 160° F. This is important, so use a thermometer to be sure. (If the dyebath gets too hot, you get browns instead of reds.) Strain out the roots, which you can soak and reuse for paler shades. Add wet, premordanted wool or silk to the dyebath, simmer at 140° to 160° F for an hour, then let the fibers cool in the dyebath. Rinse in soapy water, then in clear water. On wool and silk, madder gives several different shades of red with different mordants and additives. Multiple immersions are needed to dye premordanted cotton, flax, or other plant fibers with madder. Divide the dyebath in halves or thirds and use one portion at a time. Simmer the fibers for an hour at 120° to 160° F, cool, rinse, and dry. Rewet the fibers and simmer them again in a fresh pot of the dye, repeating as needed until the color is rich and dark. You can reuse madder dyebaths, if color remains, to make paler shades of coral, pink and beige. Use madder tops for dyeing as you use the roots, allowing four pounds of fresh or two pounds of dried tops per pound of fibers.

Several plants related to madder also produce red dyes. In Southeast Asia, dyers use the roots of mungeet, or munjista *(Rubia cordifolia)*, which is shrubbier than common madder. They also use roots from several species of *Morinda*, which are small to medium-size trees in the madder family. European and North American dyers who lack access to madder often turn to "wild madder" and other species of bedstraws *(Galium* spp.*)* as substitutes. Four species are frequently used as substitutes: the European introductions wild madder *(G. mollugo)*, lady's bedstraw *(G. vernum)*, and dyer's bedstraw *(G. tinctorium)*, and the native American species northern bedstraw *(G. boreale)*. Bedstraws have lax stems and whorled leaves like madder, but their roots are much wirier, harder to dig and clean, and less endowed with pigment. I've tried bedstraws several times out of curiosity, but I'd advise you to spend your digging energy on preparing a nice bed of madder.

Pokeberry and Other Berries

Pokeberry family. Pokeberry or pokeweed *(Phytolacca americana*, syn. *P. decandra)* is a stout perennial herb native to eastern North America. Most species of *Phytolacca* are fast-growing tropical trees and shrubs. In southern California, plants of *P. dioica*, for example, have grown to forty feet tall with a trunk three feet in diameter in less than five years! Do you get the hint that pokeweed is vigorous? New plants sprout from bird-dispersed seeds and get busy right away producing a massive root system. After that is established, pokeweeds endure for decades, sending several stout trunks eight to ten feet tall each summer. Each reddish-colored stalk bears smooth alternate leaves up to six inches long, and four- to six-inch-long spikes of small white flowers. By fall, the branches sag with clusters of juicy purple-skinned berries. In many parts of the country, pokeweed grows as a roadside weed, so you can have all the berries you want just by going out to get them. If you aren't prejudiced against it as a common weed, you might see it as a strikingly handsome plant, richly colored, and graceful in form and silhouette. As a garden plant, pokeweed makes quite a specimen. You can control its spread by gathering all the ripe berries each fall before the birds do. It is easily raised from seed or division, obtained from the wild or from herb suppliers.

Pokeweed is a more-or-less poisonous plant; the root is more poisonous and the berries are much less so. The root of pokeweed is used in folk remedies, although it is narcotic in small doses and toxic in large doses. The young shoots, gathered like asparagus in spring, are rendered edible by boiling at least twice and discarding the cooking water. Euell Gibbons thought quite highly of poke greens, and many other wild food enthusiasts enjoy them also. Children should be warned that eating the raw berries causes

Pokeweed, *Phytolacca americana*

vomiting and diarrhea, but I honestly think they taste too awful to swallow. If cooked, the berries are harmless; there are recipes for pokeberry pie.

To use pokeberries as a dye, gather them after they have fully ripened. I wear rubber gloves and use pruning shears to clip off whole clusters and toss them into a plastic pail. Get as many as you can, or pick until you get tired. You can plan to dye two to four ounces of wool with each gallon of berries. Use a potato masher to smush down on the berries and break the skins so the juice can flow. Then mix a solution of one part vinegar to four parts water and pour in enough to cover the berries. Let this sit around in a warm place for a day or two to ferment, then strain off the liquid for dyeing. Discard the residue in a sealed container; all those thousands of seeds would quickly sprout in a compost pile! Prepare clean wool for dyeing by simmering it for an hour in a one-to-four part vinegar-water solution. (Metallic mordants are optional but not required.) Remove the wool, add the pokeberry liquid to the simmering solution, and put the wool back into the dyebath. Do not bring it to a boil, but keep it at about 160° F for an hour, then set it aside to cool overnight. Remove the wool and let it dry thoroughly. A few days later, soak it briefly and rinse it several times with clear water, then dry again. This gives a brilliant crimson red. Subsequent dyebaths give softer shades. The red is lost if the solution is boiled, and becomes bluish gray if the pH is raised above 7. Many dyers malign pokeberry dye because it is not fast to bright sunlight (it fades quickly to a disappointing tan) or to frequent washing in hot soapy water. But in my experience, pokeweed colors last for years in home interiors, out of the sun; and they do not fade if washed in mild soap-plant solutions.

Other berries and fruits, both wild and cultivated, could be considered here, including elderberries *(Sambucus canadensis* and *S. nigra)*, blackberries and raspberries *(Rubus* spp.), blueberries and huckleberries *(Vaccinium* spp.), currants *(Ribes* spp.), grapes *(Vitis* spp.), plums and cherries *(Prunus* spp.), prickly pears *(Opuntia* spp.), mulberries *(Morus* spp.), and many more. To get rich colors, rather large quantities are required, as much as two gallons or more of berries per pound of wool. With blueberries, you might well choose to make pie! But if you have any mulberries, you have too many mulberries, so dyeing might be a way to use some up. For all berries, a preliminary soaking in vinegar-water solution helps to develop the color of the juice. Fermenting for several days is recommended, if your family is tolerant of such processes. Berry dyebaths should be simmered, not boiled. In acid solutions, they will dye wool or other fibers directly, without mordants, although premordanting with alum or tin, or postmordanting with iron or copper solutions, may help fix the colors. Most of the red, purple and blue pigments in the berries are in the class of compounds called anthocyanins. As dyestuffs, they are rather unstable and are subject to change as they react with oxygen in the air, particularly in the presence of sunlight. This usually leads to a faded appearance. Most are altered by washing in alkaline solutions and turn rather drab. However, for items that won't be exposed to sun or frequently washed, the berry dyes are satisfactory.

Safflower

Composite family. Safflower *(Carthamus tinctorius)* is a dye of ancient usage in its own right, but it carries the epithet "bastard saffron" because of its use as a substitute for, or adulterant of, that more expensive dyestuff, true saffron.[8] Apparently native to central Asia, safflower has been cultivated as a dye plant in China, Japan, India and Egypt. Now it is raised primarily as an oil crop. Safflower seed oil is used as salad oil, in margarine, and to make paints and soaps. Safflower is an annual plant that grows from seed to maturity in about four months. It looks like a thistle, with spiny leaves and stems. Safflower plants grow three to four feet tall, with several branches arising from a basal rosette, and bear a dozen or more flower heads. Again like a thistle, the round flower heads are protected by chaffy, prickly bracts, with a golden tuft of florets poking up through the center. The petals of these florets contain two distinct pigments, a yellow and a red. Both can be used for dyeing, but the red has always been more highly valued. Long ago, safflower red was used to dye cotton tapes used to tie legal documents together. Since then, there has been "red tape".

Safflower is easy to grow in the garden. Sow the seeds, which look like small sunflower seeds, directly in the ground in early to mid spring. If you just want to have a look at the plant, sow a few seeds in a circle and grow an ornamental clump. For a crop, plant seeds a few inches apart in two or three parallel rows at about six- to eight-inch intervals, and thin seedlings to eight-inch spacing as they begin to grow. Safflower requires full sun but isn't fussy about soil. The plants grow quickly when the weather gets warm. When they begin to bloom, go down the row every few days and pluck the fresh petals from the flower heads. Each daily harvest will yield only a small pile of petals, but gradually your supply will add up. Japanese dyers wash the petals and fold them between straw mats to ferment for a few days, then form little flower patties, or cakes, and dry them in the sun. I just spread them to dry on

---

8. True saffron *(Crocus sativus)* has always been a luxury item, used more as a spice and a cosmetic than a textile dye. It consists of tiny orange stigmas (over 60,000 to the pound) collected from the blossoms of a fall-flowering crocus grown in Europe and the Middle East. You can plant saffron corms and grow them like regular crocus plants. Get out your tweezers and kneeling pad when the flowers open and make a really special saffron-flavored dish for dinner, but don't waste it on coloring fibers.

a sheet of newspaper and keep the loose, dried petals in a storage jar. Keep picking the flowers for several weeks until the plants are exhausted.

You can use safflowers to make a yellow dye as you would use chamomile or marigolds — cover with water, simmer, strain, add your wool. But you can have your yellow and get red, too, if you go through a two-step process. Allow equal weights of petals and fibers for this. First, you extract the yellow pigment. Put the petals in a cotton bag, or wrap them up in an old handkerchief like a hobo's sack. Put this in a pan and cover with cold water, adding a cup of vinegar per gallon of water (a mild acid solution). Soak a few hours or overnight, then squeeze and wring the bag to press out all the yellow juice. This can be simmered and used as a dyebath, with or without mordants, on wool, silk and cotton.

Now rinse the petals in fresh water until all the yellow is washed out, wring the bag, and put it into a different pan. To extract the red pigment, cover with cold water, this time adding a tablespoon of washing soda or ammonia per gallon of water (a mild alkaline solution). After a few hours, squeeze and wring the bag to press out all the reddish brown juice, and throw the petals away. Now add vinegar to neutralize the dyebath. There will be bubbles, and the color will turn from reddish brown to bright red. You can use this dyebath at room temperature or heat it to 150° F, but do not boil it. Try solar dyeing — put fibers and dyebath in a big glass jar and set it in a sunny place. Leave the fibers in the dyebath several hours. Finally, fix the dye, to make it more fast and permanent, by soaking the fibers for a half hour in a solution containing equal parts of vinegar and water. Rinse and dry. Safflower dyes give lovely shades of rose, red and orange on silks and cottons, but the colors do fade as they are exposed to light, air and washings.

Sumac

Cashew family. Over a hundred species of sumac shrubs and trees grow in Africa, Eurasia and North America, and many have been used by dyers. A few are recommended for landscape use. The cutleaf sumac (*Rhus typhina* var. *laciniata*) grows ten to thirty feet tall, with multiple trunks that pose a bold, sculptural silhouette in winter. The pinnately compound leaves are quite large, up to three feet long, and finely divided into delicate, lacy leaflets. From late summer through winter, each stem is topped with a large cluster of red berries that are attractive to birds. The shining sumac (*Rhus copallina*) is a smaller shrub, growing to fifteen feet tall, with very glossy leaves and curious wings, or flaps, on the main leafstalks. It also produces large berry clusters. The dwarf and spreading fragrant sumac (*Rhus aromatica*) is good for covering banks or as a low border hedge. Its flowers and fruits are small, but its three-part leaves are fragrant. These sumacs are all very hardy to cold, tolerant of drought or poor soil, and easy to grow. Their leaves turn to vivid shades of pink, crimson and magenta in the fall. Several nurseries offer sumac plants, and they transplant readily. They also grow from seed; fresh seed sown in the fall will germinate the next spring. Related to sumac are smoke trees, or young fustic *(Cotinus coggygria* and *C. obovatus)*, whose twigs give yellow dyes. Smoke trees are also hardy shrubs, easy to grow, and are particularly attractive in midsummer when the blooms puff out like smoke. Also related are the various rash-causing species of poison sumac, poison ivy and poison oak *(Toxicodendron* spp.). The poisonous species all produce white or gray berries; the harmless species have red berries. If you are sensitive to poison ivy, learn to recognize the leaves and stems in all seasons.

In contrast with the vivid reds of the leaves and berries in fall, sumac gives disappointingly dull colors on wool — shades of tan, beige and gray with different mordants. The colors are very fast, but they start out looking like other dyes do after they have faded. Whatever red pigments sumac has aren't concentrated or stable enough to serve well as dyes. But sumac is valuable to dyers for another reason. The leaves, twigs and berries contain tannins; dried leaves have concentrations as high as ten to twenty-five percent. Some dyers add a handful of sumac leaves to dyebaths of other plants to improve the fastless of the color when dyeing wool. Sumac tannins are especially useful as mordants in the alum/tannic-acid/alum sequence outlined for cotton, flax, and other plant fibers. In the summer, use a pound of fresh leaves to make tannic acid solution for a pound of fibers; in the winter, use just eight ounces of dried leaves.

Walnuts

Walnut family. The leaves and hulls of Persian walnuts *(Juglans regia)*, black walnuts *(J. nigra)*, and butternuts *(J. cinerea)* provide good, fast brown dyes for both animal and plant fibers. Persian walnuts are native to Asia Minor but were brought to Europe by the ancient Romans, who used the dye and ate the nuts. Early American colonists quickly recognized the dye value (and food value!) of black walnuts and butternuts, both native to eastern North America. All are hardy deciduous trees that yield attractive and valuable dark-colored heartwood lumber. Late to leaf out in spring, the trees bear catkins of greenish flowers on the bare branches. The pinnately compound leaves cast a light shade during the summer, but then walnut trees are the first to drop their leaves in fall. The woody-shelled nuts themselves, familiar flavorings for ice cream and baked goods, grow inside leathery husks, or hulls.

Husks are by-products of walnut trees. Most folks complain about them and fuss about the mess, but dyers clutch after walnut hulls and stockpile

Walnut, *Juglans nigra*

them for year-round use. Black walnut hulls yield the most pigment and give the darkest colors, but Persian walnut and butternut hulls are also valuable. Butternut hulls were used to dye the uniforms of Confederate soldiers during the Civil War. All can be dried for storage or used fresh. A few dozen nut hulls will dye several ounces of fibers. Soak the hulls overnight and simmer for an hour to get medium browns, then strain off the dyebath for use. Prolonged soaking gives more intense colors, as does longer boiling, but both processes give off strong odors! The leaves, used fresh during their brief season or gathered in the fall and dried, also yield tans and browns. Juglone, the brown pigment in walnuts, is a substantive dye, which means it doesn't require the use of a mordant. However, a wider variety of shades is obtained if different mordants are used. With an iron mordant, walnut hulls give a dark brown that is almost black.

Although it is a good brown dye, the compound juglone has a poor reputation among gardeners. Exuded from the roots, in addition to leaching from the leaves and hulls, juglone is said to inhibit the growth of other plants, particularly tomatoes. I think the condemnation of walnut trees has been exaggerated; there is very little scientific evidence for negative effects of juglone. At any rate, our present home is surrounded by big old walnut trees, and the plants in my gardens are decidedly uninhibited!

Many nurseries sell young nut trees. The grafted varieties Thomas black walnut and Carpathian Persian walnut are especially desirable, as they start to bear when only five years old and yield large, tasty nuts with thin shells that are easy to crack. Growing your own can save you money. Keeping in mind how much walnut meats cost at the grocery store, can you believe that a major national herb distributor sells dried walnut leaves at $2.20 an ounce and dried walnut hulls at $1.35 an ounce? Better yet, if you have land to spare, plant black walnuts as a timber crop for your grandchildren. Good-size logs are worth over $1000 apiece.

Weld

Mignonette family. Weld, or dyer's mignonette *(Reseda luteola)*, is a hardy winter annual or biennial plant that produces a clear yellow dye. Weld grows wild in the thin soil over chalky lime rocks in England, Europe, and the Mediterranean region. It has been collected from the wild and cultivated for its dye since the days of the Romans, who used weld to dye the tunics of the vestal virgins. Flower gardeners will be familiar with weld's relative, the fragrant mignonette *(R. odorata)*, desirable for its fragrance, but weak as a dye plant. In the first season, weld grows into flat rosettes of shiny leaves with crinkly edges. Single plants may reach ten to fifteen inches in diameter. The leaves overwinter, and slender flower stalks quickly develop in the

Weld, *Reseda tinctoria*

second season. They reach two to four feet long and bear numerous tiny yellowish blooms. I say long, not tall, because usually the stalks droop and spread rather than stand erect.

To sow weld, scatter seeds in a shallow furrow and cover one-half inch deep. It helps to lay a board over the row to keep the soil from drying out before the seeds have sprouted — check from time to time and take the board off when the seedlings emerge. The seeds can be sown in early spring or in August, but normally will not flower until the second year. Weld also can be started indoors in early spring and grown in pots for six to eight weeks. Transplant with care because weld has a taproot. Space the plants about a foot apart in the garden. The first-year rosettes make a nice border along the edge of a bed. When you want to do some dyeing, go along and pick a few leaves from each plant, like you gather leaf lettuce. Weld takes full sun and prefers alkaline soil. If allowed to go to seed in the garden, a weld plant will generate thousands of seedlings that crop up in all corners and that have to be thinned out like weeds. Let it go, if you can accept the consequences, but if you prefer to keep control over what grows where, harvest weld when it flowers to keep it from spreading.

The yellow pigment luteolin is present in all above-ground parts of the weld plant (and also in dyer's broom). Traditionally, the whole plant is cut after the flower stalk has elongated and is used fresh or dried, but I have had fine results using just the leaves. The plant material should be chopped up and simmered in soft water to make the dyebath. Strain the plants from the dyebath and let the dyebath sit awhile. You will see something unusual. Unlike most dyebaths, where the colored molecules stay in solution in the water, the pigment in a weld dyebath settles to the bottom of the pan. The solution separates into clear water and yellow sediment. Hint: Stir frequently to keep the pigment dispersed when dyeing with weld!

Old dye books offer the criticism that large quantities of weld must be used to produce rich colors, but that statement is based on comparison with fustic and quercitron, two very concentrated sources of yellow pigment. By comparison with dyer's chamomile, marigold, goldenrod, or other composite plants, weld is a very rich dye source. The purity of weld's yellows is unequaled by any other herbaceous plant. Three or four weld plants gathered as large rosettes, or a single weld plant that has just come into bloom, will dye one-half pound of wool to a good, rich shade. On alum-mordanted wool, weld produces a pure lemon yellow that is extremely fast to light. Weld gives shades of gold, olive and green with other mordants on wool or silk and gives a good yellow on cotton. In all cases, the colors are best if the dyebath is made slightly alkaline by adding a small amount of lime or washing soda. Fibers dyed yellow with weld can be subsequently top-dyed with indigo or woad to achieve good greens; this two-step process has been used since the Middle Ages to create the colors Lincoln green and Saxon green.

INDIGO

Most famous of all the dyes from plants, indigo is in a class by itself. Many people have written about indigo — the legends of its ancient discovery, its value as a commercial dyestuff, the botany and identification of plants which produce it, the chemistry and techniques of indigo dyeing, and the timeless appeal of blue-dyed fabrics. If this section whets your interest, look to the suggested references at the end of this chapter.

The Chemistry of Indigo

The German chemist von Baeyer, working in the late 1800s, was fascinated with indigo and described its chemistry in utter detail. Because indigo has been studied so thoroughly, and because it is unique among plant dye pigments, I'll include a little survey of indigo chemistry here. To begin with, most higher plants produce a compound called indole (C_8H_7N), which is extremely volatile and has a very persistent odor. In very small quantities, or at a distance, indole is a desirable perfume; it adds the exotic overtones to jasmine flowers, orange blossoms and Madonna lilies. In excess, indole is the odor of putrefaction; it constitutes the disgusting stench of carrion and feces. Indole is a very reactive compound and readily combines into indole derivatives. One of these is indoleacetic acid, or auxin, a plant hormone with many functions. Auxin directs roots to grow down and shoots to grow up, bends stems towards light, regulates the development of lateral branches, initiates root formation on cuttings, and affects fruit maturation. Another indole derivative is the amino acid tryptophane, which we require in our diet and obtain from certain protein-rich foods. But digesting proteins releases indole to be excreted, and there's that smell again.

Indole is the precursor of indigo, via a few intermediate compounds. First an atom of oxygen is added to the indole molecule to produce indoxyl (C_8H_7NO), a yellowish crystalline compound that dissolves only in alkaline solutions and has a "fecal" odor. Who knows why plants make indoxyl? But some plants do, at certain times, and it is stored in their leaves. The amount present depends on the kind of plant, its stage of growth, and growing conditions (particularly temperature). In order to dissolve in the plant sap, indoxyl must combine with another substance. Usually it combines with the sugar glucose as a colorless, water-soluble compound called indican. Indican occurs in indigos of the genus *Indigofera*, in the dyer's knotweed (*Polygonum tinctorium*), in *Wrightia tinctoria*, and in *Marsdenia tinctoria*, *Lonchocarpus cyanescens* and *Strobilanthes flaccidifolius*. In woad (*Isatis tinctoria*), the indoxyl is combined with an acid to make a colorless, water-soluble compound called an ester.

Indigo, *Indigofera tinctoria*

Once leaves are cut from these plants, the indican or ester compounds are broken down, mostly by enzymes in the leaves themselves, and the indoxyl is released. This can happen in an hour or it can take several days, depending on the process used. If the leaves are being dried, the indoxyl stays in the mass of leaf tissue. If the leaves are being soaked, after the indican or ester compounds dissolve in the water, they break down and release the indoxyl there. Remember that indoxyl is insoluble in plain water; it will settle to the bottom of a container. If the water is made alkaline by adding some kind of base, the indoxyl makes a yellowish solution. As long as air is excluded, the indoxyl molecules just sit around. But within minutes of being exposed to the oxygen in the air, pairs of indoxyl molecules react and combine into single molecules of indigo ($C_{16}H_{10}N_2O_2$), also called indigotin. This is what you are waiting for, the blue stuff itself. It shows up in the drying leaves as they turn blue, and it shows up in the water if you stir it up to add air. If you dip yarn (or your hand, not an especially good idea) into the yellowish solution of indoxyl, it will turn blue after you pull it out into the air. This is the simplest way of applying an indigo dye from fresh plants.

What happens when indoxyl is transformed into indigo? Two molecules of indoxyl lose four atoms of hydrogen as they combine into a single molecule of indigo. Where do the four atoms of hydrogen go? They react with a single molecule of O_2 (two atoms), to form two molecules of good old H_2O, and you know what that is.

Once indigo has formed, it's a pretty stable compound: It doesn't react with anything in the air, it doesn't fade in sunlight, it isn't destroyed by boiling, it doesn't dissolve in soapy water. No wonder they use it to dye blue jeans! But the very stability of indigo means that it requires special handling as a dye pigment. In order to dye yarn or fabric, the pigment has to be uniformly dispersed in a dyebath. But indigo is insoluble and doesn't disperse in plain water. You can take a lump of prepared indigo and use it like a crayon to smear color onto a surface, but the stain will rub off again. And besides, it would be tedious to rub color onto thousands of yards of yarn. To dissolve indigo, you have to add a "reducing agent" to the water, something that will liberate some hydrogen from the H_2O. In the presence of excess free hydrogen, a molecule of blue indigo ($C_{16}H_{10}N_2O_2$) picks up two hydrogen atoms and turns into a molecule of leuco-indigo, or indigo white ($C_{16}H_{12}N_2O_2$), which is actually yellowish, not white. You might wonder why indigo doesn't take back four hydrogens and turn back into two molecules of indoxyl. Sometimes it probably does, to some extent. But anyway, indigo white will dissolve in water that is alkaline, making a dyebath. Anything dipped into this dyebath will get coated with indigo white, and as soon as you pull it out into the air, the indigo white will turn back into indigo blue. And that's how indigo is usually applied to fibers.

Indigo derived from plants is not pure. It includes small amounts of indigo isomers (the same atoms arranged into slightly different molecular structures), other plant pigments, and usually some sludge and organic debris. Depending on where it was grown and how it was processed, chunks, or grains, of natural indigo from *Indigofera* leaves contain between ten and fifty percent indigo blue. It may contain five to fifteen percent of the isomers indigo red and indigo brown; chemists say these pigments are worthless, but dyers think they add subtlety to the colors obtained with natural indigo dye. Synthetic indigo contains only the indigo blue isomer and is much more concentrated, as high as ninety to ninety-five percent pure. Molecules of natural indigo blue and synthetic indigo blue have the same structure. The difference between natural and synthetic indigos has to do with the nature of the impurities that are present and the concentration of the pigment in the product as it is sold. Likewise, the indigo blue pigment from one or another plant source is all the same. But extracts from different plants vary considerably in purity and strength, and this affects the colors that you end up with on the fibers you dye.[9]

Indigo-Bearing Plants To Know and Grow

Indigo Plants. Legume family. Indigo (*Indigofera* spp.) plants are perennial herbs or shrubs of the Old and New World tropics. Over three hundred species are known, many yielding the pigment indigo, but two of the most important are the Old World species *I. tinctoria* and the New World species *I. suffruticosa* (formerly called *I. anil*). These indigos grow three to six feet tall, with erect stems and few branches. They have compound leaves less than three inches long, with nine to seventeen oblong leaflets, all covered with fine, silky hairs. Indigo plants show an interesting behavior called "sleep movements": the leaves fold up and draw close to the stem at night, then unfold and spread out again at dawn. From midsummer to fall, slender clusters of tiny bronze flowers develop at the leaf axils and the ends of the branches. These develop into dry brown pods: about one-half inch long and curved in *I. suffruticosa*, and one inch or more long and straight in *I. tinctoria*. Most species of indigo are similar in growth form and foliage, but some have showier, fragrant flowers and are offered as ornamentals. All of the indigos are more or less tender to frost and grow reluctantly in cool weather. They thrive in hot, humid climates, growing best in fertile soil and full sun.

9. The relative yield of different indigo-bearing plants is often stated in simple terms, such as, "A pound of indigo is worth ten pounds of woad." These comparisons aren't very helpful in predicting how much dyeing you can do with plants that you grow. Pigment yield varies with the climate and growing season, the maturity of the plant, and the processing technique.

Dyers in India and Southeast Asia have used indigo *(I. tinctoria)* for thousands of years. Long ago, they developed a system for extracting and concentrating the pigment from the leaves of wild plants. They used it to dye cotton, primarily, and called it "nil", which led to the Arabic name *anil*, and eventually to "aniline" dyes. The Greeks and Romans, who imported cakes of the pigment, called it indicum, meaning product of India. This led to our name for it, "indigo". Familiar with the pigment, but unaware of its source, early European dyers considered it a product of the earth, perhaps a kind of stone. After all, lumps of pure indigo do seem like mineral substances, and they even develop a superficial, bronzy luster. In ancient Egypt, Greece and Rome, indigo was highly esteemed and put to various uses. It was used to dye fabric; ground up and mixed with clay to make cosmetics (eye shadow!), crayons, and paint; and applied to wounds and open sores as a medicinal treatment.

Marco Polo described how indigo was harvested and processed, based on his travels in Asia in the late 1200s, and established that it was derived from plants, not mined. In his day, some indigo from India was making its way to dyers in Venice, but most European dyers were using locally grown woad for their blues. In England, Germany and France, imported indigo did not replace domestic woad until the 1700s. Even then, the two were often combined or mixed in the dyebath, as the woad growers and processors stubbornly defended their product. Finally, when sea routes were developed and trade between East and West expanded, the increased supply and lowered cost of indigo made it irresistible to dyers.

Spanish explorers found indigo *(I. suffruticosa)* in the New World, too. Indians in Central and South America painted their bodies, dyed fabrics, and tinted clay for ceramic vessels with indigo. The Spanish, who were jealous of the profits that Dutch and Portuguese merchants were making on indigo imported from India, set up indigo production centers in Guatemala. The French followed, establishing plantations in their Caribbean colonies. The British (on whose empire the sun never set) cultivated indigo in both India and the West Indies. With an annual demand for hundreds of tons of concentrated indigo pigment, at prices much higher than most other crops, everyone wanted a share of the indigo trade.

Colonists made several attempts to produce indigo in Virginia, the Carolinas, Georgia, Florida and Louisiana; both by planting crops of *I. tinctoria* and *I. suffruticosa* and by gathering the native wild indigo *(Baptisia tinctoria)*. Most of these early American efforts were failures, usually because the growers lacked experience and the knowledge of how to properly handle the product. Only through the efforts of young Eliza Lucas (later Eliza Pinckney) did indigo become a valuable cash crop in South Carolina. From the time she was seventeen, Eliza managed the family's six-hundred-acre plantation on Wapoo Creek, six miles upstream from Charleston. She experimented with a variety of crops but was particularly determined to succeed with indigo; she used seeds her father sent from the West Indies. Eliza experienced problems growing and processing the crop the first few years, but by 1744 she was able to send six pounds of the blue pigment to be promoted in London, and she distributed seeds to her fellow planters in South Carolina. By 1770, the planters were exporting over a million pounds of indigo dye annually to Britain. But then came the American Revolution and the rise of cotton as a cash crop, and, consequently, indigo cultivation was abandoned by 1800.

There was a standard system for processing fresh indigo plants to extract and concentrate the dye. Every indigo grower had to have a set of vats and tanks and drying racks. For maximum pigment yield, the stems were cut just before the flowers opened, preferably during a spell of dry weather. Two or more crops of stems were cut each year from the same plants; the stems grew three or more feet tall each time. As soon as they were cut, the stems were carried from the fields and laid in a big vat, covered with water, and left to soak. The water darkened to a gold or olive color as the indican from the leaves dissolved and the indoxyl was released. After eight to twelve hours, depending on the temperature, all the indican had soaked out of the leaves into the water.[10] The colored liquid was drained into a lower vat, and the soggy stems were spread back on the fields as compost. Lime water was added, and the colored liquid was vigorously beaten to add air and convert the indoxyl to blue indigo. Beating continued until the head man, or "Indigo Maker", deemed that the conversion was complete. Then the vat was left alone. The indigo clumped into little specks and settled to the bottom of the vat like sludge. After a few days, the clear water was drawn off, and the residue of indigo was scooped into linen bags and hung to drip-dry. After it reached a pasty consistency, it was spread out on boards to dry and harden, and finally shaped into cakes or bricks. All that sounds like a lot of trouble, but it was the best way to reduce a bulky crop to a compact product. At best, a hundred pounds of green stems would yield only four ounces of indigo pigment. Farmers were pleased to produce sixty pounds of cake indigo per acre each year; this involved processing over twelve tons of fresh plants.

Good indigo was brightly colored and shiny, but the purity and quality of the cakes varied considerably, depending on the condition of the plants themselves and the skill of the Indigo Maker and his crew. The price dyers

---

10. This soaking process is usually referred to as fermentation. There is a chronic myth that fermentation somehow produces indigo pigment. That isn't so. All that's necessary is to get the leaves thoroughly wetted so that the indican can dissolve and break down to release indoxyl and glucose. The potential pigment is already in the leaves.

would pay for indigo cakes depended on how much dye they would yield; a pound of top-quality indigo would dye considerably more yarn or cloth than a pound of second-rate indigo. Using indigo to dye fibers required as much skill and judgment as growing and processing indigo; professional dyers took their trade very seriously. They recognized a whole series of different shades of blue, and also used indigo in combination with other dyes to obtain greens and purples. Dye books from the eighteenth and nineteenth centuries present various methods for using indigo, mostly by setting up an indigo vat. These vats were big, holding up to two thousand gallons of liquid. The liquid of choice was stale urine.[11] A vatful of urine was good for years of service – the dyer just kept adding more indigo from time to time. Woad, madder, bran, lime and ashes were also added to the vat at the dyer's discretion. The fermenting urine and other ingredients served as reducing agents to convert the insoluble indigo blue to indigo white and made the solution alkaline so the indigo white would dissolve. Regulating these processes was a tricky business. Dyers called their indigo vats "she" or "her". "Working" a vat required overnight vigils and constant watchfulness. When a vat was ready to use, a dyer would proceed to dye thirty, fifty, or a hundred pounds of wool. Home dyers did the same thing on a much smaller scale, maintaining a "blue pot" that held five or ten gallons and dyed a pound of fibers at a time.

Like me, you may be overwhelmed by quantities like twelve tons of indigo plants and two thousand gallons of urine. Instead, we'd like to grow a dozen or so plants and use them to dye a little yarn. Here's how. Both *I. tinctoria* and *I. suffruticosa* can be raised as annual crops in hot climates. They are very similar in growth and yield, but *I. suffruticosa* is more tolerant of cool weather. Choose a sunny location with good soil and prepare the ground for planting. When the soil has warmed up in late spring, soak the seeds in warm water overnight to soften the hard seed coat, then sow them one-half inch deep. Keep the bed weeded and thin the seedlings to stand twelve inches apart. They should grow vigorously and be ready to cut after ten to twelve weeks. It is possible to start seeds indoors and set out little plants, but be careful not to disturb the roots. Also, indigo plants are very vulnerable to cold air and cold soil. If they are chilled, they may stop growing and never get going again. Under favorable conditions, indigo is a hearty grower, but it doesn't recover well from little setbacks. In northern climates, it's possible to grow a few plants in containers. Start one plant in a six-inch pot or three in a twelve-inch pot. If you set them outside in summer and keep them in a south

11. Actually, urine is a very appropriate liquid to use in indigo dyeing. The urine of humans and other mammals contains a small amount of another form of indican – this one is indoxyl combined with sulfuric acid – and, by golly, it is readily converted into indigo blue pigment, just like indican derived from indigo plants. The indican excreted in urine is an end-product of protein digestion, just like the indole in feces.

window otherwise, they will grow in pots for a few years. Indigo is not susceptible to any particular insects or diseases, but is readily consumed by rabbits, deer, or livestock.

Old-time indigo growers cut the plants just as they were coming into bloom, and you should too, because that's when they yield the most pigment. For convenience, the old-timers cut and soaked the whole tops, but you can make a more concentrated solution if you strip off and use just the leaves. You can discard the stems, because they don't yield enough pigment to bother with.

Extract the indican in either of two ways:

• Pack the fresh leaves into a heat-resistant jar or container, fill it with tepid water, and put the lid on. Set this container in a kettle of water, like using a double boiler, and heat it to 160° F over two hours, then draw off the amber liquid.

• Pack the leaves into a plastic pail or garbage can, cover with water at 100° F, and seal the top with a layer of clear plastic wrap to exclude air. Set the container in the heat of the sun and leave it for twelve to twenty-four hours, then strain out the leaves.

Either way, the indican from the leaves is broken down to release indoxyl into the water. As this happens, a coppery iridescence appears on the surface of the liquid. The fresh solution can be stored for months at room temperature in plastic gallon jugs filled to the brim and tightly capped to exclude all air. Individual batches vary considerably, but the pigment extracted from a pound of fresh woad leaves should dye from two to four ounces of fibers; a pound of *Indigofera* or dyer's knotweed leaves will give enough pigment to dye four to eight ounces of fibers.

There's only a certain amount of indican in the leaves to start with, and once it has been extracted, you can throw them away. Gardening in Virginia, I found that the leaves from two dozen plants of *I. suffruticosa* were enough to dye two pounds of wool a rich navy blue color. Follow the general directions for using the fluid as a dyebath.

Woad. Mustard family. Woad *(Isatis tinctoria)* may have been the first plant cultivated for its pigment. Apparently native to the region once known as Assyria, woad has been grown and used in Europe and Britain, throughout Asia, in North Africa, and in parts of North and South America. Woad was by far the most widely used dyestuff in Europe for centuries, prior to the introduction of indigo from India in the 1600s. Then woad was used in combination with indigo for another century or so, but it fell out of use altogether after the discovery of synthetic indigo dye. Since the 1960s, dyers in Britain particularly have resurrected woad as an easy-to-grow and reliable source of

Woad, *Isatis tinctoria*

blue dye and have developed methods of using fresh woad to dye small quantities of fibers.

The genus *Isatis* includes about thirty annual, biennial, and perennial Old World herbs; more than one contain the indigo pigment. Dyer's woad *(I. tinctoria)* grows a rosette of oblong, slightly hairy, basal leaves in its first season. This rosette can be as small as six inches or as large as eighteen inches in diameter, depending on soil moisture and fertility. In mid to late spring of the second year, several stems shoot up two to three feet tall. Small leaves, with projecting "ears" at the base, clasp the upright stems. The plant bears abundant clusters of scentless, four-petaled yellow flowers which develop into purplish brown fruits. Each flat, papery fruit is about one-half inch long and contains a single seed. Dyer's woad is supposed to die after seeding, but sometimes it persists, if new sprouts develop from the base of the plant. Another species of woad *(I. glauca)* is a true perennial with larger, showier clusters of flowers. Its basal leaves are larger, smoother, and more grayish than those of dyer's woad, and its stem leaves do not have clasping bases. *I. glauca* is sometimes grown as an ornamental, but also can be used as a dye plant. A third species, *I. indigotina,* has been used for a blue dye in northern China but is not planted in North America.

The names woad and weld are often confused. The two plants have much in common, but they are definitely not synonymous. Woad gives a blue dye; weld gives a yellow dye. The name woad derives from the Anglo-Saxon "wad" or "waad". The Germanic names "weedt" or "weeda", originally applied to woad, may be the source of our term "weed". Woad is weedy: It produces a huge crop of seeds that are readily dispersed by the wind, it thrives in the disturbed soil of agricultural fields, and it grows rapidly and competes vigorously with other plants. In several areas, where it has been grown as a dye plant or, more commonly, as an ornamental, woad has become a weed problem. I have seen woad growing along roadsides in several states, but particularly in Virginia and the mountainous regions of the West. Some states list woad as a "noxious weed" that infests fields of hay and small grains. I'm not saying that you should be afraid that woad will take over your garden, but I strongly encourage anyone who grows woad as a dye plant to cut down the flower stems before the fruits ripen and to leave only enough to collect seeds for the next crop. The seeds from one woad plant will supply you and your friends for several seasons.

The pigment yield from woad plants grown in fertile, well-cultivated soil is much, much greater than that from plants found along a roadside. I grow woad in a row in the vegetable garden, in soil well-enriched with compost and manure, and deeply tilled. Woad appreciates full sun and grows more rank if there is plenty of moisture from rain or irrigation. I've not had any trouble growing woad, although it can be affected by the same pests and diseases that affect cole crops in general. Woad can be sown in the garden in late September or October to overwinter as small seedlings. Space plants twelve to fifteen inches apart. They will develop good root systems the first winter, produce leaves throughout the summer, and then flower the following spring. Or, woad can be started in very early spring for harvest the first year. I sow a few dozen seeds indoors in February or March and set them out at the same time I'm planting cauliflower, broccoli and cabbage; or I sow the seeds outdoors about the time I plant peas. With such an early start, woad grows quickly, and I can begin picking leaves in June or July.

Historically, dyeing with woad was not a do-it-yourself project. Woad processing was a medieval industry, on the scale of thousands of tons annually. From the thirteenth to sixteenth centuries, particularly in parts of Germany and England where the soil and climate were favorable, acres and acres of woad were planted. Growing woad was one occupation; using it as a dyestuff was another. The problem was processing the leaves so that they could be stored and transported. Simple drying, unfortunately, does not preserve the pigment, so more elaborate methods were developed. First, the freshly cut leaves were ground between rollers or grindstones into a mushy pulp, and then the pulp was spread out in a uniform layer on the ground or the floor of a shed to dry. A blackish crust formed as the woad dried. Workers were fussy about sealing up any cracks or crevices in the crust, lest worms or maggots should generate in the woad and spoil it (everyone believed in spontaneous generation in those days). After it had dried a week or two, the woad was kneaded into a uniform mix and then carefully shaped by hand into balls or loaves. The size and weight of these balls was regulated by the woad processing guilds; they usually contained two handfuls of woad and weighed over a pound. The balls were spread on racks to dry, outdoors in good weather or inside during rainy spells. After two to four weeks, the balls were judged ready if they had a good violet color and an agreeable smell when broken apart. The next step took place in a special barn, called a couching house, which had a smooth brick floor and brick-lined walls. Wagonloads of woad balls were ground into powder, which was heaped three or four feet thick on the barn floor and then sprinkled with water. Of course, the woad began to heat up and ferment right away and released clouds of stinking vapors. The unlucky fellows whose lot it was to be woad workers had to turn the whole pile each day, shoveling and pitching it from one side to the other so that the mass would ferment evenly. After several weeks, the pile shrank to about one-tenth its original bulk. The dark residue that remained was packaged into bales weighing one hundred-fifty to two hundred pounds and sold as woad dye.

Centuries have passed since woad was grown and processed on that scale. Chances are that you just have a few plants, or a few dozen plants, and want to dye yarn for a skirt or a sweater. You can try making woad balls, etc., but I recommend using an extract from the fresh leaves, gathered during the warm months between June and October when they contain the most pigment. The yield of dye is much less in the winter and when the plants start to flower and go to seed. You can harvest several times over the summer.

Under good conditions, each woad plant may produce half a pound of leaves over a season. Two pounds of woad leaves will give enough dye for four ounces of fibers. Go down the row and pluck handfuls of leaves from around the bottom of each plant, and more new leaves will grow up through the center. Promptly chop or shred the fresh leaves and stuff them into a container with a tight-fitting lid. Pour almost-boiling water over the leaves to scald them. Fill the container to overflowing and add the lid to exclude air. After forty-five minutes or so, remove the leaves and squeeze them dry. The indoxyl will have been extracted into the reddish brown fluid in the container. Now follow the general directions for dyeing with fresh indigo. For more information on using woad, check Jill Godwin's *A Dyer's Manual*. She explains different methods and hints at many variations. Based on years of research and experimentation, her directions are clear and reliable.

Dyer's Knotweed. Buckwheat family. *Polygonum tinctorium* is often called indigo or Japanese indigo, but to avoid confusion with the *Indigofera* indigos, I'll side with those who call it dyer's knotweed. Dyer's knotweed is a vigorous annual plant native to Southeast Asia and used as a source of indigo pigment in Japan, Indonesia and other countries. Although European and American dye books from the 1800s described the plant and acknowledged its value, it wasn't cultivated outside the Orient until recently. Dorothy Miller's book *Indigo from Seed to Dye* is about *Polygonum tinctorium*. She introduced the plant to dyers in the United States.

Dyer's knotweed is just one of dozens of species in the genus *Polygonum*; others possibly yield indigo also, but in minute quantities. It has smooth, pinkish stems with swollen joints (like knots in a string, hence the name knotweed), and branches readily into a full, bushy plant. The simple alternate leaves are less than one inch wide by three to four inches long, dark green on top, and grayish blue on the bottom. In late summer and fall, slender clusters of tiny pink flowers grow on the end of each branch. As in indigo, the compound indican is present in the leaves but not the stems or other parts of dyer's knotweed.

It's easy to grow a crop. I'd compare growing dyer's knotweed to growing green peppers; they require similar conditions. Plant a patch in fertile soil with full sun. You can sow the pinhead-size seeds one-half inch deep in rows eighteen inches apart when the soil is warm. Thin seedlings to twelve inches apart. For an earlier start, sow seeds indoors six weeks before the last frost.

Grow the seedlings in separate pots; they transplant with ease. Set the little plants out after frost and watch 'em grow. Although dyer's knotweed can survive drought, poor soil and crowding, it's much more productive if you supply plenty of water and nutrients, and space the plants at least a foot apart. From seed sown in mid spring, single plants can spread to fill a square yard by late summer, but they die after the first killing frost in fall. Dyer's knotweed will grow faster and yield more pigment in hot humid climates than in cool or dry regions, but it is adaptable enough to be worth trying almost anywhere in the United States. You can harvest leaves from mid or late August until frost.

Pick or strip the green leaves off the stems, starting from the base of the plant. Grown under favorable conditions, six dyer's knotweed plants can produce more than two pounds of leaves over a season. The pigment content declines after the plants are covered with flowers. Watch carefully as the flowers fade from pink to tan. When the seeds enlarge inside the chaffy bracts, pick them off to dry and save. Watch out for birds and rodents which eat the seeds. Dyer's knotweed must self-sow in nature, but it doesn't sprout up like a weed each spring in my garden. If you want to save seeds, but anticipate a hard frost before Halloween, root a few tip cuttings from the plants and grow them in a pot indoors to flower and bear seeds on a sunny windowsill.

Historically, dyer's knotweed has been processed in either of two ways. For export from Java, it was treated like indigo. The plant tops were cut off at the ground before flowering and soaked in large vats. The colored liquid was drained off, aerated, and treated with lime water. Blue indigo pigment settled to the bottom, and the sediment was dried and shaped into bricks. The pigment obtained in this way was equivalent in both quantity and quality to that extracted from indigo. For domestic use in Japan, however, dyer's knotweed was treated like woad. Whole stems, or just the stripped-off leaves, were spread to dry in the sun, rewet and piled in a layer or a heap to ferment for about three months, and occasionally stirred to keep the mass uniformly blended. Once bacteria had reduced the leaves to a dark blue paste, it was shaped into balls or patties and dried for storage. Later the balls were ground up and mixed in a vat of water with small amounts of bran and lime or ash added. After a few weeks' fermenting, the dyebath was ready to use.

The simplest way to use fresh dyer's knotweed at home is to gather a quantity of fresh leaves and pack as many as you can into a container. A pound of dyer's knotweed leaves will dye from four to six ounces of fibers. Cover with warm water and put the lid on. As with indigo leaves, you can either heat the vessel to 160° F over two hours' time or let it sit in the hot sun for a day. When the leaves look coppery instead of green and the surface of the water is iridescent, pour off the colored fluid to use for dyeing and follow the general directions. I recommend Dorothy Miller's and Jill Goodwin's books for information on other ways to process your dyer's knotweed crop.

Other Indigo-Bearing Plants. In addition to the *Indigofera* indigos, woad and dyer's knotweed, there are several other plants which yield indigo. A few are perennial legumes native to North America. Some species of *Baptisia* are called wild indigos. *B. tinctoria*, at one time identified as *Sophora tinctoria*, was mentioned as an indigo source in records from South Carolina and Virginia in the 1700s and 1800s. Once widespread in the eastern United States, it is now found occasionally in sandy soil along roadsides or in forest openings. It has greenish stems, tiny leaflets, and bears numerous yellow pea-like flowers. *B. pendula* is often grown in perennial gardens and has larger leaflets and azure flowers. Several other species grow in nature and also are valued as choice garden ornamentals to plant in full sun. They are slow for the first year or two from seed, but then live for decades. All develop into impressive clumps, sending up dozens of stalks each spring and dying back in the fall. They have quite large root systems and don't transplant well, so decide ahead of time where to establish a plant. If grown in hot weather and harvested just before flowering, wild indigo leaves will contain indigo, but in much lower concentrations than *Indigofera* leaves. And with *B. tinctoria* in particular, because the foliage is sparse, it takes a lot of plants to yield a pound of leaves. I tried it once and could only pluck two pounds of leaves from a small pickup truckload of stems – and that was enough to dye one ounce of yarn a pale bluish gray. Another plant, bastard or false indigo, *Amorpha fruticosa*, also may produce a little bit of indigo pigment, but not enough to fuss with. Both wild and false indigos have various insecticidal and medicinal properties. They may be more useful for those purposes than they are as dye plants.

A "dye oleander", identified as *Nerium tinctorium*, is occasionally included in lists of indigo-bearing plants written by dyers. Note: The common ornamental oleander *(N. oleander)* does *not* contain indigo. I have looked and looked for references to *N. tinctorium* in botanical literature, trying to learn more about it, but could never find it listed. I was ready to declare it a mythical plant, a vegetable unicorn. In looking for it, though, I found another plant, and gradually, through correspondence with the American Oleander Society and the Botanic Survey of India, I've found some interesting information. *N. tinctorium* is a name that botanists no longer use; very few of them ever did use it. The plant once called *N. tinctorium* is properly known as *Wrightia tinctoria*, and like common oleander, is in the dogbane family. In contemporary botanical literature, it is not assigned a common name in English. I think the name "dye oleander" has caused enough confusion already and should be laid to rest, so I'll resist the temptation to apply it to *Wrightia*.

Sir George Watt was an authority on the useful plants of India who wrote several major treatises in the early 1900s. In his book *Commercial Products of India,* he lists several sources of indigo. Most intresting is his report that people in India have used the leaves of *Wrightia tinctoria* as a source of a blue dye, or indigo, "since remote times". In fact, he suggests that this may have been the first plant used as an indigo source in India, the original "nil" or "anil". It is a small tree that occurs almost all over the plains and foothills of India, with deciduous opposite leaves three to four inches long. From March to July, it bears large terminal clusters of flowers with five white or creamy yellow petals opening from a spiraled bud, followed by pairs of slender pods up to twenty-five inches long. *Wrightia tinctoria* is described in gardening encyclopedias as an attractive ornamental for tropical climates or greenhouses. I am experimenting with it as a houseplant to grow in a sunny window.

I found information on using *Wrightia tinctoria* leaves in an old French book on dyeing. The leaves should be gathered when about three months old. If picked at the right time, they develop a bluish tint as they dry; immature or overripe leaves yield very little pigment and aren't worth using. The leaves should be chopped, put into a kettle, covered with water, and brought to a rapid boil. The water should be poured off as soon as it boils to avoid contaminating the indigo solution with various other pigments from the leaves. After it cools, the liquid can be processed like other fresh indigo extracts.

Another indigo source is *Marsdenia tinctoria,* a coarse vine in the Milkweed family that grows naturally and in cultivation in Southeast Asia and Indonesia. Its leaves give a blue dye, and its stems contain useful, strong fibers. *Strobilanthes flaccidifolius,* in the acanthus family, is a Southeast Asian shrub whose leaves are harvested two or three times a year for indigo. It grows several feet tall and has opposite, toothed leaves with a thin, papery texture. Another species, *S. dyerianus,* is sometimes offered as a greenhouse ornamental with iridescent purply-silvery leaves, but it is named for a Mr. Dyer, not for dyers in general, and isn't an indigo source. In parts of Africa, the shrubby *Lonchocarpus cyanescens* in the legume family provides indigo. Its leaves are dried and then fermented in sunken vats of wood ash water until ready for dyeing. These three indigo-bearing plants could be grown in other tropical regions or (for demonstration) in greenhouses, but seeds are not commercially available.

Using Indigo from Fresh Plants

Dye books give dozens of recipes for using commercially prepared indigo, and, for that matter, if you buy a little cube of indigo pigment from a dye supplier, you'll probably receive directions on how to use it. So rather than repeating that information, I will offer some methods for using the dye prepared from fresh leaves of indigo, woad or dyer's knotweed. Dyeing with the indigo pigment is quite different from dyeing with other plant dyes. While dyebaths from other plants are prepared by simmering, indigo dyeing proceeds at temperatures between 80° F and 120° F. You *can* simmer a bath of these leaves and use it to dye premordanted wool, and you'll get lots of interesting colors — pinks, lavenders, tans, grays and browns — but you don't get blue that way. With most plant dyes, the color of the dyebath resembles the color of the dyed fibers — a brown dyebath gives brown yarn — but an indigo dyebath is yellow, and the yarn doesn't turn blue until you take it out. And finally, the fastness and stability of most plant dyes depend on a chemical union formed directly between the dye and the fiber molecules or with a mordant of some kind. The indigo pigment is very stable, but it doesn't react with the fibers, it just adheres to their surface, forming a mechanical but not a chemical bond. Indigo will dye fibers that haven't been mordanted, and it will stick to synthetic fibers as well as to plant or animal fibers. It will also stick to itself; the traditional way to achieve intensely saturated shades of blue is to build up successive layers of pigment on the fibers by dipping them into the dyebath over and over again. Indigo doesn't fade over time or change from dark to pale blue, but indigo-dyed fabrics (such as blue jeans) gradually fade as the dye molecules are rubbed off the fibers, like chalk marks are erased from a blackboard.

You can dye wool, silk, cotton, flax or other fibers with indigo, as loose fibers, yarn, woven or knitted fabrics. Two things are important: The fibers to be dyed must be immaculately clean, and they should be thoroughly wet. If they aren't clean, the indigo will stick to the dirt, grease, or whatever is on the fibers instead of to the fibers themselves. If they aren't wet, they will carry air bubbles into the dyebath, and that causes uneven dyeing. Each time before you add fibers to an indigo dyebath, soak them in water and squeeze out all the air. Then gently lower the wet fibers down under the surface of the dyebath and arrange them loosely so the solution can penetrate. When you withdraw the fibers from the dyebath, give them a *very* quick squeeze right at the surface, then immediately move them away from the vat as the color begins to develop. Hang yarn or fabric on a clothesline or spread fibers on a screen or rack. Turn them every so often to expose all sides to the air.

The preceding sections, on growing indigo, woad and dyer's knotweed, explain how to collect and treat the leaves of each plant to produce a tan fluid, which is the indoxyl solution. You can use the indoxyl solutions from each of these plants interchangeably; they all yield the same indigo blue pigment and can be handled in the same way. Try the following methods of using the solution.

Direct Dyeing. The simplest way to use the fresh solution is called direct dyeing. The indoxyl released from the leaves into the water settles onto the surface of the fibers, and when they are withdrawn into the air, the indoxyl reacts to form indigo. For this method, it's very important to keep air out of the dyebath. Remove the soaked leaves with a minimum of disturbance and splashing, don't stir or agitate the fluid, and keep the vessel covered. Add wet fibers to the dyebath, work them under the surface to be sure all the air is expelled, then leave them to soak in a warm place for an hour or two. Gently draw the fibers out of the dyebath and watch the yellow color turn to blue. Amazing! Let the fibers dry in the air for an hour or two, then if you want to intensify the color, rewet them and put them back in the dyebath again. You can alternately dip and air the fibers as many times as you want to, until the color is dark enough or you get tired. Sooner or later you'll have used up most of the potential pigment, and then it's time to pour the solution down the drain and start again with fresh leaves.

There are two problems with direct dyeing. First, the indoxyl is not really dissolved in the dyebath water, it's suspended there until it settles out. Since it isn't uniformly dispersed in the fluid, it may not get uniformly deposited on the fibers. You can correct this by adding enough of an alkaline substance to bring the pH of the dyebath up to about 9—start by adding a tablespoon of ammonia, or a tablespoon of baking soda, or a teaspoon of washing soda per gallon of water. Although insoluble in plain water, the indoxyl is soluble in an alkaline solution, so this treatment solves the problem of even dispersal and deposition. The other problem with direct dyeing has to do with the clarity and fastness of the blue color obtained this way. Instead of clear, pure blue, the fibers may turn out grayish blue, or bluish lavender, or brownish blue, but these are nice colors, too. Some dyers report that direct-dyed indigo blues aren't very fast to light or washing, but I've been satisfied with my samples.

Vat Dyeing. The indoxyl solution can be treated to produce the indigo blue pigment, and then the indigo blue can be reduced back to indigo white to make the dyebath. Why bother? Because the end result is more satisfactory, and it solves the problems of lack of clarity and fastness that are associated with direct dyeing. The transformation of indoxyl to indigo blue has a little more leeway and allows for more varied by-products than the transformation of indigo white to indigo blue. The extra steps of creating and then reducing the pigment purify the final product and improve the color and quality of the dye.

Starting with the reddish tan fluid, then, containing the indoxyl extracted from indigo, woad, or dyer's knotweed leaves, the first step is to add enough of an alkali to bring the pH up to about 9. Start by adding a tablespoon of ammonia, or a tablespoon of baking soda, or a teaspoon of washing soda per gallon of water. Test with pH paper, and add as little as possible, especially if you plan to dye wool or silk fibers. Then, to convert the indoxyl to indigo blue, you need to expose it to oxygen from the air. Beat the liquid vigorously with an eggbeater or whisk, or pour it back and forth from one container to another. The liquid will turn dark blue-green within a few minutes, but you aren't done yet. Keep beating or pouring for at least ten minutes, until the froth no longer turns blue. Rest a few minutes if you get tired or are interrupted, but then go back and aerate the liquid a little more, until you are sure you have done a thorough job.

Now you've got indigo blue. It makes a good stain and will color anything it comes in contact with. But it won't stay in solution in the dyebath and settles down to the bottom. So the indigo blue has to be reduced back to indigo white, which will dissolve in the alkaline solution, and that, at last, will be the dyebath. There are many ways to proceed, but here are four possibilities:

• Mix equal quantities of indigo blue liquid and stale urine. (Collect urine in advance — yours or the whole family's — and let it age in a closed container for a few weeks. Yes, this smells bad, although the urine doesn't really smell much worse than the indigo itself.) Anyway, combine the fluids in a large vessel, put the lid on, and let it sit in a very warm place (100° F) for about two weeks. The bacteria that ferment the urine liberate hydrogen from urea, and thereby reduce the indigo blue to indigo white. When the color of the liquid changes back to a golden tan, you can add wet fibers for dyeing. Alternately soak and air the fibers for an hour or more at a time until the blue is dark enough to suit you. Let the fibers dry, wash in soapy water, and rinse until the smell goes away.

• For each gallon of indigo blue liquid, add either a cup of bran or one-quarter cup of chopped dates or raisins. Cover the container and put it in the warmest place you've got (again, 100° F or body temperature is best) for a few days. As bacteria ferment the starch or sugar of the bran or dried fruit, the indigo is reduced. When the liquid changes to tan, add the fibers and proceed with the dyeing.

• For each gallon of indigo blue liquid, add a tablespoon of dry yeast and one-quarter cup of sugar. In a day or so at 80° F temperatures, as the yeast grows and feeds on the sugar, it will use up all the available oxygen and then split oxygen from water molecules, liberating hydrogen that will reduce the

indigo. Again, when the fluid turns tan, you can add the fibers for dyeing.
• The fastest way to reduce the indigo blue to indigo white is to add a chemical reducing agent. You can purchase either sodium hydrosulphite or Spectralite™ from dye suppliers, or you can use Rit Color Remover, which contains sodium hydrosulphite. Sodium hydrosulphite, in particular, has a limited shelf life and deteriorates over a year's time, so purchase a small quantity and use the chemical while it's fresh. To use, start with a tablespoon of Spectralite or two tablespoons of sodium hydrosulphite per gallon of fluid. Sprinkle the powdered chemical on the surface and let it sink down by itself. For best results, the dyebath should be heated to about 100° to 120° F. Within an hour or two, the color should change from dark blue-green to yellow-tan. If it hasn't changed by that time, add a little more chemical and wait a while longer. When the color of the fluid has changed, proceed with dyeing.

SUGGESTED READING

Dye Plants

A fascinating introduction to the broad subject of color and dyeing is *Color: A Survey in Words and Pictures from Ancient Mysticism to Modern Science* by Faber Birren (Secaucus, New Jersey: Citadel Press, 1963). To learn more about the origins of dyeing, start with "Dyeing Among Primitive Peoples", "Primitive Dyeing Methods", and "Some Problems of Primitive Dyeing" by A. Buhler *(CIBA Review* 68 [1948]: 2478-512). A survey of dyeing and a dictionary of historically important dye plants are given in *The Art of Dyeing in the History of Mankind* by Franco Brunello, translated by Bernard Hickey (Cleveland: Phoenix Dyeworks, 1978). More information on traditional dyestuffs is given in "Dyestuffs in the 18th Century" by Susan Fairlie *(Economic History Review* 2d ser., 17 no. 3 [April 1965]: 488-510), "Dyestuffs in the Nineteenth Century" by E.J. Holmyard, pp. 257-87 in *A History of Technology*, vol. 4, edited by Charles Singer (Oxford: Clarendon, 1958), and *Ancient and Medieval Dyes* by William F. Leggett (Brooklyn: Chemical Publishing, 1944).

For readers with some training and interest in chemistry, descriptions of molecular structure and pigment properties are given in *The Chemistry of Natural Coloring Matters* by Fritz Mayer, translated and revised by A.H. Cook (New York: Reinhold, 1943), and *The Biochemistry of Natural Pigments* by G. Britton (Cambridge: Cambridge University, 1983). The chemistry of indigo, in particular, has been described in utter detail; for example, see *Heterocyclic Compounds with Indole and Carbazole Systems* by Ward C. Sumpter and F.M. Miller (New York: Interscience, 1954).

Old references on the cultivation and use of indigo include "Indigo", pp. 974-78 in the *U.S. Patent Office Report: 1845* (Washington: U.S. Patent Office, 1845), "Indigo", pp. 255-61 in the *U.S. Department of Agriculture Report: 1873* (Washington: U.S. Department of Agriculture, 1873), *On Indigo Manufacture: A Practical and Theoretical Guide to the Production of the Dye* by J. Bridges-Lee (London: Thacker, Spink, and Co., 1892). In French are two valuable works: *Observations generales sur les plantes qui peuvent fournir des couleurs bleus* by Nicholas Joly (Paris: Montpelier, Boehm, et cie., 1839), and *Art de l'Indigotier* by G. Samuel Perrottet (Paris: Bouchard-Hazard, 1842).

Indigo as a crop in colonial America is discussed in "Eliza Lucas Pinckney — Colonial Gardener" by Marcia Bonta *(American Horticulturist* 64, no. 10 [October 1985]: 7-12), and "The Indigo of Commerce in Colonial North America" by D.H. Rembert *(Economic Botany* 33 [1979]: 128-34).

Indigo and the Antiquity of Dyeing by Fred Gerber (Ormond Beach, Florida: Fred Gerber, n.d.) discusses the *Indigofera* indigos. *The Woad Plant and Its Dye* by J.B. Hurry (London: Oxford University, 1930) covers *Isatis tinctoria. Indigo from Seed to Dye* by Dorothy Miller (Aptos, California: Indigo Press, 1981) is about *Polygonum tinctorium. A Dyer's Manual* by Jill Godwin (London: Pelham, 1982) gives directions on using all of these indigo-bearing plants.

The cultivation of madder is well described in two old reports: "Madder", pp. 311-24 in the *U.S. Patent Office Report: 1844* (Washington: U.S. Patent Office, 1844), and "Madder", pp. 339-46 in the *U.S. Department of Agriculture Report: 1865* (Washington: U.S. Department of Agriculture, 1865). Also see "The Cultivation of Madder" and "The History of Turkey Red Dyeing" by G. Schaeffer *(CIBA Review* 39 [1941]: 1398-416).

Two older handbooks for using dyes from plants are *Experimental Researches Concerning the Philosophy of Permanent Colors,* in 2 vols., by Edward Bancroft, M.D. (Philadelphia, 1814), and *The Dyer's Companion* by Elija Bemis (reprint of the 1815 edition; New York: Dover, 1973). They are of great historical interest, although few dyers today work with such large quantities of fibers as are indicated in the older book.

More recent sources are "Dye Plants and Dyeing" edited by Ethel Jane Schetky *(Plants and Gardens,* the Brooklyn Botanic Garden Record 20, no. 3, 1964), and "Natural Plant Dyeing" edited by Palmy Weigle *(Plants and Gardens,* the Brooklyn Botanic Garden Record 29, no. 2, 1973). Other practical handbooks include *Natural Dyes and Home Dyeing* by Rita J. Adrosko (New York: Dover, 1971), *Dyes from Plants* by Seonaid M. Robertson (New York: Van Nostrand Reinhold, 1978), *Nature's Colors* by Ida Grae (New York: Macmillan, 1974), and *A Handbook of Dyes from Natural Materials* by Anne Bliss (New York: Charles Scribner's Sons, 1981).

Several books on dye plants have a regional focus, such as *Craft of the Dyer: Colour from Plants and Lichens of the Northeast* by Karen Leigh Casselman (Toronto: University of Toronto, 1980), *Hopi Dyes* by Mary-Russell Ferrell Colton (Flagstaff, Arizona: Museum of Northern Arizona, 1965), and *Tintes Naturales* by Hugo Zumbuhl (Huancayo, Peru: Hugo Zumbuhl, 1979).

The various textile magazines regularly feature articles on using dyes from plants; for example, see "Annatto" by Anne Bliss *(Handwoven* 5, no. 5 [Nov.-Dec. 1984]: 82-84), and "Dyes of Mexico" by Michele Wipplinger *(Spin·Off* 9, no. 3 [Fall 1985]: 32-35).

SOAP PLANTS FOR CLEANING TEXTILES

No doubt about it, doing laundry has always been an unpopular chore, the sort of task you put off as long as possible. But the next time you stuff a load of dirty clothes into the automatic washer, think about the alternatives. Have you ever knelt on the rocks beside a river to rinse out socks on a camping trip? Imagine doing all your wash that way. Throughout human history and in much of the world today, people have washed clothes, diapers, bedding, and all of their other fabric goods by scrubbing and beating, with or without the benefits of soap, in the nearest river. Washing in tubs or basins, using warm or hot water, making suds with soaps of various kinds, adding bleach or starch or fragrance: these all are advances from the most basic and primitive riverbank laundry. One traditional laundry method makes use of plants. There are several kinds of plants known as soap plants; chopped up and added to water, they produce a sudsy lather. This soap is gentle but effective for removing soil and grease. Using soap plants to clean textiles is an old-fashioned technique that is both satisfactory and fun to do.

CLEANING WITHOUT SOAP

The simplest thing to do with dirty clothes is to soak or rinse them in plain water. Merely rinsing, or even boiling, clothing in water doesn't remove accumulated body oils and grease, but it does remove dust and dirt and carry off the salts from perspiration. If the water is perfumed a bit, the rinsed clothes will smell better. In post-medieval Europe, distilled essences from fragrant plants such as rosemary or lavender were recommended for freshening clothes and bedding. Sometimes stale garments were revived with steam from brewing herbs or fumigated with the smoke from burning resins and incenses. These treatments at least disguised the odors of uncleanliness. Perhaps they were also needed to overcome the smell of "cleanliness": Read on!

From antiquity until the nineteenth century, people in Europe thought that boiling clothing and other fabrics in stale putrid urine from animals or humans was one of the best laundry techniques. Urine releases quantities of ammonia as it decomposes, and ammonia is an active cleanser. To have an adequate supply, households collected and stored their own urine; professional launderers set collection vessels in public places. Raw wool was cleaned with stale urine in preparation for dyeing, carding and spinning, and fresh pig dung was also widely esteemed for cleaning woolen goods. Both urine and dung actually do remove some grease from fibers and fabrics, because the alkaline ammonia dissolves animal fats, but in excess they give wool a peculiar, brittle texture, in addition to an abominable stench. Despite these disadvantages, the use of urine for washing wool persisted even after soap was used on cotton and linen fabrics, partly because it was cheap and abundant, and partly in adherence to tradition.

The use of alkaline substances as cleaning agents was developed by the Egyptians and practiced by other cultures in Biblical times. Although urine was used for wool, natural alkalis from plant sources were used on linen and cotton fabrics. Perhaps this helps account for the Egyptians' distinction between wool, which was considered "unclean", and linen, which was a symbol of purity. Wood ashes are rich in potassium carbonate (or potash) and potassium hydroxide, which dissolve in water to make wood lye, a caustic liquid. The ashes of marine algae such as kelp, glasswort *(Salicornia* spp.), and saltwort or barilla *(Salsola kali)* are particularly rich sources of sodium carbonate and sodium hydroxide or common lye.[1] Sodium carbonate can also be mined from mineral deposits; it is now called washing soda. The Egyptians called these natural sodium salts "natron", and used natron solutions for laundry, bathing, purification, and all sorts of washing, bleaching and fulling activities.

Strong alkaline solutions remove greasy soil, perspiration acids, and various stains, but are quite harsh on human skin and hair and on wool and silk fibers. Cotton, linen and other cellulose fibers tolerate alkalis better, and can be simultaneously cleaned, bleached, and strengthened by soaking or boiling in washing soda or lye solutions. Throughout the Middle Ages in Europe, linens were subjected to a process called bucking, which involved soaking or even boiling the textiles in a solution of lye extracted from wood ashes. The various stages of soaking, rinsing and drying each required several days, and proper bucking took a week or more to complete, but the sparkling white color and remarkable cleanness of bucked linens were especially note-

---

1. Once known as barilla and used as a source of alkaline salts, *Salsola kali* was accidentally introduced to the United States in a shipment of grain seeds, and has since become a widespread weed in the Western states. Each fall the branches curl into a ball and the plant snaps off its root to roll away in the wind — it's tumbleweed!

worthy in those days of darkness and plague. In more recent centuries, wood lye solutions were combined with soap to maximize its cleansing power. Even today, washing soda is sold as a booster to use with detergents, especially for cleaning cotton clothing and towels.

Several "dry" cleaning processes have been practiced around the world for centuries.[2] Dry dust and loose dirt can be removed by shaking or beating textiles; carpets and rugs, for example, release clouds of gritty dust when beaten. Vacuum cleaning is the modern equivalent of this old technique. Oils and grease that stick to fibers can be removed if fabrics are first rubbed with finely ground absorbent powders, and then beaten or vacuumed. The ancient Egyptians used soapstone dust or fuller's earth in this way to clean woolen robes and blankets. The English and Scots used powdered oatmeal flakes to freshen tweed garments before the days of solvent dry cleaning. The Navaho Indians use a dry white clay to clean wool fleece, yarns and rugs in their desert homeland where wash water is scarce. Fuller's earth is a very absorbent fine clay that is still recommended for removing grease spots from upholstery, carpets or garments. In far northern climates, fresh snow can be used to clean rugs without actually wetting them. The snow is scattered on the rug and thoroughly brushed into the pile, then snow and dirt are together shaken loose.

ABOUT SOAP

Soap is not a naturally occurring compound, but it is produced from simple natural ingredients: an alkaline solution (usually lye in water) and some melted fat. Soap is formed when sodium or potassium ions from the alkaline solution react with organic fatty acids. This process is called *saponification.* A basic recipe for soap goes something like this: Mix eight pounds of melted grease with eighteen quarts of strong lye water (made by pouring rain water through wood ashes to extract the lye). Stir well and bring to a boil, then set aside for several weeks to age and mature. The product will be a soft, jelly-like soap.

By using different raw materials, various soap products can be made. The fats can be waste animal fats of all kinds: beef tallow, lard, goat fat, mutton tallow, goose grease, whale blubber or whatever. Vegetable oils are also suitable: olive, palm or coconut oils are preferred, but oil from castor beans, flax seeds (linseeds), hemp seeds, or even turnip seeds will do. In theory, the

---

2. Solvent dry cleaning, using benzene, gasoline or carbon tetrachloride to remove grease and dirt without actually wetting the fabric, was not invented until 1857 and has become popular only in recent decades.

saponification process yields an odorless soap even if the raw fat is rancid or pungent; in fact, foul old grease makes soap that smells bad. The alkaline solution can be made from different ingredients. Lye from wood ashes is rich in potassium hydroxide, which makes soft, creamy soaps. Ashes from salt-worts and seaweeds contain more sodium hydroxide and make hard, solid soaps. Adding other ingredients, such as salt, resin, and perfume oils, leads to a variety of plain and fancy soaps.

Apparently soap has been made and used in the Far East since ancient times, but it was not exported and little is known of its early history. The origins and spread of soap making in the Mediterranean region are better known, and the use of soap in Europe has been traced through references in classical literature and historic documents. In parts of Asia, in Africa, and in North and South America, soap was not known until it was introduced by European colonists. Native peoples in these continents made use of whatever soap plants grew locally to make suds for washing themselves and their clothes, even though they did not produce any form of saponified soap.

Before the time of Christ, the Phoenecians, Sumerians and Egyptians all used mixtures containing soap ingredients, but they didn't recognize the soap itself as a product. The Phoenecians mixed goat fat and wood ashes; the Sumerians mixed palm and castor oil, sodium or potassium lye, resin, and salt; the Egyptians mixed their natron minerals with castor oil. Although these cultures performed the process of soap making, they did not emphasize soap as a cleanser, and used alkaline solutions of natron or common wood ashes for most bathing. The Greeks and Romans knew of soap, but they didn't make much use of it either. Roman men and women used soap as hair pomade, but preferred to bathe with scented water. Throughout the Mediterranean civilizations, laundering was a trade practiced in special workshops, not done in private homes, and professional launderers used inexpensive urine and ashes rather than exotic soap.

During the Middle Ages and up until the seventeenth century, soap was rare in Europe, and served few functions. Luxurious scented soap balls were desired by upperclass ladies and gentlemen for their personal bathing. More caustic and often strong-smelling soaps were recommended for medicinal purposes, and washing body and clothes with soap was proposed as a cure for certain diseases. When soap of higher quality was eventually produced in greater supply and the relationships between personal cleanliness and health were better known, soap at last entered into the daily life of common householders. In Europe and North America, the widespread use of soap for bathing and laundry dates back less than three hundred years.

SURFACTANTS AS CLEANING AGENTS

Soaps, detergents and saponins all function as surfactants, which are compounds that make a foam of suds and reduce the surface tension of water. The appearance of suds indicates the presence of surfactants. They increase the ability of water to wet and penetrate a fibrous surface, and reduce the repulsive forces between water and grease or oil. Surfactant compounds have a particular molecular structure: one end is hydrophilic and attracts water, and the other end is hydrophobic and repels water. This structure is the key to their cleansing properties. When dirty fabrics are soaked in sudsy water, the surfactant molecules get oriented with the hydrophilic end toward the water and the hydrophobic end toward greasy or oily spots on the fibers. With agitation, the oily materials roll up with the surfactants into spherical clusters of molecules called micelles. All the oil and grease molecules are surrounded by surfactant molecules, with the hydrophobic ends in the center and the hydrophilic ends sticking out. The micelles trap insoluble materials and carry them into solution. The grease is emulsified, or suspended in tiny particles in the water, and can be washed away. Any dirt clinging to the grease is dislodged from the fabric at the same time. Basically, soap and detergents and plant saponins all clean in this way, gathering oily dirt into micelles which drain away with the rinse water.

Soap is a typical surfactant. The molecules of soap combine the properties of the grease and of the alkali. The grease component makes the hydrophobic end of the molecule, and the alkali component makes the hydrophilic end. In solution, soap molecules act at the interface between water and fabric, pulling particles of soil off the fibers and forming micelles. Soap works best in an alkaline solution, so lye or washing soda is often added to improve the performance of laundry soap. Soap also works best in "soft" water, such as rain water, without dissolved minerals. In "hard" water, the high concentrations of dissolved calcium and magnesium salts react with soap to form scummy blobs. It takes a lot of soaking, scrubbing and rinsing with hot water to flush away the gray slime that settles out when soap and hard water coagulate. Soap is a good product for washing cottons and linens in hot soft water, or in combination with an alkalizing agent, but it does not serve well in all circumstances.

When automatic washing machines came along to replace the scrubboards and washtubs of our grandmothers, synthetic detergents were developed and introduced as replacements for soap. Boiling clothes with soap and lye solution was a hard job for the laundress and a harsh treatment for the fibers. Detergents are easy to use, effective even in hard water and at lower temperatures, and don't form troublesome calcium curds. First introduced as laundry products, detergents have since been designed especially for dishwashing, shampooing and other cleaning jobs. Inexpensive detergents that dissolve in cold water, work on all types of natural and synthetic fibers, remove heavy grease and soil, and rinse away easily are taken for granted in most modern American homes, but synthetic detergent is a recent invention and is still rare in most of the world. Most detergent compounds are large molecules with long names: Sodium alkyl sulfates or alkylbenzene sulfonates. These compounds are surfactants, and thus have cleaning properties. In addition, early detergents included plenty of sodium triphosphate to tie up or "sequester" the calcium in hard waters, but the excess phosphate was soon implicated as a source of water pollution. Newer detergents combine biodegradable surfactant and sequesterant ingredients in order to maintain good cleaning power and minimize environmental side effects.

A third category of surfactant compounds serves well for cleaning fabrics. Certain plant parts, such as the fruits of soapberry trees, the leaves and stems of soapwort, and the roots of yucca, make a sudsy froth when mixed with water. The compounds in these plants that have soap-like properties are called saponins and function like other surfactants. A single plant may have a mixture of different saponin compounds, and the saponin content of different plant parts often varies with the stage of growth, the time of year and the growing conditions. Although saponins occur in plants from more than ninety families, their function in the plant kingdom is unknown. Some have antibiotic or antifungal properties that may protect plants from infection, but others do not. If taken internally, most saponins are toxic to animals and cause hemolysis, or rupture of the red blood cells. Although saponins were formerly used to enhance the sudsiness of bottled beer and root beer, and were sometimes prescribed as herbal medicines, these uses are not recommended.

All soap plants can be used in either fresh or dried form to produce suds. The plant parts should be ground, pounded, chopped or cut into small bits to release the saponins, and then agitated in lukewarm water until suds form. The solution does not store well and loses its effectiveness in a day or two, so a fresh batch must be prepared for each use. Fabrics can be soaked in the solution, scrubbed or sloshed about as needed, and then thoroughly rinsed. Although the cleaning effect may be improved with hot water, cold water can be used and boiling is not recommended as it breaks down the saponin compounds. Compared to soaps and detergents, saponins are mild cleaners. They remove light oils and grease spots, smoke films, and dust; however, they are less effective on heavy grease and grime. The properties of saponins are particularly well suited for cleaning fragile textiles, heirlooms, naturally dyed fabrics, and baskets. Saponin suds are nonionic and nonalkaline, do not damage dyes and fibers, and do not leave deposits. Saponins used to be preferred to soaps for cleaning the textiles in museum collections. Since the fifties and sixties, however, many institutions have used specially formulated synthetic products.

Pure soaps, detergents and saponins are all unscented, and fabrics cleaned by washing with unscented surfactants are odorless. Nearly all modern washing products are perfumed, but traditionally the cleaning process was followed by a separate treatment to add a desired fragrance (see chapter 4).

WASHING DIFFERENT FIBERS AND FABRICS

The different fibers used by spinners and weavers require special handling. Raw fibers must be prepared for spinning by cleaning processes which remove dirt, grease, wax or other sticky compounds. Fibers must be thoroughly clean so they will dye evenly and absorb color well. Woven fabrics benefit from finishing treatments that include washing. Completed garments, table linens, rugs, blankets and bedding, hangings and other textiles need regular cleaning in a manner appropriate to their fibers, dyes, and construction.

Cotton is the easiest fiber to prepare for spinning, because the cotton fibers are almost pure cellulose and are remarkably clean when pulled from the boll. If the seeds and stray bits of vegetal matter are removed, cotton is ready to spin. Once spun and plied, cotton threads and yarns are often boiled in a solution of soap and washing soda. This removes the thin coating of waterproof wax that coats the fibers and permits better dye penetration. The process of mercerization goes further, and involves treating cotton with a concentrated alkaline solution, as high as twenty percent sodium hydroxide (also called caustic soda or lye) in water. Mercerized cotton is strong and lustrous; many industrial mills produce mercerized cotton thread and fabrics as a matter of course. It is possible to mercerize cotton goods at home, but the concentrated lye solutions require informed and cautious handling. Because cotton is not damaged by either high temperatures or high alkalinity, cotton fabrics are effectively cleaned by hot water and soap. However, for removing light soil or grease spots from fine cotton fabrics, saponins from soap plants work very well. Cotton fabrics are often starched to create a stiff, glossy finish. Starch from wheat, potatoes, corn, rice and other food plants is used in the final rinse or sprayed on the clean fabric, then pressed to a high luster. Starch washes out and must be reapplied with each laundering.

Like cotton fibers, flax fibers are almost pure cellulose and are tolerant of being boiled in soapy water with plenty of lye. Undyed linen fabrics, such as fine towels, table linens and bed sheets, have been passed down through generations, enduring and even improving over decades of weekly washing. Dyed linens may fade, however, if washed too vigorously, and special linen pieces deserve gentle handling. Again, a warm solution of soapwort suds might be just enough to clean the fabric without altering the colors or texture.

Soft and rigid baskets made from plant fibers, leaves and stems often benefit from an annual dip in a mild solution of saponins. Baskets collect oil and grime from the atmosphere and from use. Strong soap or detergents may leave a residue that is hard to remove without scrubbing. Plain water doesn't remove greasy soil. Saponins are good cleansers for baskets because they clean quickly and thoroughly but rinse off easily. Soak small baskets briefly, then shake or agitate in a tub of suds solution. Use a sponge to wipe suds over the surfaces of large baskets. Rinse with a spray of warm water and dry in a warm airy place or outdoors in the sun and breeze.

Raw silk requires a special treatment called "degumming", to remove the silk-glue or sericin from the surface of the fibers. Sericin is a form of protein; the interior of the silk fiber is also a protein called fibroin. If raw silk is heated to 205° F in soft water with plenty of soap and a little ammonia, the yellowish sericin will dissolve and can be rinsed away, leaving the silk fibers white, soft and glossy. Degummed silk absorbs dyes well and has a desirable luster and texture. The degumming process requires heat and alkalinity. Soap works well for degumming, but saponins do not. After the initial treatment, however, silk should not be washed in hot soapy alkaline solutions again or it will be dulled and weakened. Silk fabrics can be washed in detergent suds in neutral water, or with saponin suds. Wash silk at temperatures that are comfortably warm to your hands. Adding white vinegar to the wash or rinse water preserves the fine qualities of silk. Wash silk garments frequently to rinse out perspiration salts which stain and damage the fibers. I think that saponins are especially good for cleaning silks without reducing the brilliance of the dyed colors or altering the texture and feel of the fabric.

Wool is the most popular fiber among modern handspinners, and wool yarns are widely used in weaving and knitting. Of all fibers, wool is most affected by the washing process. Wool *is* washable, and washing can and should improve the texture and feel of woolen goods. Take care not to treat wool harshly, not to overheat it or subject it to sudden temperature changes, and not to rub or wring wet wool. Always rinse wool well after washing, and add a little white vinegar to the final rinse water to remove any traces of alkalinity.

Raw fleeces, as they are shorn from the sheep, may yield only fifty percent of their weight in clean wool after the grease, dirt and suint (dried perspiration salts) are washed away. Sooner or later it is necessary to thoroughly clean or "scour" the wool. Some spinners prefer to spin the greasy fleece and wash the spun yarn, but throughout the history of wool spinning it has been traditional to scour and often to dye the wool before spinning. Either way, the process requires soaking the wool in a solution that can dissolve the waxy greases and salty suint. Curiously, when a dirty fleece is soaked in hot water, some of the salts and greases react in a saponification process, so in a sense wool comes with the ingredients to make its own soap and be self-cleaning. But to fully scour wool, something must be added to complete the grease removal. Although stale urine and strong soap have had their advocates, the alkalinity of those agents is destructive to the wool fibers. Modern liquid detergents work well for scouring wool. Good strong solutions of saponins from soapwort or other soap plants are also very effective. Water at about 140° F (too hot for bare hands, but definitely not up to simmering temperature) will help dissolve the wool grease and remove the dirt. Use more warm water to rinse away the grease and dirt after scouring; spread the wool to air dry.

Wool needs to be scoured only once, and further washings of wool yarn, fabrics, or finished pieces can and should be milder. Wool is subject to felting, which is an irreversible interlocking of the fibers. A little felting may be a good thing, and handwoven woolen fabrics can be improved by a vigorous washing or "fulling" in hot soapy water, which draws the weave together into a thick, dense texture. Accidental felting is another matter. Too much heat, agitation and alkalinity all cause felting; to avoid reducing a size fourteen sweater to a size nine, wash wool gently in cool water with a nonalkaline cleanser. I think that handspun, handwoven, naturally dyed wool fabrics deserve special treatment. To clean such treasures gently, try slow soaking in a warm bath of soap-plant suds followed by several rinsings in clear soft water.

SOAP PLANTS TO KNOW AND GROW

Like most of you readers, I live within easy driving distance of a well-stocked supermarket, and can choose from a whole aisle of soap and detergent products. Why, then, grow soap plants? The ones that I list here are attractive enough to grow as ornamentals, and many gardeners plant them for that reason. But the sudsing properties of leaves, roots and berries never fail to fascinate me, and each year I make a few batches of suds from different soap plants and try the solutions on fleece, yarns and fabrics. Soap plants are fun to use and work fine, to gently clean special textiles.

Some of the plants in this category are restricted to mild climates; others, particularly soapwort, are quite hardy throughout the United States. This list includes a variety of herbaceous and woody plants, both native and exotic.

First the major soap plants are listed separately, and then other sources of soap plants are grouped at the end of the chapter.

Soapbark

Rose family. Few nurseries sell live plants or trees of soapbark (*Quillaja saponaria*), but the dried bark is commonly stocked by suppliers of herb products. Native to mountainous regions in Peru and Chile, soapbark is a tree that can grow up to sixty feet in height. It has attractive, leathery, ever-green leaves and clusters of three to five white flowers that open out at the tips of the branches in spring, and are followed by star-shaped fruits. Young trees are slender and erect, but older trees have gracefully spreading branches. Soapbark is sometimes planted in the southern states and California, but is not hardy where temperatures fall below 10° F. In cold climates it can be grown as a greenhouse plant, or set outside in summer and brought in for the winter. With annual pruning, the trees can be kept small enough to live for years in a large pot or tub.

As the name suggests, the saponins of soapbark are in the tree's bark, which can be used fresh or dried. Strip fresh bark from pruned branches; do not wound a living tree. Dried bark is sold in small flat flakes, less than one-quarter inch thick, that are brownish and corky on one side and white and smooth on the other. A cup of bark flakes makes a generous suds in a gallon of water. The suds are odorless and nonirritating and clean all kinds of fabrics. The bark is still used as a laundry soap in Peru, and was formerly used in this country and abroad for cleaning old tapestries and other museum textiles.

Soapberry

Soapberry family. Western soapberry (*Sapindus drummondii*), wingleaf soapberry (*S. saponaria*, formerly *S. marginatus*) and nearly forty other species of soapberry plants are all tropical trees or shrubs. The genus name *Sapindus* combines the Latin roots for "soap" and "Indian", referring to the West Indies natives who used the berries as soap. Wingleaf soapberry is com-mon in the Caribbean Islands and southern Florida. Western soapberry grows along the Mexican border and through Texas up into Kansas. Both varieties are planted as ornamental landscaping trees in the south, and do well even in poor soil conditions, but are not hardy in the north. Both grow rather slowly into trees thirty-five to fifty feet tall, with pinnately compound deciduous leaves and terminal clusters of tiny white flowers. The ripe fruits look like yellow cherries, each with a single black pit-like seed inside. The fruits mature in September, but hang on the tree through the winter, gradually shriveling and turning black and leathery. A single tree will yield at least a gallon of fruits each year. Soapberries are not usually marketed by herb dealers, so you must grow your own or harvest them from wild trees. The berries can be gathered from the trees throughout the winter, or gathered and dried for storage. A handful of fresh or dried berries makes a good lather in two quarts of water.

Like other plant parts that contain saponins, soapberries are inedible, and birds and wildlife leave them alone. As soap substitutes, the berries make a mild but efficient cleanser. The pulp of the fruits can be mashed up in water to make a good suds, then the sudsy water can be strained off for use. The solution cleans oily or greasy soiled fabrics well, and is easily rinsed out. Soapberry suds are odorless and nonallergenic.

Soap Plant

Lily family. On dry hills and open woodlands along the California coast grows the soap plant *(Chlorogalum pomeridianum)*, a robust and vigorous native perennial. Each year when the rainy season starts, the bulb puts forth a new rosette of slender leaves two and one-half feet long. At this stage the soap plant looks like a large tuft of coarse grass. The flowering stalk shoots up six to ten feet tall, bearing a panicle of small white blossoms. Later the seeds mature and the plant dies back in the hot dry weather of late summer, leaving the bulb hidden underground. Soap plants grow readily from seed, although the seed is not listed in many catalogs. Transplant seedlings with care, as the young roots are brittle. Because the plants and even the bulbs are damaged by hard frosts, in most parts of the United States it is necessary to raise soap plants like dahlias, cannas, or other tender plants, setting the bulbs out in late spring and digging them back up in the fall. Plant the bulbs three to four inches deep in groups of five to seven at the back of a bed, in full sun and well-drained soil of average fertility. Plants reach flowering size in a few years and the bulbs can be used for soap at that time.

The saponins of soap plants are concentrated in the egg-shaped bulbs, which grow as big as five inches long. Covered with a mat of stiff black hairs on the outside, the bulbs are creamy white inside and smell like onions. Indians and early settlers alike used the fibrous coating to make brushes or for stuffing material, and used the crushed or grated bulb to make lather for bathing, shampooing, and washing clothes. Although the raw soapy bulbs taste bad and are poisonous to humans, they are reported to be potentially edible and nutritious. An old recipe calls for peeling the bulbs and wrapping them in, of all things, poison-oak leaves, then baking them for a day or more in a pit oven. I wonder if anyone actually ate bulbs treated this way, or if it was just something with which impatient parents used to threaten foul-mouthed children, as in, "If you ever say that word again, I'll wash your mouth out with soap plant. . . ."

As a cleanser, soap plant bulbs can be used fresh or dried. Grate a few tablespoons of fresh bulb into a quart of warm water and shake well to generate suds. The bulbs get hard as stones when they dry out, so it's best to cut or slice them while they are still fresh and let the pieces dry, rather than drying whole bulbs. To use the dried bulb, soak a handful of chunks in warm water for a few hours; when the pieces soften, pound and knead them to release the saponins into solution.

Soapwort

Pink family. One of the best known, easiest to grow, and most widely used soap plants is the soapwort *(Saponaria officinalis)*, also called fuller's herb, crow soap, latherwort and bouncing bet. The name *Saponaria* derives from the Latin word for soap, and soapwort was used by professional launderers and fullers in the days of the Roman empire. Native to the Mediterranean region, it was early introduced to Europe and England, and later brought to North America, where it is now widespread as an attractive roadside weed. In addition to its use in cleaning fabrics, soapwort has been used as dish soap, as shampoo, and in the treatment of skin infections and poison ivy. However, it is most closely associated with wool and has been used to wash wool on the sheep before shearing, to scour raw fleeces in preparation for dyeing and spinning, to full and finish woven fabrics, and to clean and restore old textiles.

Soapwort is a herbaceous perennial, growing to three feet tall each summer with simple opposite leaves on slender sprawling stems. Terminal clusters of pinkish or white flowers with five petals bloom over a period of several months, releasing a spicy fragrance in the evening to attract its hawkmoth pollinators, which dart from flower to flower like tiny hummingbirds. A variety with double flowers is a favorite plant for old-fashioned flower gardens, but the single-flowered variety is more commonly seen nowadays. Soapwort is tolerant of sunny or shady exposures and of moist or dry soils; it is rarely affected by insect or disease problems, and is perfectly hardy everywhere in the United States. It starts easily from seed or by division, grows quickly, and spreads to form a solid patch, but I don't consider it aggressively weedy. Established plants persist for decades with no care. I can recall seeing thriving patches of soapwort along railroad tracks, on vacant lots or behind abandoned farm homes.

A related species, the rock soapwort *(S. ocymoides)*, is a dwarf trailing plant that grows well in rock gardens or as a ground cover or edging plant. Only eight inches tall, it spreads into a dense bushy mound twelve inches

Soapwort, *Saponaria officinalis*

wide, with softly hairy leaves. Each plant bears scores of small neon-pink flowers in late spring. Like soapwort itself, rock soapwort produces saponins and can be used to make good suds. Both varieties grow vigorously and you can cut them back several times a year to harvest the leaves and stems for soap. A two-foot by four-foot patch of either soapwort will supply enough suds for gallons of wash water.

All parts of soapwort contain saponins, and I have tried rhizomes, stems, leaves, flowers and seeds at different times of the year. I think that the greatest concentration of saponins is in the leaves in midsummer, but the rhizomes in fall and spring are also good sources. Either stems and leaves or rhizomes can be harvested and dried for storage without diminishing the saponin content. Fresh leaves give the water a greenish tinge, but this is not a stain and easily rinses out of fabrics. To prepare a soap solution, chop the plant parts into small pieces, soak them briefly in warm water, then stir or agitate until suds form. Dried rhizomes may need to soak for an hour. Use about one-quarter cup of fresh or dried soapwort per quart of water, and make a fresh batch for each washing. Newly mixed solutions are odorless, but after a few days they begin to ferment and smell.

Compared to actual soap, the suds produced by soapwort saponins are milder and gentler to fabrics. Soapwort suds are neutral rather than alkaline, which is especially important when dealing with wool or silk, as the protein fibers are vulnerable to alkaline damage. Soapwort can be safely used to restore brilliant color and resilient texture to old vegetable-dyed tapestries made with wool or silk yarns. Delicate fabrics can be stretched on a smooth surface and gently sponged with suds, or mounted between layers of fiber-glass screen and briefly soaked in suds solution, then carefully rinsed and dried. If a fabric will not be harmed by water, I believe it can safely be washed in soapwort suds. When in doubt about cleaning valuable pieces in private collections, check first with a textile specialist trained in conservation techniques; several museums and institutions have consulting services.

Yuccas and Agaves

Agave family. Yuccas, sometimes called soaproot or soapweeds, are tough native plants that spread to form large clumps and live for decades, even centuries. The long-lasting leaves have been used both in basketry and as sources of fiber for spinning (see chapter 1). Several species grow wild in different parts of the United States, and yuccas are also popular as garden plants. All yuccas grow best with plenty of sun in gritty soil that drains quickly. They are propagated by seed or by division of the offsets that are readily produced by most species. Young plants grow slowly for several years before reaching flowering size, and before they are large enough to have their roots harvested

Yucca, *Yucca filamentosa*

for soap. Once you have a clump established, you may be understandably reluctant to sacrifice it; however, in the parts of the country where yucca grows wild, it is abundant enough that you will do no harm by harvesting a few roots from an existing patch.

The stout rootstocks contain saponins that were used as soap by the native Indians who introduced yucca to early Spanish settlers in the Southwest. Gathering yucca roots is no easy task! Even approaching a dense clump of yuccas is forbidding, as each leaf is tipped with a needle-like spine. The plants often grow in hard rocky soil which bends the tines of digging forks. Start at the perimeter of a clump and scrape away dirt until you expose the main rootstock. It will be surprisingly large, as big as your arm or leg, and quite woody. An ax is useful for chopping a section of root away from the rest of the clump. While you are sweating over the task of gathering yucca roots, you might rest a while and wonder how Indians were able to manage without metal tools.

Yucca roots can be dug at any time, and used fresh or dried for storage. Once you have excavated them, yucca roots are easy to prepare into soap. Chop off a handful of root chips with an ax or knife, and put them to soak in cold water. Pound with a hammer or knead with your hands until the roots soften into a shredded mass, and agitate to make suds. Strain off the liquid and dilute it with extra water before you use it. The Navahos and other Southwestern Indians hold yucca soap in particular esteem and use it for ritual cleansing and purification rites, as well as for everyday washing of wool. Sometimes yucca root suds seem to leave a slight residue on fibers that can be mildly irritating to the skin, so follow a yucca washing with generous rinsing in plenty of fresh water.

Lecheguilla and other agaves *(Agave* spp.), discussed in Chapter 1 as fiber plants, contain saponins in the pulp and epidermis of their spiny succulent leaves, and in their thick roots. The sudsing properties of the leaves are obvious when they are being pounded, scraped, and rinsed during fiber processing. In the parts of rural Mexico where the lecheguilla is harvested for its fibers, the sudsy residue of leaf spines and pulp is used to scour dishes. Freshly dug rootstocks, called amoles, are pounded and added to warm water to make a soap solution for shampoo and laundry use. Agave saponins are effective cleansers but also have an astringent property that can irritate skin.

Other Plants Used as Soaps

In the Pacific Northwest and British Columbia, Indians used the leaves of mock orange *(Philadelphus lewisii)* as a source of soap. This and several other species of mock orange *(Philadelphus* spp.) are attractive deciduous shrubs with very fragrant four-petaled flowers in late spring. The leaves of all mock oranges, if crushed, produce a sticky mucilage that becomes foamy when rubbed between the hands or mixed in water. The flowers and bark also yield saponins, and all were used for personal bathing and laundering clothes. Farther south along the Pacific coast, the attractive shrubs of the genus *Ceanothus* have provided soap substitutes occasionally used by Indians and settlers. Ceanothus contains saponins in its dense clusters of blue, pink, or white flowers, which make a fragrant cleansing lather.

Like the fruits of soapberry trees, the shiny brown seeds of horse chestnut (*Aesculus hippocastanum*), introduced from Europe, and of the native buckeyes (*Aesculus* spp.) contain high concentrations of saponins. The nuts of horse chestnut were formerly used for washing wool in France and Germany, and were briefly recalled to that use during World War II.

In rural villages of India, Africa, and Australia, the fruits of a shrubby perennial plant called withania (*Withania somnifera*) are still used as soap. Withania is an interesting plant to grow, and seeds or plants are available from some herb nurseries. Its stems and foliage are plain-looking, but the fruits puff out like little Chinese lanterns. Experienced gardeners and botanists will immediately recognize that withania is a member of the nightshade family. The entire plant is useful: the fruits are saponin-rich, the dried roots are sold in India as tranquilizers for adults or unruly children, the leaves are used in Africa to repel body lice, and the pulverized plant is applied to wounds as an antibiotic. In gardens, it grows quickly from seed and can be treated as an annual, growing one to two feet tall in full sun and moderately rich soil.

Two native North American plants with surprisingly massive roots are the pokeweed (*Phytolacca americana*) and the wild gourd or calabazilla (*Cucurbita foetidissima*). Both are sources of saponins. Pokeweed, also listed in Chapter 3 as a dye plant, has a fleshy taproot that once was used in folk medicine but is now recognized as quite poisonous. Ground or chopped into small pieces, it generates a rich lather in water. Pokeweed is hardy everywhere, grows easily from seed, and may already be a weed in your neighborhood. The wild gourd is a coarse perennial vine native to the arid Southwest, with a man-sized root that sends out twenty-five-foot-long runners in every direction. Each year it bears a crop of small round gourds that smell bad and taste worse, but the fleshy pulp of the gourds is rich in saponins and can be used as a soap or scouring agent. Wild gourds grow quickly as annuals even where they are not hardy as perennials. The plants are fun to grow if you have enough room.

One final plant that is sometimes considered a soap plant is the European pennyroyal (*Mentha pulegium*), discussed at length in Chapter 4 as a moth repellent. Pennyroyal does not contain saponins, but does produce an essential oil that is recommended by some spinners for cleaning greasy and dirty fleece. A solution of fresh or dried pennyroyal in warm water may help to break down the waxes and hardened greases of old or stale fleece, and certainly gives a fresh smell to the cleaned wool. Use at least two cups of pennyroyal flowers and stems for each pound of wool. Leave the wool to soak several hours or overnight in the solution, then rinse well. Much of the dirt and grease will be removed by this treatment, but I don't think that pennyroyal is as effective a cleanser as soapwort or other saponin-rich plants.

SUGGESTED READINGS

Soap Plants

Cleaning without soap and the early use of soap are described in *Textiles*, Vol. 4 in *Studies in Ancient Technology*, by R.J. Forbes (2d. ed.; Leiden, Netherlands: E.J. Brill, 1964), and in "Historical Facts Concerning the Production and Use of Soap" and "Some Old-Fashioned Ways of Cleaning Textiles," by G. Schaeffer *(CIBA Review* 56 [1947]: 2014-23 and 2034-37).

Soap plants native to North America are listed in "Food and Fiber Plants of the North American Indians" by J.J. Newberry *(Popular Science Monthly* 32 [1887]: 31-46), and *Useful Wild Plants of the United States and Canada* by Charles Frances Saunders (New York: McBride, 1926).

Recipes for making soap at home are given in *Soap—Making It, Enjoying It* by Ann Bromson (New York: Workman, 1972), and *Making Homemade Soaps and Candles* by Phyllis Hobson (Charlotte, Vermont: Garden Way, 1974).

For practical information on cleaning fibers, finishing fabrics, and caring for textiles, refer to "Another Look at Wool Scouring" by Lee Raven *(Spin•Off* 9, no. 4 [Winter, 1985]: 25-28), *The Final Steps* by Beverly Gordon (Loveland, Colorado: Interweave Press, 1982), and "Principles of Fragile Textile Cleaning" by James W. Rice, pp. 32-72 in *Textile Conservation*, edited by Jentina E. Leene (Washington: Smithsonian Institution, 1972).

FRAGRANT PLANTS TO SCENT AND PROTECT TEXTILES

Many modern housekeeping aids play on the sense of smell. Many products, such as laundry detergent, furniture polish, glass cleaner, and even toilet tissue, are perfumed. We have learned from television commercials to expect fresh laundry to have a certain smell, which we think of as smelling "clean". Bathroom products are supposed to smell "sanitary". Unscented detergents, soaps, cosmetics and other products are available, but they are uncommon. More than we realize or admit, we are affected by the smells around us. Nowadays we are accustomed to perfumes that are carefully calculated and synthesized in chemistry laboratories. Historically, fragrant plants were used singly or in simple blends to scent garments and textiles and to improve the home atmosphere. Aside from their aesthetic value, it was widely believed that spicy, pungent, penetrating aromas served as repellents and disinfectants, protecting against contamination, disease and vermin. Perhaps the powers of fragrance were exaggerated through superstition and hearsay, but some traditional beliefs have been confirmed by modern research. Some plants have fragrances that have long been used to perfume linen, cotton and wool fabrics; other aromatic plants are used to protect woolens from moth damage.

TRADITIONAL SACHETS

When the Mole and the Water Rat spent the night at the Badger's house in *The Wind in the Willows*, they "tumbled in between the sheets in great joy and contentment," because "the two little white beds looked soft and inviting, and the linen on them, though coarse, was clean and smelled beautifully of lavender." For centuries, lavender has been the traditional perfume for linen cupboards and bedding. Sachets of dried lavender flowers or drops of lavender water penetrate fabric with a welcome fragrance. Lavender not only smells fresh and clean, it actually has a sanitizing effect. The essential oil of lavender is an antibiotic that destroys the bacteria that cause tuberculosis and typhoid fever. Its function on bedding was more than cosmetic; it also helped prevent infectious diseases from spreading. Lavender was especially popular in Britain, where the climate favored its growth, and where fine linens were produced. Vast plantations of lavender surrounded the town of Mitcham in Surrey from the early 1600s, yielding gallons of distilled lavender water and oil for use in soaps and perfumes. Writing in 1629, the British herbalist, Parkinson, claimed that "Lavender is almost wholly spent with us, for to perfume linnen, apparell, gloves and leather. . . ."

With the expansion of trade routes in the seventeenth and eighteenth centuries, luxurious textiles were imported to Europe from the Far East. Fine cotton muslins from India were more delicate than any fabrics produced in Europe. They were greatly desired for dainty gowns and cool summer garments. These muslin fabrics bore a characteristic perfume, known as mousseleine, which came from the dried roots of a tropical grass. Called vetiver or khus-khus in India, the grass's roots had a cool, sweet fragrance. Long after mills in Great Britain began to spin and weave their own cotton goods, mousseleine perfume continued to be used to give the cotton fabric the scent of the original imported muslins.

Similarly, when delicate brocaded cashmere shawls from Kashmir were introduced to Britain in the early nineteenth century, an exotic perfume was their mark of authenticity. Packed in the shipping trunks with the imported shawls were sachets of dried patchouli leaves, widely used in India as a perfume and as a moth repellent. Patchouli has an intense, heavy fragrance, too powerful for some tastes. It was so unlike any perfume known in Britain in those days that it served well to distinguish genuine shawls. Those original shawls were very rare and expensive and symbolized great luxury and status. Later the designs were copied by drawloom weavers in Paisley, Scotland. At first, the counterfeit cashmeres, or paisleys, could pass on the market, if they were convincingly perfumed. Eventually, however, when so many paisley shawls were produced that they became commonplace rather than luxuries, patchouli went out of favor.

TEXTILE PEST REPELLENTS

"The roots of Avens, taken up in autumne and dried, do keepe garments from being eaten with Mothes, and make them to have an excellent good odour. . . ."

Gerarde, Herball, *1597*

"The Galls of a sumac will keep moths from garments and woolen clothes, giving unto them a good scent, and therefore it is much used to be laid in Wardrobes, Chests, Presses, and the like."

Coles, Nature's Paradise, *1657*

These examples from old herbals repeated advice based on centuries of experience in using plants around the house. Wool moths must have been a serious concern in days when most clothing and domestic textiles were either wool or linen. Judging from the numerous references to wool-moth repellents, anxious homemakers were desperate to protect their handspun, handwoven or knitted garments, blankets, carpets, cushions, and draperies. Until commercial mothballs became widely available in the twentieth century, nearly every book of housekeeping advice included a recipe for a moth repellent preparation. Dozens of different plants were recommended for use in sachets that would both scent and protect woolens.

In fact, the concerns of scenting and protecting woolens were closely related. By our standards of regular dry cleaning and frequent washing, most of the clothing and textiles in earlier centuries were filthy and rank. Dirty clothes and bedding are particularly attractive to insects. So, with soiled wool in every household, wool moths and carpet beetles had a heyday. But, as mentioned in the last chapter, soap was not widely available, and cleanliness was not highly valued, until more recently in history. Homemakers used aromatic herb products instead, in an effort to cover up odors with perfumes and to confuse and repel insect pests.

Modern research supports the age-old belief that moths can be discouraged by fragrant plants. In answer to the question of why plants smell as they do, biologists have found that many fragrant compounds serve a definite role in repelling insects and other herbivores. Over millions of years, plants have developed a whole arsenal of chemicals to protect themselves. Each case is different; compounds which repel one insect species may actually attract others. Compounds which are toxic to insects may be harmless to mammals. But insects in general have remarkable abilities to detect specific odors, even in minute concentrations, and much of insect behavior is regulated by these chemical stimuli. This sensitivity enables insects to locate members of the opposite sex for mating, to find appropriate sites for laying eggs, and to identify potential food sources. As any gardener knows, insects do very well locating their preferred food! Each summer, potato beetles find potato plants, onion flies find onions, cabbage loopers find cabbages; all respond to the scents of the plants' foliage. Perhaps clothes moths find wool in a similar way.

The Insect Pests of Stored Fiber Products

Cotton, linen, and other plant fibers are mostly cellulose. Although subject to degradation by mildew, they are rarely attacked by insects. In dark, damp conditions, crickets, termites, silverfish and cockroaches may chew holes in these fabrics, but they do not prey primarily on textiles. Wool, mohair, alpaca, camel down, angora, and other animal hair products, however, are fibers that are vulnerable to a specialized group of insects. These insects have the ability to digest the protein keratin, which is the chief component of wool and hair, skin and leather, feathers, horn, and tortoiseshell (but not silk). Keratin's function is to provide a tough outer covering for warm-blooded animals. Keratin contains a small but significant amount of sulfur.[1] The insects that can digest keratin need that sulfur in their diet, and they may have a sensitivity for the scent of sulfur that helps them locate potential food sources. In nature, these insects feed on dead carcasses and in the nests of birds and mammals. In our homes, they feed on woolen goods, such as clothing, upholstery, carpets and blankets.

The insects to watch for are clothes moths and carpet beetles. Both go through four stages of development: eggs, larvae, pupae and adults. Although they can be detected and destroyed at any stage, only the larval forms damage fibers. After hatching from eggs laid in secluded places, these larvae, like little caterpillars, chew through several times their own volume of wool as they grow. To supplement the protein in their diet, they seek the salts and oils of urine, sweat and grease deposits on raw wool or soiled garments. Easily disturbed by light, ventilation and movement, these insects are most likely to cause damage in neglected or out-of-the-way spots. Wool clothing that is worn frequently won't be damaged by moths, but stored goods are vulnerable to infestation.

As adults, clothes moths are small, buff-colored moths with a wingspan of less than one-half inch. They fly about aimlessly when disturbed and are not attracted to light. They may be seen any time of the year, but most commonly in summer, when humidity is high. Male clothes moths may fly from one building to another; females never go far from their birthplace. After mating, the females lay one hundred to one hundred fifty tiny white eggs and then die. These eggs hatch within a week into hairless white larvae with dark heads. The larvae grow from one-sixteenth inch to one-third inch long over a period of six weeks to four years, depending on weather conditions. Webbing clothes moth larvae make silken threads over the fabric as they graze. Case-making clothes moth larvae make a little sack, or case, which they drag

---

1. We detect the sulfur content of keratin when it burns — it has the nasty smell of burned hair or burned wool. Other proteins, such as meat or egg, also smell bad when burned, but not *as* bad as keratin does. It's the sulfur that makes the difference.

around behind them. These threads or sacks may be your first hint of moth infestation. Clothes moth larvae stay in one place as they grow, moving only a few inches, if at all, as they feed. When ready, they pupate for one to four weeks and emerge as adults. The life cycle may be as short as two months or as long as four years. If undisturbed, a single female could produce more than one million offspring in a year, with the potential of eating up to one hundred pounds of wool. If that fact doesn't motivate you to clean your closets, nothing will.

Carpet beetles are mentioned less frequently than clothes moths but are just as damaging. Adults are small, hard-shelled beetles, about one-eighth inch long, with mottled spots on a black background. They become active in May and June and fly around windows and are attracted to lights. They may venture outdoors to feed on the pollen of spring flowers. After mating, the females lay eggs in dark places where dust collects: in furnace ducts, in crevices of upholstered furniture, in carpeting, or in cracks in the floor. Larvae hatch in a week or two, crawl to a suitable source of food, then begin to eat and to grow. The larvae are covered with bristles, or hairs, that look fuzzy. They grow to be one-fourth inch long over a period of one to three years. Carpet beetles are somewhat more omnivorous than clothes moths, and eat grains and flours, organic debris, and leather, as well as fibers.

There are two kinds of clothes moths and four kinds of carpet beetles to guard against. In different parts of the country, one or another of these six insects might be more abundant. Any can be easily transported, though, in shipments of raw materials or in finished textiles. Although moths and beetles do not fly or crawl long distances on their own, they often catch a ride to new surroundings. Tiny larvae are especially likely to accompany woolen goods in transit and enter your home undetected. Take a close look at newly purchased yarns, sweaters, rugs or blankets, especially if they have been imported from other countries or if they have been stored for long periods in warehouses where they might have become infested.

Wool moths have a look-alike: the Indian meal moth. It is slightly smaller, it is attracted to light, and its larvae feed on stored grains and seed products. Carpet beetles are closely related and very similar to dermestid beetles, which are notorious for infesting kitchen cupboards and pantries and feeding on all kinds of dried foods. Watch for Indian meal moths or dermestid beetles if you save seeds from year to year, but these insects don't attack fiber products.

Advice on Storing and Protecting Wool and Woolens

If you have fleeces, yarn, clothing, heirloom textiles, and other special fiber products to protect, you'll want to observe the following good housekeeping tips. Frequent inspection for insects and conscientious efforts to prevent infestation will protect your supplies, your completed projects, and your favorite pieces from insect damage.

• At least once a year, take everything out of the drawers and closets and vacuum thoroughly. Clean all dusty corners and crevices, clean under and behind furniture. Carpet beetles, particularly, may linger in dark crannies until you vacuum them out of their hiding places.

• Carefully look at everything you have taken out. Do you see any eggs, any telltale silky threads or cases of clothes moth larvae, any holes or damage? Inspect garments inside and out. Untwist skeins of yarn. Unfold blankets and carpets. Take tapestries and fiber art pieces off the wall. Even if you don't see any signs of insects or damage, it's a good time to take things outside for a few hours in the sun and fresh air. Shake or brush away the dust and lint, loosen the folds, and let the wind blow over them. Moth and beetle larvae are creatures of darkness and seclusion. They literally lose their grip and fall to the ground when confronted with sunlight and open air.

• If you find any eggs or larvae, destroy them at once. You can use commercial sprays which contain pyrethrins. Or, you can have things dry cleaned, which kills insects in all life stages. If a textile or garment is washable, you can drown eggs or larvae by keeping the entire article submerged at least twelve hours. Depending on where you live and the time of year, you may be able to kill pest insects by exposing them to extreme heat or cold. Eight or more hours at temperatures below 10° F or above 110° F will suffice. But remember, wool is a good insulator. Allow plenty of time for heat or cold to penetrate to the interior of the piece. Put infested articles outside during a winter cold spell, or in a hot, parked car in the heat of summer. No matter which method you choose—chemical insecticide, dry or wet cleaning, exposure to heat or cold—act rapidly to prevent the larval insects from doing more damage.

• Always, before storing any wool product, be sure it is clean. I can't emphasize it too strongly: Dirty wool is much more attractive to pests than clean wool. Garments are most likely to be damaged at the collar line, underarm, or other spots where perspiration or oils have accumulated. Check blankets, cushions and rugs for spots or stains. Wool that is "flavored" by neglected spills and soiling is often the target of moth damage.

• For long-term storage, place your yarn, garments, blankets, rugs, fiber supplies, clean wool fleeces, and other textiles in wooden chests of drawers, in clean paper bags, in cardboard cartons, or in cotton pillowcases or sacks. Moths and beetles are less likely to lay their eggs on paper or cotton than directly on wool. Larvae also are stopped by a cellulose barrier and usually will not penetrate such containers to get at the wool within. Plastic bags are less desirable for long-term storage, as they don't "breathe", but even plastic provides some barrier against insects. Open storage of yarn in baskets, of sweaters in drawers, of blankets on shelves, and of garments in a closet, invites insect visitors. Use repellent sachets to protect stored woolen goods that are not enclosed.

Plant Products as Insecticides and Repellents

Before going on to the use of plant products to control insect pests, I will review the chemical means of pest control. Chemical insecticides are commonly available and widely used in today's world, but many people use them without understanding just how they work. For decades, the products most widely used for protecting stored goods have been mothballs, or crystals made of paradichlorobenzene or naphthalene. In terms of chemical structure, these compounds are quite similar to benzene, DDT and lindane. I suspect that they carry similar potential health hazards, but they may not be a threat to humans "if used as directed". Mothballs gradually evaporate, changing from a crystalline white solid to an invisible vapor. In a tightly enclosed space, where the concentration can build up to a critical level, these vapors kill moths and beetles in all life stages. If incorrectly used, they may be ineffective. In open areas, where the vapors cannot accumulate to a high enough level, living insects may still feed away, undisturbed. Even though you may detect a strong odor, the mothballs may not be doing the job. The odor itself may be repellent to moths and beetles, but the manufacturer doesn't claim it to be. Mothballs are designed to kill, not just to repel. For repellent purposes, herbal products work as well and smell much better.

Other products, called antifeedants, are designed to repel insect larvae from treated fibers. If applied during the process of dyeing yarn or fabric, at one to three percent of the weight of the fiber or cloth, antifeedants provide lifetime protection from insect damage. Advertised as permanent mothproofing, this process is routine practice in some textile mills. The chemical products are sold under various trade names and can be applied by some dry cleaners, but they generally are not recommended for home use. I believe that antifeedant compounds, applied before installation, are best used for treating wool felt for piano hammers, wool upholstery fabrics, wool carpeting, and wool tapestries or wall hangings. For mothproofing clothing, I prefer other means of protection.

Plant products can be used in many ways to protect stored woolens from clothes moths and carpet beetles. First, extracts of insecticidal plants will kill these insects on contact. Some commercial mothproofing products include either pyrethrum or rotenone. Both of these chemicals are derived from plants. Second, larval insects can be killed by toxic vapors, particularly in an enclosed space. Nicotine from tobacco, pulgeone from pennyroyal, and cedar oil from eastern red cedarwood are examples of volatile products that kill larvae. Third, many essential oils are insecticidal; they also may deter larvae from feeding on treated fiber products. Finally, adult females may be repelled from depositing eggs on woolens that are protected by aromatic sachets of certain dried herbs.

When an infestation is discovered, toxic extracts of plants can be used to kill insects outright. Pyrethrum, a chemical extracted from the open flowers of a kind of daisy, is the active ingredient in several aerosol insecticides sold for home use. Although it kills eggs, larvae and adult insects on contact, it is safe to use around children and pets. Special paper bags treated with pyrethrum are used to store grain and commodities and to protect them from weevils; similarly, dried pyrethrum flowers are included in herbal moth control products. Rotenone, which is derived from the roots of several species of tropical legumes, is another popular insecticide sold for home use. Applied as a very fine powder or dust, or in an oil solution, rotenone kills on contact and also may have some repellent effect. Rotenone is an ingredient in some commercial mothproofing products. Using insecticides may be necessary only to eliminate an infestation in carpeting, upholstery or mounted tapestries. In most other cases, where clothes moths and carpet beetles are discovered, they can be killed by washing or dry cleaning the infested goods or by exposing them to heat or cold.

Nicotine from tobacco is one of the most potent insecticides derived from plants. Liquid nicotine sulfate is sold to gardeners for killing aphids and other soft-bodied insects, but it is a dangerous chemical to handle and highly toxic to humans and other mammals. There is a safer way to use nicotine to control moths. You can raise a few tobacco plants from seed in your garden, and then gather and dry some leaves. The tobacco used for this purpose is not the same as smoking tobacco, nor is it the sweet-scented flowering nicotiana. For insecticidal purposes, grow Indian tobacco *(Nicotiana rustica)*. Its crushed, dried leaves contain up to ten percent nicotine by weight and give off a vapor which will kill young moth and beetle larvae in an enclosed space. I have heard that some Indian tribes still use tobacco in this way to store their woolen rugs and blankets.

Essential oils are highly concentrated, intensely fragrant, volatile liquids that are distilled from flowers, leaves, and the wood of aromatic plants. These oils are widely used to scent perfumes, cosmetics and cleaning products. They often are sold in small bottles at natural food stores, and are available by mail order from specialty herb suppliers. They are precious and expensive, because large quantities of plant parts must be processed to yield only a spoonful of oil. In their concentrated form, many are insecticidal. The essential oil of cedar, particularly of the eastern red cedar, evaporates slowly from freshly cut wood surfaces. In a cedar chest, these vapors accumulate and are toxic to young larvae of clothes moths and carpet beetles. To be effective, a cedar chest should have a tight-fitting lid and remain closed for several days at a time. Over a year or more, the oils near the surface of the wood will evaporate, so the chest must be renewed by sanding the interior surface. Fresh cedar oil really does have insecticidal properties, but the oil in heirloom cedar chests may be exhausted. An old cedar chest, or for that matter, any tight-fitting wooden box or chest of drawers, can be improved for mothproof storage by treating the interior with an application of essential oil. Cedar oil is a favorite choice, but the essential oils of eucalyptus, pennyroyal and lavender also are toxic to moth and beetle larvae. Treat an inexpensive pine chest from an unfinished furniture store in this way to substitute for a more expensive solid cedarwood chest.

Essential oils also serve as antifeedant compounds, deterring larvae from feeding on treated fibers. I add a few drops of oil of cedar, eucalyptus or pennyroyal to the final rinse water when I am washing fleece, yarn, fabrics or knitted garments. Let the wool soak awhile so that the oils can lightly coat each fiber. These rinses impart a slight gloss and a fragrance to clean wool and provide some protection, too.

Herbal moth repellents usually consist of dried herbs, packaged in small cloth bags as sachets. Sachets can contain a single herb or a blend of several different herbs. They may include dried flowers, seeds, fruits, leaves, roots and wood chips. I have a list of over forty-five plants that have been recommended for sachets, but I don't know how many are actually effective. Scientific plant testing for active insecticidal properties is an expensive and prolonged process. It involves isolating a particular compound, defining its chemical structure, and testing its effectiveness under controlled laboratory conditions. In a related field, this kind of testing has given twentieth-century recognition to several traditional herbal medicines. Some researchers are starting to take an interest in natural pest control products.

I believe that, most likely, an effective herbal repellent confuses and disorients the egg-bearing adult female so that she cannot locate a potential food supply. Instead, she lays her eggs in an inappropriate place. Given the limited motility of very young larvae, particularly clothes moth larvae, the offspring are unlikely to locate a food supply if the female doesn't target in on one. The sulfur content of keratin protein may be an olfactory clue to a female moth or beetle searching for animal fibers; any strongly fragrant herbal product that masks the wool odor may be a potential repellent. These herbs may have no effect on eggs or larvae that are already present. They will neither kill the insects nor reduce their appetite. I think they are best used in combination with good housekeeping measures, to prevent new infestations, but not to control existing problems. Enjoy the natural fragrances, but don't expect too much. Use repellent herbs to protect *clean*, properly stored wool.

HARVESTING AND DRYING FRAGRANT PLANTS

The quality of dried herb products depends on the soil and the climate in which the plants were grown, the timing of the harvest, and the method of drying. Most herbs produce the best fragrance when grown in well-drained soil of moderate fertility, with plenty of sun and clear, dry air. Drying your own fragrant plants is a satisfying way to extend the pleasures of the growing season, but for the best results it's important to gather and process herbs properly.

Herbs with fragrant leaves and stems are most intensely scented when the weather is hot and dry. The concentration of essential oils increases in sunny weather but is diluted by rain or wet growing conditions. The time to harvest plants such as camphor basil, rosemary, santolina, southernwood or tansy is during a spell of clear, dry weather. Early morning is the best time of day, because the oil content is highest before the sun's heat strikes the leaves. Herbs can be harvested throughout the growing season, but harvesting is like pruning and affects a plant's subsequent growth. For annuals, pinch out the tips in early and mid season to make bushier plants; gather the whole plant in fall before frost. For perennials, it's best to shear once or twice in midsummer; leave the new growth which follows to mature and harden before winter. Most herbs are usually gathered just as the flowers begin to develop, although mints and pennyroyals should be picked in full bloom. The best time to harvest lavender flowers is just as the buds show full color and the flowers begin to open. Pick pyrethrum flowers the day they open. Roots and rhizomes, such as sweet flag, are usually dug in the fall, after the leaves of the plants die down. The leaves of evergreen trees and shrubs, such as eucalyptus, sweet gale, balsam fir or juniper, are best in midsummer, after the year's new growth has begun to harden and mature.

Depending on your climate and facilities, you can dry herbs by different methods. To prepare materials for drying, rinse or shake off any soil and pick off dead or discolored leaves. Plants like pennyroyal or sweet woodruff, with small leaves and slender stems, can be dried as sprigs. The leaves can be separated easily from the stalks after drying. For larger plants, like tobacco or patchouli, pick off and dry individual leaves and discard the coarse stems. Scrub the soil off sweet flag rhizomes and vetiver roots, and then cut and slice them into short, thin sections. Make a label for each plant as you harvest it! With practice, you will learn to recognize dried materials by smell. At first, though, they're pretty much a lot of hay unless you've labeled each batch.

To dry bundles of herbs, gather the cut ends of several stems together and tie them firmly with string. Keep the bundles small, no larger than a broomstick in diameter. Hang them upside down to dry, in a warm airy place, out of direct sunlight. An attic is ideal, but an enclosed porch or spare room with good air circulation will do. Space the bundles well apart so that air can flow around and between them. A circulating fan or air conditioner can help if there is no natural air flow. If daytime temperatures reach 90° to 100° F and the air is dry, the bundles will dry in just a few days. At cooler temperatures or in humid climates, they will take several weeks to dry. When the leaves crackle and break easily from the stem, the herbs are dry enough to store.

A variation of drying herbs in bundles is to place each bunch in its own brown paper bag. Tie or clip the bag around the plant stems and hang it up to dry. This works well with rosemary, santolina and evergreen leaves. The bag regulates the drying process by protecting the herbs inside from changes in air temperature or humidity. The bag also retards evaporation of volatile oils and prevents bleaching or fading of color. Herbs in a bag can be dried on an air vent without blowing away, and they will perfume the whole room as they dry. Bagged herbs dry in just a day or two in a car parked in the summer sun.

Some herbs are hard to bundle; flowers, small stems or individual leaves can be dried on trays or racks. Window screens set on blocks work fine, or you can make shallow trays by tacking fiberglass screen or fine nylon netting onto wooden frames. The important thing is to support the trays so that air can circulate underneath as well as over the drying material. If your trays are in a breezy spot, cover them with a layer of light netting or cheesecloth to keep the stems and leaves from blowing away. Spread the herbs in a thin layer to start with, then stir or turn daily until the leaves are crisp and dry.

For faster results, especially in humid climates, artificial drying is quite effective. This is also a good way to finish off air-dried herbs in preparation for storage. Fresh leaves and stems dry in just a day on a rack in the oven at 100° to 110° F. In a gas oven, the pilot light produces just enough heat. Use the lowest possible setting in an electric oven and check the temperature with a thermometer to make sure it doesn't overheat. Artificial drying that is too rapid usually results in a loss of color and scent, but some people report good results in using a microwave oven to dry their herbs. Fold the herbs in a paper towel and dry for one or two minutes on the highest power setting. Food dehydrators, designed for drying fruits and vegetables, do a fine job with herbs but may have limited capacity. One cloudy summer, I improvised a drier by arranging a set of stackable plastic storage trays over a small electric fan with a built-in heating element. You can even pack leaves loosely in a cloth bag and tumble them on the air cycle setting in the clothes drier! Artificial drying needs close supervision. Overdrying reduces the quality of the dried products. Dry only until the leaves are crisp, and then stop.

Although bundles of dried herbs are decorative and ornamental, they don't store well. Their fragrance rapidly dissipates in the open air, they gather dust, and tiny crumbs of leaves and stems are always dropping off onto the floor. To preserve dried materials at their best, process them as soon as they are dry. Working over a large tub or bowl, break all the leaves off the stems and crumble large leaves into smaller pieces. Sift the leaves through a one-quarter inch mesh screen to remove bits of stem. You will notice that freshly dried herbs are intensely fragrant. As you break the leaves, essential oils are released from the exposed surfaces. Be careful not to inhale too much dust while handling the dried plants; the concentrated oils may make you sneeze or give you a headache. Pack the dried leaves in glass, ceramic or metal containers. These containers will keep moisture out and keep fragrance in. Paper, cardboard and plastic containers are less satisfactory. Be sure to label each dried plant by name.

Although most articles written about drying herbs claim that home-dried products are vastly superior to purchased ones, sometimes things don't turn out that way. If grown in rich damp soil, herbs may not develop good fragrance. Lush foliage may yield a disappointing dried product. In cool rainy weather, the scent may be weak. If plants are dried too quickly, particularly in direct sunlight or in an overheated drier, much of the fragrance is lost. But if leaves are packed in storage jars before they are fully dry, they will mildew. Drying can be a pleasure, or it can be a frustration. In some situations, it seems nearly impossible to produce home-dried herbs that are as good as commercial ones. Fortunately, the mail-order suppliers of fragrant sachet ingredients and prepared herbal moth repellents offer a variety of products at very reasonable prices.

Preparing and Using Herbal Moth Repellents

Once you have a supply of fragrant plants that you have dried or purchased, you can prepare your own moth repellent sachets. Plan to work in a well-ventilated area. You will need a sieve or screen to sift out coarse particles, a rolling pin or mallet to crush hard materials, a measuring cup, and a basin or bowl to mix ingredients. Use a notebook to record the ingredients that you blend, and label each mixture so that you can repeat your favorite combinations and modify others in the future.

When you prepare, measure and blend ingredients, you may find it hard to compare different mixtures. Your sense of smell will be overwhelmed by so many rich and intense fragrances. For this reason, it's good to start out with simple blends of only three or four ingredients, and follow recommended formulas. Prepare a mixture, let it sit for a few days while your nose rests, then sniff it to see if you like it. Some plants have a raw smell when they first are dried but develop a more pleasing aroma over time. Most blends benefit from aging a few weeks, and then remain stable until the scent gradually weakens.

Making moth repellent products differs from making aromatic potpourris. Potpourris are intended to hold their aroma a long time, even for decades. They also are designed to look attractive and include inert but colorful dried flowers. Potpourri blends are usually scented with spices and essential oils. Special fixatives, such as powdered orrisroot, are added to the dried flower petals and other ingredients that go into potpourri. The fixatives absorb essential oils and retard evaporation so that the potpourri's fragrance will be released slowly. Good potpourri looks lovely and lasts a long time. Moth repellents, on the other hand, are usually packaged into sachets, so the ingredients are not chosen for color or appearance. To be most effective, repellents should give off a generous fragrance. Only the most aromatic ingredients are included, and no fixatives are used. It helps to give sachets a little squeeze from time to time to release a fresh burst of scent. After a year or two, repellents lose their effectiveness and must be replaced.

For best protection, package repellent products in small bags or envelopes and distribute them throughout your drawers, closets and storage chests. Sachet blends can be packed into tiny bags of closely woven fabric; stitch or tie them firmly shut. For special sachets, decorate the bags with lace, ribbons or embroidery. These make lovely gifts. For everyday protection, plain cotton muslin is fine; paper bags and envelopes are also suitable. Each packet can hold as little as a few tablespoons or as much as a pint of sachet, but several small bags will serve to distribute the fragrance more widely and uniformly than a single large bag. In a closet, hang small bags from hooks or hangers and place one or two on the floor. Use a bag for each drawer in a bureau. Place bags between layers of blankets stored in a chest.

Try these different plants and plant combinations in your sachets:

• For sachets with a single distinctive scent, choose one of the following: camphor basil leaves, pennyroyal leaves, eucalyptus leaves, red cedarwood shavings, lavender flowers, southernwood leaves, patchouli leaves. Combine equal parts of the dried fragrant plant with finely ground, dried pyrethrum flowers (which are unscented) to increase the repellent's effectiveness without altering the aroma.

• For a sweet mixture, combine equal parts of southernwood, wormwood and tansy.

• For a sharper, more penetrating aroma, combine equal parts of camphor basil, lavender and rosemary. Add a small amount of purchased camphor or cinnamon if you choose.

• For a man's wardrobe, use a mix of two parts red cedarwood shavings, two parts Indian tobacco, one part sweet woodruff, and one part sweet flag. Add a few purchased tonka beans to this mix if desired.

• For a woodsy mix, combine the leaves of California laurel or sweet gale, needles of balsam fir or juniper, cedarwood shavings, and sassafras roots in equal parts.

• For a more complex mix, combine two parts lavender, two parts southernwood, one part rosemary, one part pennyroyal, and one part wormwood. Add one tablespoon of powdered cloves to each two cups of herbs and mix well.

As you gain experience in preparing dried materials and mixing sachets, you may invent your own combinations with your favorite fragrant plants. There are many plants to choose from which blend into effective and pleasant repellents.

FRAGRANT AND INSECTICIDAL PLANTS TO KNOW AND GROW

Camphor Basil

Mint family. Camphor basil *(Ocimum kilimandscharicum)* is one of many fragrant plants in the basil genus; indeed, the name *Ocimum* is derived from the Greek verb "to be fragrant". It grows as a perennial shrub up to ten feet tall in eastern Africa and is cultivated in Kenya for camphor production. It branches readily and assumes a full, bushy shape. Its mature stems are reddish and ridged, but the leaves and new shoots are grayish green and covered with a soft, silvery down. Leaves are opposite, one-half inch wide by two and one-half inches long. From July to October, white flowers, in spikes up to six inches long, tip each branch and are very attractive to honeybees.

Pure camphor is a white crystalline substance with an intensely penetrating odor. It has long been used as a home cold remedy and disinfectant. It is also insecticidal and a good moth repellent. Camphor is extracted from the leaves of camphor basil and from the wood and bark of the camphor tree *(Cinnamomum camphora)*. It is present in smaller quantities in the leaves of the California bay laurel *(Umbellularia californica)*, the leaves of Carolina allspice *(Calycanthus floridus)*, the berries of spicebush *(Lindera benzoin)*, and other plants. Lumps of camphor and camphorwood chips can be purchased from some suppliers.

Camphor basil is easily raised from seed or propagated by cuttings. It can overwinter outdoors only in frost-free areas, so plan to start new plants each year or overwinter rooted cuttings as pot plants. Start seeds inside, six weeks before last frost, and set plants out at eighteen to twenty-four inch spacing. The plants will grow three to five feet tall in a single season. Camphor basil can be shaped by pruning or left to bush out naturally. For an attractive patio specimen, set a single plant in a large pot or tub. Several plants in a row make a nice hedge or can serve as a background planting. Harvest by pruning during the growing season or collect the entire plant before fall frosts. Wrap a brown paper bag around bundles of stems and hang them up to dry, then shake the dried leaves off into the bag and just pull out the woody stems. One summer I collected a whole grocery sack full of dried leaves from only three camphor basil plants! The dried stems are fragrant, too, and make an aromatic kindling for your fireplace.

Coumarin-Scented Plants

This category includes an assortment of unrelated plants that all contain the chemical coumarin. Although they may be unscented when fresh and green, as they dry and age, these plants develop a sweet fragrance likened to vanilla or new-mown hay. This fragrance is very popular for sachets and was long used as a perfume to scent pipe tobacco. Coumarin is poisonous if ingested and causes fatal internal bleeding in mammals. Whether or not it is insecticidal is unknown, but coumarin-scented plants have traditionally been considered effective moth repellents.

These plants have all been introduced from Europe but are well adapted to North American soils and climates. Both sweet vernal grass *(Anthoxanthum odoratum)* and holy grass *(Hierochloe odorata)* are low-growing, inconspicuous plants, easily raised from seed or division, and tolerate a range of growing conditions. Pick whole leaves by snapping them off at ground level and dry them in bundles. The dried leaf blades are very desirable for weaving into fragrant baskets or crumbling into sachets. Sweet woodruff *(Galium odoratum,* formerly *Asperula odorata)* is a shade-loving ground cover with whorls of shiny leaves and clusters of tiny, star-like white flowers in spring. It is hardy and spreads quickly to fill a bed. Pick and dry whole stems in summer. Sweet woodruff retains its bulk well as it dries and doesn't shrink away like some herbs do. Sweet clover *(Melilotus officinalis)* grows in abandoned fields and along roadsides over much of the United States. It reaches four feet in height but seems delicate because of its sparse foliage and slender flower clusters. Pick and dry whole plants just as the flowers fade. Strip the tiny leaves off the coarser stems when dry. Coumarin is also concentrated in the leaves of a native eastern wildflower, known as vanilla leaf or deer's tongue *(Trilisa odoratissima).* Although not commonly cultivated, deer's tongue has been collected in quantities from wild stands and used as a flavoring for pipe tobaccos. It has a rich aroma and is very desirable in sachets.

Eucalypts

Myrtle family. In their native Australia, hundreds of species of eucalypts, or gum trees *(Eucalyptus* spp.), grow as small to large trees. Many have two kinds of foliage: juvenile leaves, which are opposite, rounded and pliable; and mature leaves, which are alternate, oblong and stiff. The flower bud has a curious little hat that drops off to reveal a brushy tuft of stamens when the flower opens. In Australia, there are eucalypts in the arid desert regions, in the lush rain forest, in the mild lowlands, and in the bleak and windy mountains. Promoted as miracle trees (although critics feel that the merits of eucalypts have been exaggerated), fast-growing species of eucalypt trees have been introduced throughout the tropics to act as windbreaks in reforestation projects, to reduce soil erosion, and to provide firewood and timber resources.

Blue gum trees *(E. globulus)* were planted on a large scale in California in the early 1900s. A few other species are common in California and Florida landscaping. In the last few years, specialty seed catalogs have listed quite a few species of eucalypts. This is a new opportunity for gardeners around the country. I'm raising a few kinds and am pleased at how easily they germinate and how quickly they grow. In full sun and average garden soil, some species grow to be six feet tall their first year and can be treated as annual bedding plants. Others make satisfactory pot plants for the house or greenhouse. Some are hardy to about 20° F, but most are tender to frost. They tolerate a range of soil types and are resistant to drought. Nearly all have strong-scented foliage and yield essential oils which are antiseptic and insecticidal. The silver dollar gum *(E. cinerea)* and blue gum *(E. globulus)*, which produce the shiny, round gray leaves so popular with florists, are relatively hardy and grow as much as six feet a year. Both tolerate repeated hard prunings but will outgrow their containers in a few years. The lemon scented gum *(E. citriodora)* and dwarf blue gum *(E. globulus* "compacta") are longer-lasting pot plants. These have distinct and pure fragrances. All eucalypt leaves dry easily and retain their scent and effectiveness well. Many also provide vivid pigments for natural dyeing. Quite a range of colors can be obtained from leaves of different species and with different mordants.

Indian Tobacco

Nightshade family. The first New World explorers were introduced to tobacco by pipe-smoking Native Americans. "Tabaco" was the word for smoking pipe in the language of the West Indies tribes. In eastern North America, Indians cultivated and smoked the potent Indian tobacco *Nicotiana rustica,* and in Central and South America they grew the milder smoking tobacco *N. tabacum.* Both were introduced to Europe in the sixteenth century and were

Eucalyptus, *Eucalyptus cinerea*

popularized by the Frenchman Nicot, for whom the genus is named. At first, tobacco was recommended as a "heal-all", an herb for healing cuts and wounds, but the fashion of pipe smoking spread rapidly on the continent and in England. By 1612, there was so much demand for "Spanish leaf" that John Rolfe began the first tobacco plantation in Virginia. The rest, as they say, is history.

Not long after tobacco was popularized as a smoking herb, its insecticidal property was discovered. Since the seventeenth century, tobacco dusts and sprays have been used to control soft-bodied insects on fruit trees and vegetable crops and as sheep dips to control ticks and mites. The active compound is nicotine, which is produced in the roots and transported to the stems and leaves of tobacco plants. Top-quality smoking tobacco contains as little as one percent nicotine by dry weight; Indian tobacco yields as much as ten percent nicotine. In pure form, nicotine is a colorless liquid that evaporates quickly at room temperature. It kills insects on contact by paralyzing their nervous systems. Readily absorbed by inhalation or through the tongue, eyes or skin, nicotine is also highly toxic to humans and other mammals.

Indian tobacco is easy to grow. The tiny seeds germinate in a week in warm soil and grow rapidly. Start them in a prepared seedbed outdoors in late spring, or, for a head start, on a windowsill, six weeks before last frost. Do not start them under artificial lighting, because exposure to long days (over fourteen hours of light) will induce premature flowering. When the plants have several leaves, thin seedlings or transplant to individual pots. Set plants out at eighteen to twenty-four inch spacing in deep fertile soil and full sun. Indian tobacco can grow up to five feet tall, with leaves six inches wide and twelve inches long. It attracts quite a lot of attention in any garden. The plant is quite brittle in texture and covered with sticky viscid hairs. Beginning in August, hundreds of one-half inch yellow, scentless flowers develop at the top of each plant, followed by round seed capsules that can contain as many as 200,000 seeds per plant. This is worth seeing, but for a better dried product, cut the tops off tobacco plants in July so that all the nicotine produced by the roots will be concentrated in the large lower leaves.

Harvest leaves individually, starting at the base of the plant as they begin to yellow, and hang them in a warm, dark place to dry. You may prefer to wear rubber gloves when handling fresh or dried tobacco. As soon as the leaf blades are dry enough to crumble, break them up into bits, sift out the stalks, and seal the flaked leaves in glass jars. Some of the nicotine is lost in this initial drying, particularly if artificial heat is used. The remaining nicotine is released more slowly. Label the jars clearly as poisonous. Keep the jars sealed until you take out small quantities to add to sachet blends. Exposed to open air, nicotine evaporates completely and disappears into the atmosphere, so tobacco sachets must be replaced every six months to be effective.

Indian tobacco, *Nicotiana rustica*

My first crop of Indian tobacco flourished untouched during a season when grasshoppers devoured my corn and beans in adjacent rows. One afternoon at the end of the summer, I uprooted tobacco plants as big as I am and hung the whole plants to dry in an open shed. Two days later I went to check on them and found the plants were chewed to shreds, and the floor was covered with a thick layer of dead grasshoppers. I'll never know what attracted those suicidal grasshoppers to feast on wilting tobacco, but the experience convinced me of Indian tobacco's potency as an insecticide.

Lavender

Mint family. English lavender *(Lavandula angustifolia*, formerly *L. officinalis, L. vera,* or *L. spica)* is a shrubby plant two to three feet tall. It has twisted woody stems; narrow gray leaves about two inches long with smooth edges and a downy texture; and long-stemmed spikes of tiny lavender, pink or purple flowers. Its name comes from the Latin "lavare", because the Romans used lavender to scent and disinfect their public baths. English lavender grows wild on mountainsides of the Mediterranean region but has been popular in English gardens since the 1500s. Hidcote, Munstead, Twickle, Waltham, Alba and Jean Davis are different varieties chosen for their growth habits or flower colors. Spike lavender *(L. latifolia)* and French or Spanish lavender *(L. stoechas)* are also popular garden plants.

Although all parts of a lavender plant are fragrant, the flowers have the strongest aroma. Tiny drops of essential oil sparkle on the surface of developing buds and flower stalks. Oil of lavender and distilled lavender water are widely used in cosmetics and perfumes, so the fragrance is a familiar one. But there's a world of difference between a bar of lavender soap and your own lavender plants in bloom on a sunny day. When I smell lavender, I remember a bicycle trip I took years ago through southern France. Small stills were set up outside each country cottage, and whole families were at work gathering wild lavender and distilling lavender water. One kind woman explained the process to me and tucked a bag of dried flowers in my baggage as a souvenir. Its perfume is still delightful after more than a decade.

Lavender prefers a coarse sandy soil and needs alkaline conditions. Be sparing with peat moss, leaf mold or compost. Full sun is essential, and a south-facing exposure, protected from winter cold and dampness, is ideal. It is easiest to begin with purchased plants, and many nurseries offer several varieties. You can propagate lavender by tip cuttings taken in late summer and rooted in coarse sand. Seeds need a cold treatment to overcome dormancy, and seedlings grow slowly for the first year. Young plants raised from cuttings or seeds should be overwintered in a cold frame, but established plants are hardy to 0° F. In mild climates, lavender is an excellent landscape

Lavender, *Lavandula officinalis*

plant. In cold climates, potted plants can be set outside in the summer and brought back indoors for winter protection. Blooms are produced on each year's new growth, so do not prune in spring or summer. After the blooming period, prune to desired size and shape. Collect stalks of flowers for drying after most of the buds have opened and tie in bunches to dry in a shady place. Rub the stalks between your hands to break off the dried flowers for use in sachets.

Native Trees

A few North American native trees have fragrant leaves or wood that are recommended for use as moth repellents. Most effective is the magenta-colored heartwood of the eastern red cedar *(Juniperus virginiana)*. This wood releases an essential oil that is toxic to clothes moth eggs and larvae. If the vapor is contained in an enclosed space, it gets concentrated enough to actually kill insects. Cedar chests are perhaps the best natural means of protecting woolens from damage. It takes centuries for an eastern red cedar to get big enough to mill into wide boards, but lumberyards regularly have narrow cedar boards and chipboard made of compressed cedar shavings. All cedar-wood products need periodic renewal: Sand to expose a fresh surface or apply cedar oil to replace the oil that has evaporated.

The flat scaly needles and fleshy blue berries of eastern red cedar and other junipers are also aromatic; I particularly prefer the aroma of Rocky Mountain juniper needles *(J. scopulorum)*. Junipers are tolerant of a variety of soils and climate conditions and are versatile evergreens for garden use. Most nurseries have several varieties and sizes of junipers in containers ready for easy transplanting. You will find upright junipers, spreading junipers, and junipers with colored foliage. The fragrant needles of balsam fir *(Abies balsamea)*, alpine fir *(A. lasiocarpa)*, and grand fir *(A. grandis)* can be collected from these attractive evergreen trees in the areas where they grow wild, but they don't grow well as landscape plants. Their needles, which dry easily and hold their scent well, are commonly stuffed into small pillows and sold as souvenir items. They are recommended as moth repellents.

The glossy leathery leaves of California laurel *(Umbellularia californica)*, an attractive broad-leaved evergreen tree native to the Pacific coastal regions, have a spicy pungent smell and are insecticidal. Also in the laurel family are sassafras *(Sassafras albidum)* and spicebush *(Lindera benzoin)*, deciduous hardy trees with fragrant leaves, bark and berries. All add a pleasant woodsy character to sachet mixes. They also contain amounts of camphor and other repellent compounds. Evergreen needles and leaves of all these native trees, as well as bark and twigs, can be used as dyestuffs. They yield shades of rosy tan and brown on wool, and make pleasantly fragrant dyebaths.

Eastern red cedar, *Juniperus virginiana*

Patchouli

Mint family. True patchouli (*Pogostemon cablin*) and Java patchouli (*P. heyneanus*) are small shrubby herbs native to India, Malaysia, and the East Indies. Both grow into rounded bushes three to three and one-half feet tall, with the square stems and opposite leaves that are characteristic of the mint family. The leaves can be as large as two inches wide by four inches long, are slightly downy or hairy, and release an intense fragrance when crushed. Pale lavender or white flowers form in one- to three-inch spikes on the tips of all the branches under the short day conditions of winter months. Patchouli is primarily a tropical crop. Bales of dried leaves and stems are imported by perfume manufacturers in England, Europe, and the United States. Both the essential oil of patchouli and the dried product are available through herb distributors and in natural food stores.

Commercial perfumists prefer the fragrance of true patchouli to that of Java patchouli, but for home use, either is delightful. Plants can be obtained from herb nurseries, but I know of no source for patchouli seeds. After danger of frost is past in the spring, set out a patchouli plant in moist fertile soil in sun or partial shade. Pinching out the tip encourages branching, and the plant will form a low mound eighteen inches in diameter by fall. Patchouli also grows well in a container but will need generous watering and light weekly feedings during the summer months. In July or August, root tip cuttings under a plastic tent to start plants for wintering over, for patchouli is not hardy outside. Rooted cuttings can be kept in four-inch pots over the winter. After a spurt of blooming in fall, the plants drop their yellowing leaves and go dormant until spring. Keep them warm and barely moist during this time. Cut the tops back to short stubs and water well to initiate new growth in March or April.

The best fragrance comes from young leaves, so harvest from the tips of the branches. In midsummer, you can pick off several leaves at a time each week or two and dry them in a brown paper bag in a warm shady place. Freshly picked, the leaves have an intense aroma. Curiously, this disappears at first after drying, but the scent of the dried leaves improves with age. After a few months, the characteristic fragrance will develop. Patchouli may not be an effective insecticide or moth repellent, but it is a desirable perfume for woolen goods. In a blended sachet, it mixes well with more active herbal ingredients.

Pennyroyal

Mint family. European pennyroyal (*Mentha pulegium*) was known to the ancient Romans, who named it *pulegium* for its ability to dispel fleas. It grows in rich moist soil throughout Europe and Great Britain, both wild and

Patchouli, *Pogostemon cablin*

European pennyroyal, *Mentha pulegium*

in cultivation. Although its stalks of tiny lavender flowers reach up to six to twelve inches in July and August, for most of the year, it creeps over the ground and threads among the grass, noticed more for its penetrating scent than its appearance. The folk name for pennyroyal, "Lurk-in-the-Ditch", well describes its growth habit. It has reddish stems and opposite leaves that are rounded and less than one-half inch long.

American pennyroyal *(Hedeoma pulegioides)* was used by native Americans as a medicinal herb long before European colonists discovered and used it. Unlike European pennyroyal, American pennyroyal grows in dry sandy soil in open woods and fields throughout the northern and eastern states. Related species grow in Texas and the southwest. American pennyroyal is a slender, erect plant with many thin branches, narrow opposite leaves less than three-quarters of an inch long, and a few pale blue flowers in summer. It is easy to overlook; hikers are likely to step on it, unaware, and then wonder where the mint-like odor is coming from.

The chief constituent in the pennyroyals' essential oils is pulgeone. Both pennyroyals have many traditional uses. Pennyroyal tea has been recommended for colds, headaches, indigestion, toothaches, menstrual disorders, and other ailments. Although pleasant and flavorful by the cupful, too much pennyroyal tea can be harmful. The concentrated oil is highly toxic. European pennyroyal was formerly used to purify the water supplies stored aboard ships, as it has disinfectant properties. It is sometimes used in scouring wool fleeces and woolen goods (chapter 3). Both European and American pennyroyal have several applications as insect repellents. Fresh or dried leaves of either plant, or drops of pennyroyal oil, can be used to repel mosquitoes, to repel fleas from dogs and cats, to repel weevils from pantries, and to repel wool moths and carpet beetles.

European pennyroyal grows quickly from seed or can be propagated by cuttings or division. Sow seeds indoors six weeks before last frost, or directly in a prepared bed after frosts are past. Set out or thin seedlings to six inches apart, as they will spread and form a low mat. European pennyroyal needs fertile, moist soil, but grows well in either sun or shade. It makes a nice edging or ground cover, makes a lawn fragrant when planted in the grass, and trails gracefully from hanging baskets or window boxes. It is hardy to about 10° F if protected with a mulch, or you can root cuttings or bring in clumps of rhizomes to overwinter in a cold frame, unheated garage or cellar. Since the plants flower within several months of sowing seed, European pennyroyal can be raised as an annual. Harvest the upright stems of European pennyroyal when the plants are in full bloom and hang in bunches to dry. The yield from dried leaves is not great: a patch three feet square will produce only a few cupfuls. The fragrance is powerful and penetrating, though, and is particularly effective as a repellent.

American pennyroyal is an annual that grows readily from seeds sown in fall or early spring and reseeds itself from year to year. Grow it in a sunny spot, in well-drained acidic soil of low to moderate fertility. Because it reaches only a foot in height, it makes a good, inconspicuous filler between showier plants. Uproot and dry whole plants when they come into bloom, leaving just a few to set seed for next year. American pennyroyal shrinks to less than ten percent of its fresh volume when dried, but both leaves and stems crumble into valuable sachet material.

Pyrethrum

Composite family. There are two different daisy-like plants known as pyrethrum. The first, also known as painted daisy (*Chrysanthemum coccineum*, formerly *Pyrethrum roseum*), is native to Iran and the Middle East. It forms a rosette of finely divided leaves that look like carrot greens. Painted daisy plants bear red, pink or white daisy-like inflorescences, three inches in diameter, on stalks up to two feet tall. The second, also known as dalmatian insect flower (*Chrysanthemum cinerariifolium*), is native to Yugoslavia. Its foliage is similar to that of the painted daisy, but is more silvery, and its inflorescences are white, only one and one-half inches in diameter, on stalks up to fifteen inches tall. Both are perennials, native to sunny, dry mountainous habitats. Painted daisy pyrethrum has been used as an insecticide since ancient times. It is widely offered today as an ornamental plant. Dalmatian insect flower pyrethrum produces a higher yield of insecticidal compounds, but it is more difficult to raise and is less attractive.

The active ingredients of pyrethrums are called pyrethrins, and are produced in the yellow disk flowers in the center of the daisy inflorescence. The red, pink or white ray flowers, leaves, stems, and roots are all devoid of insecticidal properties. Pyrethrum inflorescences should be picked just as they open from the bud to obtain the maximum concentration of pyrethrins. Finely ground, dried pyrethrum flowers were sold as "insect dust" in Europe and the United States in the 1800s to kill houseflies and other insects around the home or on domestic animals. Used in this way, the active compounds evaporate rapidly. The vapors paralyze insects on contact, but the dust rapidly deteriorates and becomes harmless when exposed to light and air. More effective, longer-lasting products are made by first extracting the pyrethrins with kerosine or oil solvents and concentrating the solution, and then adding ingredients known as synergists (often sesame oil is used), which are not insecticidal, but increase the potency of the pyrethrins. These products are recommended for household use because they are harmless to people and pets.

Both painted daisies and dalmatian insect flowers can be raised from seeds, but the seedlings are slight and not vigorous. The plants are intolerant of excess moisture or humidity, shade, or competition from neighboring plants. Both roots and tops succumb to fungus infections in wet conditions, causing the plants to falter and die. To do well, they should be spaced twelve inches apart in a bright sunny spot where the soil is neutral or alkaline, coarse, and well-drained. Purchased plants and divisions will bloom the first year, but seedlings will not bloom until their second year. Under ideal conditions, a single plant can yield over sixty flowers each year. The flowers are attractive in the garden or as cut flowers, but if you want to use them in moth repellent products, gather them each day as they open. Dry them on screens or racks. As soon as the flowers are dry, store them in a tightly sealed jar in a dark place so they will retain their effectiveness. Grind the flowers into a fine powder before adding to other sachet ingredients. Discard and replace pyrethrum sachets at least twice a year.

Rosemary

Mint family. Rosemary *(Rosmarinus officinalis)* is native to the Mediterranean area. Its name, "Ros marinus", is Latin for "dew of the sea". One of the most popular herbs for culinary, cosmetic and symbolic uses, its recorded history dates back over three thousand years. It grows in both upright and prostrate forms. Rosemary can be raised as a ground cover or a shrub in the South or as a potted plant in the North. The needlelike leaves are up to one inch long, glossy and resinous, and high aromatic. The grayish stems arch gracefully into attractive shapes. Clusters of pale blue or white flowers appear in late winter on the older wood of untrimmed plants. Whether grown outdoors or indoors, the many forms of rosemary make delightful and beautiful plants.

Oil of rosemary is obtained from the leaves and stems, preferably, but not necessarily, collected when the plant is in bloom. The scent of the dried leaves lasts so well that the plant is a traditional symbol of constancy or of remembrance. Dried rosemary leaves can be used alone or in mixtures with other plants for repellent sachets. Harvest leaves by trimming off and drying newly grown branches two or three times during the summer and fall, or wait until the flowering season and collect stems with leaves and flowers both present. Rosemary dries well in a paper bag or on a rack. The leaves cling tenaciously to the twigs until both are thoroughly dry, then break off readily.

Rosemary can be raised from seed, but the seedlings are tiny and grow slowly for months. Tip cuttings, rooted in early summer, can be potted or can be transplanted into the ground in time to get established before winter. In the

South, if you choose a permanent location with plenty of sun and well-drained alkaline soil, your rosemary can climb or spread to six feet tall or four feet wide. In northern states, or where temperatures drop below 25° F, it will be necessary to bring the plants inside for protection. You can sink the plant, pot and all, into a bed for the summer, then lift it out in the fall. Prune the plant well before bringing it in. You can grow an upright form of rosemary as a standard tree in a large tub, or a prostrate form in a hanging basket. Give either form plenty of light and good air circulation. Use a potting mix with a bit of ground limestone and add a good measure of coarse sand.

Southernwood

Composite family. Southernwood *(Artemisia abrotanum)* is a shrubby plant native to southern Europe. It rarely flowers in cultivation, but it is an attractive plant with very delicate lacy foliage on slender stems. The species name, *abrotanum,* is Greek for elegant and refers to the graceful appearance and pleasing fragrance of the foliage. Long popular among European and English gardeners, it was brought to the United States with the early colonists, and now is widely planted as an ornamental and useful herb.

Different varieties of southernwood have been selected for their strong citrus or camphor overtones. According to herb lore, ladies used to carry sprigs of southernwood to church and sniffed the penetrating aroma to prevent drowsiness during long sermons. The same herb also has been prescribed as a cure for sleeplessness, however, and as an aphrodisiac! In France, southernwood appropriately is known as "garde-robe" for its use as a wool moth repellent. The dried leaves retain their scent and effectiveness for six months to a year. Southernwood can be used alone or in blended sachets.

Because southernwood rarely flowers and sets seed, it is propagated by cuttings. Begin with a purchased plant, then increase your stock by rooting three-inch tip cuttings in the spring. Southernwood tolerates poor soil but prefers plenty of sun. It makes a nice hedge and can grow to four feet tall, or it can be pruned each spring into a tidy ball-shaped plant. Do not prune or harvest after midsummer, to ensure that new growth has time to harden before winter. In mild climates, southernwood is almost evergreen, but in the North, it yellows and dies back in the winter. The plants are quite hardy and long-lived in most gardens. Harvest by cutting off branches in spring and summer and drying them in bunches or in paper bags. The feathery leaves yield only a small amount of dried material, but the aroma is strong.

Sweet Flag

Arum family. Originally native to Asia, sweet flag *(Acorus calamus)* now is widely distributed in marshy soil throughout Europe, Great Britain and North America. The Latin name derives from the Greek word *kalamos*, for reed. The common name "flag" refers to a number of slender-leaved plants that thrive near water. The leaves of sweet flag grow one inch wide by four feet long, have a distinct midrib and crinkly edges, and smell of a mixture of citrus and vanilla. Formerly, these plants were used as "strewing herbs", spread over the floors of cathedrals, castles and even cottages to sweeten the air. When woven into mats or used in basketry, the leaves keep their fragrance for years. Because the thick spongy rhizomes of sweet flag also have a spicy and invigorating scent, they are valued as a fixative to blend with other fragrant ingredients. Both the leaves and the rhizomes of sweet flag have been recommended as moth repellents, but their effectiveness as an insecticide has not been confirmed. I value sweet flag for its use as a perfume.

Regular sweet flag, a variegated form of sweet flag, and a narrow-leaved species all can be obtained from herb nurseries. All forms are propagated by division of the rhizomes. Although it prefers moist swampy soil, sweet flag will grow in any good garden soil with adequate watering, in full sun or in the shade. Fresh leaves appear in a flush of growth in the spring and die back in the fall. The flowers, which appear in June only on established plants growing in standing water, look like little thumbs projecting from the sides of the leaves. Seeds rarely set. Harvest and dry the leaves at any time after they appear. Dig up sections of rhizome in late fall, cut off the hairy rootlets, scrub them clean with a stiff brush, and cut them in slices to dry. Do not peel the rhizome, as much of the essential oil is in the outer layers. Alone or in blends, sweet flag gives a welcome fresh scent to stored goods.

Tansy

Composite family. Tansy *(Tanacetum vulgare)* is a perennial plant with dark green, fern-like leaves and clusters of yellow, button-like flowers. Native to Europe, tansy was introduced to the United States by the early colonists and has spread to become weedy in some parts of the country. The aromatic leaves are finely divided and grow to six inches long; the leaves of the cultivar 'Fernleaf' tansy are especially curly and attractive. Flowering stems reach three feet tall by early summer, and flowers open from July to September. Cut flowers dry well and hold their color nicely in winter bouquets. A tansy plant spreads rapidly by its rhizomes to form a large clump. It is a long-lasting, trouble-free ornamental plant.

The foliage of tansy is dotted with small shiny glands that release an aromatic oil. This oil contains thujone and smells of resin and balsam. It is insecticidal and repellent, recommended to repel moths from wool and fleas from pets. Despite, or perhaps because of, its bitterness, tansy tea was widely administered as a medicinal tonic in Victorian days. Tansy was added to cakes and puddings at Easter and eaten to "purify the body". These uses were dangerous. Tansy is toxic, and an overdose can be fatal. Do not take tansy internally! I am careful to process my dried tansy leaves outdoors, with plenty of fresh air; I find that inhaling tansy dust gives me a headache.

Tansy is easy to start, either by raising seedlings or by division. Seeds sown in early spring will grow into large plants that bloom the first year. Give tansy full sun and average soil of moderate fertility. If you clean away the dead leaves and stems of the previous year's growth each spring, your tansy patch will last for decades. It is very hardy and resistant to pests and diseases. Harvest leaves at any time during the summer or fall. Hang them in small bunches to dry. The dry leaves will crumble into a very fine powder. Once established, a single tansy plant will yield several cupfuls of dried leaves each year. Tansy also is recommended as a dye plant. With different mordants, the tops and leaves produce shades of yellow and green on wool.

Vetiver

Grass family. Vetiver grass, vetivert, or khus-khus (*Vetiveria zizanioides*) is a tropical grass that forms round clumps up to eight feet tall. It is native to India and Southeast Asia but has been introduced to the Caribbean Islands, Florida and Louisiana. I have seen vigorous plants at the National Herb Garden in Washington, D.C. The stout erect stems, long slender leaves, and graceful flower panicles are all scentless, but the fibrous spongy roots smell of sweet violets. In India, the roots are woven into screens and hung in front of windows, then sprinkled with water on hot afternoons. The fragrance is released as the water evaporates. Dried roots are used to scent cotton and linen clothing. Oil of vetiver is used in perfumes and, curiously, is added as a flavoring ingredient in canned asparagus.

Vetiver seeds are rarely available, but herb growers sell small plants they have propagated by division. Set plants out in late spring. Rich, moist soil and a sunny exposure in a hot climate are best for vetiver. Dig clumps in fall to collect the roots for drying, and pot up a healthy section of the plant to save. In most of the United States, vetiver plants must be wintered over in containers in a greenhouse or in the house, since both tops and rhizomes are killed by hard frost. Scrub roots clean before drying, spread them on screens or racks in a warm room, and give them plenty of time to dry thoroughly. The dried roots can be crumbled or ground into a powder to release the fragrance.

Wormwood

Composite family. Wormwood *(Artemisia absinthium)* is a bushy perennial herb native to northern Europe, with ribbed stems, finely divided gray leaves, and inconspicuous yellowish flowers. The entire plant is covered with silvery hairs which give wormwood a silky appearance. Although it is hardy, tolerant, and makes an attractive ornamental, for two thousand years it has been used for its bitterness, not for its beauty. The leaves of wormwood yield a strong-scented oil that attracts dogs, repels insects, and causes headaches and nervousness in humans. Extracts of wormwood have been used to expel "worms", or intestinal parasites, from humans and domestic animals, and to repel clothes moths and other household insect pests. Wormwood has been recommended as a digestive tonic, a cure for overeating or indigestion, but pure wormwood oil is quite poisonous. Although it still is used as a flavoring in vermouth, the dangers of wormwood were made obvious in the early 1900s, when thousands of French people became addicted to the wormwood-flavored liqueur absinthe. They gradually suffered paralysis and insanity, and eventually died.

I treat wormwood with caution, for it is a powerful herb. Growing easily from seeds or rooted cuttings, it will make a bushy plant up to three feet tall and two feet wide in its first year. Although the tops die back in winter, the roots are very hardy. Prune off the dead growth each spring and divide the clump every three or four years or when it gets too dense. Wormwood will grow in any garden soil and is tolerant of sun or shade. Unfortunately, other plants are not tolerant of wormwood; some researchers believe that the oil produced by wormwood's foliage inhibits the growth of neighboring plants. I have not noticed this, but many herb gardeners put wormwood in a bed by itself, just in case.

Pick large leaves or cut whole stems for drying at any time during the summer. Tie in bunches and hang to dry, noting that the stems retain moisture much longer than the leaves. If necessary, finish the drying with artificial heat to achieve a crisp texture. Crumble and sift dried wormwood outdoors. Work quickly to finish the job with minimal inhalation of the strong odor. Wormwood can be blended in sachets with other ingredients, to combine its insecticidal properties with the pleasant fragrances of less potent herbs.

Wormwood, *Artemisia absinthium*

SUGGESTED READINGS

Fragrant Plants

The insect pests of stored fiber products are described in "Textile Pests and Their Control" by H.J. Hueck, pp. 76-97 in *Textile Conservation*, edited by Jentina E. Leene (Washington: Smithsonian Institution, 1972), "Clothes Moths and Carpet Beetles: How to Combat Them" (Home and Garden Bulletin No. 24. Washington: U.S. Department of Agriculture, 1953), and "Wool Digestion and Mothproofing" by D.F. Waterhouse, pp. 207-62 in *Advances in Pest Control Research*, Vol. 2, edited by R.L. Metcalfe (New York: Wiley-Interscience, 1958).

Plants with insecticidal properties and the uses of botanical pesticides are discussed in "The Significance of Botanical Pesticides" by Steve Hart *(The Herbarist* 37 [1971]: 51-55), *Pest Control with Nature's Chemicals* by Elroy Rice (New York: Academic Press, 1983), and *Naturally Occurring Insecticides* by Martin Jacobsen (New York: Marcel Dekker, 1971). "The Use of Plants in Control of Agricultural and Domestic Pests" by D.M. Secoy and A.E. Smith *(Economic Botany* 37 [1983]: 28-57) is a listing of plants that are reported to have pesticidal properties. *Insecticidal Materials of Vegetable Origin*, edited by H.J. Holman (London: Imperial Institute, 1940), is the classic reference on this subject.

The botany and cultivation of fragrant plants are presented in *Scented Flora of the World* by Roy Genders (New York: St. Martins, 1977), and *The Fragrant Garden* by Louise Beebe Wilder (reprint of the 1932 edition; New York: Dover, 1974). A popular but somewhat outdated reference on herbs is *A Modern Herbal* (in two volumes) by Maude Grieve (reprint of the 1931 edition; New York: Dover, 1971). *Herbs and Spices* by Julia Morton (New York: Golden Press, 1976) is a small book with accurate and up-to-date information.

For ideas and information on herb gardening, consult *Park's Success with Herbs* by Gertrude B. Foster and Rosemary F. Louden (Greenwood, South Carolina: George Park Seed Company, 1980), *The Herb Garden* by Sarah Garland, in cooperation with the New York Botanic Garden Institute of Urban Horticulture (New York: Penguin, 1984), *The Rodale Herb Book* edited by William Hylton (Emmaus, Pennsylvania: Rodale, 1974), and *Herbs: How to Select, Grow, and Enjoy* by Norma Jean Lathrop (Tucson: Select, 1981). Periodicals about herb gardening include *The Herbarist, The Herb Grower,* and *The Herb Quarterly.*

PLANT MATERIALS USED TO MAKE TEXTILE TOOLS

It's natural, I think, for people who work with their hands to develop a fondness for particular tools. Out in the garden, my trustworthy digging fork is as comfortable to me as old shoes. Each year I gladly resharpen my favorite old pruning shears, the same ones that have cut so many bouquets and have tidied so many straggling branches. In my spinning and weaving studio, I weave one project after another on the same loom, although I've tried many others. It's a matter of finding a tool that feels right, that is sturdy and reliable, that functions smoothly. Satisfaction and fulfillment come from owning and using good tools.

When a craft's tools are handmade, their appeal is even greater. What gardener can resist handmade pottery planters? What weaver can resist handmade wooden shuttles? Gardeners and weavers alike choose handwoven baskets for storing and displaying their materials. Because they are so often unique and individual, antique tools of all kinds are popular among collectors and decorators. Old used tools speak both of the hands that made them and of the hands that used them. People who wouldn't think of learning to spin will buy an old spinning wheel to admire and display, and may think of all the yarn that has been spun on it. For a spinner, using an antique wheel is an affirmation of tradition, a reminder of countless grandmothers and great-grandmothers who also spun.

Looms and spinning wheels are simple machines compared to modern mechanisms such as computers and cars, but even so, they're big steps up from the humble tools of our ancestors. Spinning and weaving are ancient crafts, and the most basic textile tools — spindles, shuttles, looms — have been used around the globe for thousands of years. Often these simple tools are little more than parts of plants, but weavers have made clever use of the materials nature has provided.

SPINDLES AND OTHER SPINNING TOOLS

Although fibers can be twisted by rolling them between the spinner's hands or between palm and thigh, the spun yarn must be wound into a ball or onto a stick for tidy storage. When the stick itself is rolled or spun to insert twist into each new length of yarn, it is called a spindle. Handspindles fashioned from sticks have been found on archeological sites around the world. These hand-spindles are still used in remote lands. The basic spindle is nothing but a smooth straight twig. Adding a round whorl, carved of wood, stone, shell or pottery, adds weight and increases the momentum of the spinning spindle. A hook or notch at one end of the stick helps secure the attachment of the yarn. Different cultures have developed various methods of spinning with a hand-spindle: Some people stand or walk and drop the whirling spindle at their side, others sit and roll the spindle against their leg or twist it in their palm, and others use a shallow dish to support the rotating spindle and take the weight off the yarn.

Although these methods are slow compared to spinning on a belt-driven spinning wheel, they have been used to spin exquisitely fine yarns from all kinds of fibers. The ancient Egyptians spun linen threads so fine that they could be spaced closer than five hundred to the inch for the warp and weft of woven fabrics. (For reference, the very finest contemporary shirt fabrics rarely have more than one hundred threads per inch.) In ancient India, spinners worked twelve hours a day for sixty days to spin a single ounce of cotton into five miles of thread, and weavers made fabrics so fine they were transparent. All this, mind you, with spindles (and looms) made from mere sticks.

The finest yarns are spun from fibers that have been carefully prepared for spinning. Short cotton or wool fibers are prepared by picking, or teasing, to loosen the tangles and to expand the fibers into a fluffy mass. This can be done by hand or with carding devices. Short fibers are readily picked apart by the teeth on a pair of cards. Since the Middle Ages, cards have been made of wire teeth set in a leather backing and mounted on a wooden frame. Earlier models might have been designed with thorns or spines instead of wire teeth; a card excavated from an ancient English lake village had thorns from the Glastonbury thorn tree (Crataegus monogyna) set into a thick leather pad. "Bowing" is another way to decompress a wad of fibers. If a pile of cotton or wool is twanged with a strung bow, the vibrations relax and separate the fibers. Short fibers are fluffed up for spinning, but long wool and most plant fibers are stretched out into smooth parallel alignment instead, by drawing them through combs with long sharp teeth. Either short or long fibers can be arranged on a distaff for storage, so the spinner can draw conveniently from a ready supply of prepared fibers as she spins and spins. Like spindles, distaffs can be simple sticks. A distaff modeled from a forked branch will support a mass of fibers, like a tree crotch supports a bird nest.

REEDS AND OTHER WEAVING TOOLS

On all but the simplest looms, the warps are spaced evenly by a device called a reed. The reed fits into the beater of the loom, and it serves not only to separate the warp threads, but also to pack each new shot of weft firmly into place. Reeds are rectangular in shape, four or five inches high, by as long as the loom is wide. Like a comb, a reed can be fine-toothed or coarse-toothed, with either thin or wide spaces between the teeth. Reeds are designed to have an exact number of spaces, or dents, per inch; this can be as few as two or three or as many as sixty to seventy. The most commonly used reeds have from six to twenty dents per inch. Weavers usually purchase a variety of reeds to meet their requirements for weaving finer and heavier fabrics. Most modern handlooms come equipped with a reed in the beater; the teeth are made of steel or stainless steel wires or bars.

Originally, however, the teeth of reeds were made from thin strips of plant stems. These strips, split and smoothed to uniform thinness, were secured in a wooden framework and positioned between the turns of a cord. The diameter of the cord determined the spacing of the teeth and the number of dents per inch. Sometimes, different colored strips were inserted to mark off the inches, like lines on a ruler. Now, it's easy enough to say that a tool is called a reed because it has been made from sections of split reed plants. But what are reed plants? As it turns out, several large grasses are called reedgrass, giant reed, cane or bamboo, and their common names have been used interchangeably. Even the scientific names of these plants have been changed and reassigned several times in the last century.

Although I've been looking into the origin of the term reed and the history of reed making, I can't say I've learned where reeds were first made and used, or what exact species of plants provided the raw materials. Studying the tools used by early American handweavers, I was surprised to learn that few reeds were made at home by amateurs. Looking at various old reeds that I've picked up at country auctions, I thought that reed making was like basketry or chair caning. I imagined that in colonial days any small town would have at least one old fellow who knew how to fabricate loom reeds. But textile historians point out that reed making was a highly specialized craft, carried out in workshops and factories. Even the self-sufficient and resourceful weavers who did build their own looms usually purchased their reeds. At first, immigrant weavers brought reeds with them when they came from the Old Country, and passed them down through their families. Later, loom reed factories were built in New York, Philadelphia, and other cities and towns. The Englishman John Kay invented metal-toothed reeds in the early 1700s, but reeds made from plant stems were less expensive and remained popular with home weavers through the 1800s.

Other weaving tools have been made of many different materials, depending on what was available. For looms, good solid hardwood is preferred by modern weavers, for strength and durability as well as appearance, but it's pointless to discuss looms in general as there are so many local variations in materials and traditions. Shuttles can likewise be made from whatever hard, straight-grained wood is on hand. Some writers claim that early American handweavers and weaving mills depended on oak or hard maple for loom construction and dogwood or persimmon for shuttles, but I have seen plenty of exceptions and have concluded that most people simply used what they could get. Throughout the years that weaving persisted as a household activity, weaving tools were not highly standardized. Colonial handweavers didn't necessarily build their own looms; often local carpenters or cabinetmakers made and sold looms. But the smaller tools and accessories often were homemade and were as unique and individual as their owners. Old weaving tools frequently are displayed at local history museums, and it's fun to try to figure out what functions they served. Chances are the museum curator doesn't know for sure: Once I saw a bobbin rack with corncob spools for holding the yarn — and there was yarn wound on them — labeled, "A rack for drying corncobs".

TEASELS FOR FINISHING WOOLENS

Freshly woven woolen cloth may seem nice enough as it comes off the loom, but its texture and appearance are greatly improved by a series of finishing treatments. "Fulling", or vigorous washing in warm soapy water, is the first step. It draws the yarns together, filling in the spaces of the weave to make a denser fabric. During fulling, a piece of cloth may shrink as much as twenty-five percent in length and width, but, at the same time, it gets much thicker. After fulling, the surface texture of wool fabrics is enhanced if the cloth is brushed to bring loose fibers to the surface and to raise a soft nap. For this brushing, no man-made substitute works quite as well as the spiny heads of a plant called the fuller's teasel. The teasel's flexible hooked spikes scratch gently at the cloth, yielding to irregularities rather than snagging and tugging. Named from the Anglo-Saxon verb *taesan* (to pluck or pull), the fuller's teasel is an ideal natural tool.

Murals on the walls at Pompeii, illustrating everyday life in the days of the Roman Empire, show the work of spinning, weaving and finishing fabrics. The Romans had learned their finishing techniques from the Egyptians, and in those days, proper finishing of fabric was taken seriously and done by professional members of the fuller's guilds. The murals show workmen using brushing tools made from teasel heads fitted into a wooden frame with a handle. The raised nap was then carefully trimmed to a uniform length with huge blades or shears. The finishing of wool was considered a very important process and was done with great skill and care. From ancient times through the Middle Ages and up until the nineteenth century, fulling, brushing and pressing were all done by hand.

Leonardo da Vinci invented a nap-raising machine in 1490 that used wire teeth instead of teasels, but his idea wasn't appreciated by the fullers' guilds. Three hundred years later, when hand wool finishing was outmoded by the Industrial Revolution and the building of water-powered mills in England and the United States, mills still raised a nap on the wool by passing the cloth against rotating drums fitted with teasel heads. It took a lot of teasels to keep these mills supplied, and for a few decades in the mid 1800s, teasels were a commercial crop in upstate New York. Old U.S. Department of Agriculture reports quote yields of up to two hundred thousand teasels per acre, valued at two to three dollars per thousand. The crop was harvested by men who picked as many as twenty thousand teasels a day, then dried, trimmed and sorted, and sent them off to foreign and domestic mills. By the late 1800s, however, nearly all mills began to use wire bristles instead of teasels. Today there is one mill in the United States that uses a teasel-equipped drum to custom brush handwoven fabric.

You don't have to join a fullers' guild to grow and use your own teasels. It takes two years for the plants to grow and mature, but after you have collected and dried a handful of teasel heads, you can insert them into a frame and try brushing. Large and small, old and new teasels all have different effects. You can combine and mix them in your brushing tool for an all-in-one treatment, or you can use them separately to see how each works on your fabric. As old teasels break down, you'll need to discard and replace them, so teasel tools are designed to be easy to refill.

The nap of a fabric is affected by the fineness or coarseness of the wool fibers themselves, the way the yarn was spun and the way the fabric was woven, and by the way the cloth was brushed. Fine wools make a softer nap than coarse wools, and softly spun yarns yield more fibers to the nap than firmly or tightly spun yarns. If the same yarn is woven in either plain or twill weave, you'll find it easier to raise a nap on the twill fabric, where longer sections of yarn appear on the surface. Brushing fabric while it is slightly wet will yield a smooth close finish, and brushing dry fabric will yield a more upright nap. I've had the best results by washing and rinsing newly woven wool fabric, spinning it in the automatic washer to remove excess moisture, then spreading the damp cloth on a smooth table or workbench for brushing. I brush in one direction and then the other, on either or both surfaces of the still-damp cloth, until it looks and feels the way I want it to. Then I press the cloth with a steam iron and a pressing cloth to smooth out wrinkles in the fabric, and then leave it to rest and dry. I have brushed blankets and throws, scarves and shawls, and jacket and coat fabrics. Wool is the most common material for brushing, but angora, alpaca, cashmere and mohair brush up just as well, and cotton makes a nice flannel. Knitted items also can be brushed after they are steamed and blocked, sometimes with unexpected results. I have one sweater whose fuzziness is so appealing that every time I wear it complete strangers come up and ask to touch it.

PLANTS TO KNOW AND GROW FOR USE AS TOOLS

The plants in this chapter's list are rather easy to obtain because they are popular ornamentals. They all are attractive, trouble-free and hardy, and interesting to grow. Many gardeners choose and enjoy these plants even though they never intend to fabricate a reed, spin on a spindle, or brush up a nap with a teasel tool. If you *do* choose to try using these products, you'll value the plants even more.

Reed, Cane and Bamboo

Several different species of tall grassy plants with hollow stems all go by the common names of reed, cane or bamboo. All are striking ornamental plants, but before you dig and plant, choose a site with care. These grasses get very tall, spread to form large dense patches, and live forever. If you have a spare corner, though, consider growing your own supply of useful reedy stems. These plants all are propagated by root division, not from seed. Starter plants are available from several nurseries. It's best to set them out in early spring. They prefer full sun and moist soil and benefit from a heavy mulch for the first year or two while their root systems are becoming established.

Reed, or common reedgrass (*Phragmites australis*, formerly *P. communis*), is normally considered to be a marsh plant; it grows in wet soil near streams and lakes in temperate climates around the world, and is tolerant of brackish, or salty, as well as fresh water. But common reedgrass also will grow in dry upland soils, and I have seen healthy patches in vacant lots, on highway median strips, and on highway shoulders. Common reed is the hardiest of these large grasses and grows as a wild plant throughout the United States. Reedgrass gets introduced to an area when its tiny tufted seeds land and germinate on a spot of moist soil. Some biologists think that reedgrass and other marsh plants have been aided in their dispersal by their seeds riding along in mud stuck to the feet of migrating shorebirds. At any rate, once a reedgrass begins to grow, it can spread by stout, creeping rhizomes or rootstocks to form large stands, eventually covering acres of marshland and enduring for centuries. These huge patches are especially attractive when a wind blows through them, twisting the stems so that all the leaves align in the same direction and waving the fluffy plumes of flowers. Reedgrass grows ten to fifteen feet tall and has a dozen or more smooth flat leaves, two inches wide by twelve to sixteen inches long, spaced along each upright stem or culm. The leaves are tough and flexible and useful in weaving mats or baskets. The dried stems, harvested in autumn, have been used to make thatched roofs, light fences, screens and lattices, mats, and baskets. These stems are very durable. A reedgrass roof will last through a century of rainy British weather. Reedgrass matting, made by prehistoric Indians more than a thousand years ago, has been retrieved from dry caves in the Southwest.

Giant reed *(Arundo donax)* is very much like common reedgrass, but the culms are taller and thicker in diameter. Also, giant reed is less hardy and is damaged by late frosts after new growth appears in the spring, so it is grown only in southern Europe and in the southern United States. Giant reed has been widely planted along irrigation ditches in Texas and California, where it helps to control erosion and serves as a windbreak. A form with white- or yellow-striped leaves is offered by several nurseries. It makes an excellent ornamental grass, preferring moist soil and full sun, but tolerating almost any conditions. In Italy, giant reed is raised in managed stands called canebrakes and is harvested for use as garden stakes, for use in light construction, and for making baskets. Perhaps the most important use of giant reed is in making reeds for clarinets, oboes, and other woodwind instruments. This is an outgrowth of earlier uses of the plant for making flutes and panpipes.

The stems of both common reedgrass and giant reed die back each fall. These old dead stems will eventually decay, but quite a bit of litter can accumulate in a clump of these big grasses. The obvious solution is to cut the stems back to the ground and use them in basketry, weaving, tool making, or even as garden stakes. Save the fluffy tops for dried arrangements. The new growth will be healthier, and the clump will look tidier, if you clear away the old stems at least every other year.

Cane *(Arundinaria gigantea)* is a hardy native bamboo. Huge dense colonies of cane, called canebrakes, once filled river bottomlands from Virginia to the Ohio Valley and southward into Florida and Texas. The canes were used for fishing poles and woven into baskets and mats. Early explorers reported on the abundance of cane and measured some culms that were as thick as three inches in diameter and up to twenty-five feet tall. I've never come upon a canebrake that lived up to that description, though, because the young shoots are very attractive to cattle and other domestic animals. Centuries of grazing have long since destroyed most of the aboriginal canebrakes. Cane looks like a large grass with purplish stems and rough-edged leaves up to twelve inches long. The roots are hardy to -20° F if protected by a thick mulch. The plant is a long-lived perennial. Other species of *Arundinaria*, native to China and Japan, are similar in growth and hardiness but sometimes considered more attractive than our native cane.

Bamboo is the raw material for countless crafts and construction projects in the Orient and throughout the tropics. If you have the space (these plants can be quite invasive and spread quickly if not controlled), you might try either the golden bamboo *(Phyllostachys aurea)* or the giant timber bamboo *(P. bambusoides)*. Both of these bamboos are surprisingly hardy. The stems and leaves of older shoots are evergreen if not frozen hard, and new shoots grow up each spring. The roots can survive temperatures as low as -20° F if thickly mulched. Golden bamboo can be trimmed to any height or left to grow to fifteen feet tall. It has yellowish stems one to two inches in diameter and plenty of green leaves five inches long. Giant timber bamboo will grow to seventy feet tall and will reach six inches in diameter! I once stayed a few days in a cabin that was dwarfed by a dooryard planting of giant bamboo, and I was surprised by the sounds it made. In breezy weather, all the hollow stems ring like wind chimes as they sway and clang together.

I think that the stems of any of these plants — reed, giant reed, cane, or bamboo — could have been used to make loom reeds. All of them have stems that are easily split into thin strips, with a fine texture that can be shaved or sanded to a smooth finish. Perhaps the makers of reeds for looms sought out one or another desired raw material, or perhaps they didn't distinguish between these alternatives. Maybe other researchers will be able to learn more about the reed makers of the past. Modern weavers and gardeners will use the useful stems of reed plants for all kinds of indoor and outdoor projects, even if they never do make a reed.

Spindle Tree

Staff tree family. Spindle tree *(Euonymus europaea)* is a slender small tree or shrub native to Europe but frequently planted in North American gardens. It was named not by common usage, but by the botanist William Turner in 1568, who wrote, "I coulde never learne an Englishe name for it. The Duche men call it in Netherlande, 'spilboome', that is, spindel-tree, because they use

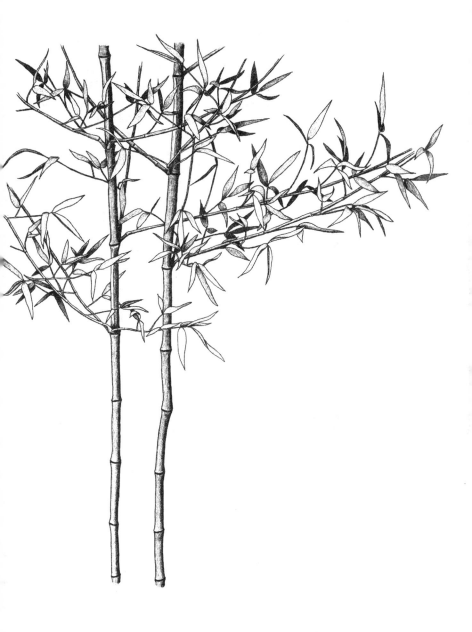

Golden bamboo, *Phyllostachys aurea*

to make spindels of it in that country, and me thynke it may be as wel named in English seying we have no other name." Actually, the twigs and wood also were used for knitting needles and were made into bird cages. They really are no better suited for spindles than many other straight-grained stems or stalks, but the name spindle tree has persisted. First applied to the single species *(E. europaea)*, the name was later applied to the spindle tree genus *(Euonymus)*.

Spindle tree grows rather slowly, reaching a height of fifteen to twenty feet after several years. The opposite leaves are two to four inches long, smooth and oblong, and slightly toothed along the margins. They turn a bright yellow-orange in fall. The flowers are small and inconspicuous in early summer but develop into remarkable fruits, with fleshy neon pink hulls that open to reveal shocking orange berries. Many gardeners grow spindle tree for these showy and ornamental fruits, which open just as the leaves develop their richest fall color. The opposite branches of the tree make an attractive silhouette in winter. The twigs of spindle tree are straight and slender, square in cross section, and quite strong. The wood itself is pale yellow and close-grained.

Other species are sometimes called spindle tree, including the native American spindle tree or burning bush *(E. atropurpurea)* and the winged spindle tree *(E. alata)*. Like the European spindle tree, these are attractive garden specimens, hardy to 0° F or colder, and not particular about soil or exposure. Container-grown plants are available from many nurseries and easily adjust to transplanting. Spindle trees are normally propagated by cuttings, rather than from seed. All species of *Euonymus* are notoriously susceptible to attack by scale insects. Scale insects rarely kill plants, but they do disfigure and distort the growing shoots. Unfortunately, it seems that being infested with scale is the normal condition of a spindle tree, and the best a gardener can hope for is a series of remissions, but never a permanent cure. To help control scale, lightly spray dormant oil on spindle trees in the spring, before the buds swell. Two or more sprayings with insecticidal soap during the growing season also will help.

The leaves, bark and fruits of spindle trees are all poisonous. The attractive berries, in particular, are fiercely purgative, so warn children not to touch or taste them. There is no danger in handling or using the twigs, however. Although many other plants serve just fine as spindle sources, it is fun to grow this small tree that earned the recognition and name of spindle tree.

Fuller's Teasel

Teasel family. The fuller's teasel *(Dipsacus sativus*, formerly *D. fullonum)* is a native of southern Europe and has been cultivated and used since the days of the Roman Empire. It has been planted in northern Europe and England, the United States, Pakistan, and other countries where wool is woven and finished. The head of the true fuller's teasel is uniquely equipped with small hooked spikes that are stiff but flexible. No man-made substitute works quite as well for raising the nap on fabrics. The wild teasel *(D. sylvestris)*, also a native European but now a common and widespread roadside weed in the United States, is no substitute for the fuller's teasel. Common teasels are similar in growth and habit, but differ in the most important way.[1] The spines on common teasel heads are weak and straight, rather than strong and curved, and they are absolutely useless as finishing tools.

Many seed companies sell fuller's teasel seeds, for the dried heads are popular in winter arrangements. Sow seeds in early spring. When started under lights or in a greenhouse, transplants are ready to set out after eight weeks. To sow directly, scatter seeds on well-prepared soil and cover lightly. Teasels develop best on deep rich soil and need full sun. By June, transplant or thin seedlings to their permanent spacing of twelve to eighteen inches apart. A young teasel plant seems to grow leaves slowly, because it first develops a good taproot, but by midsummer the top growth also makes good progress. Teasel leaves spread into a flat rosette the first summer. This can be as small as eight inches in diameter or as large as thirty inches, depending on soil fertility and moisture. I boost the plants with a dose of vegetable garden fertilizer to encourage vigorous growth, because larger plants yield a bigger crop of teasel heads. After the first season, nutrients produced in the leaves are stored in the taproot, and the plants go dormant over the winter. Teasels are hardy in most of the United States, especially if the crowns are covered with snow or protected by mulch.

The second year, flowering stems up to six feet tall shoot up over the flat old rosette. These stems have prickly spines along four ridges and are clasped by pairs of large opposite leaves with toothed margins. Sometimes rain water collects in the cups where the leaf bases are joined together. The name *Dipsacus* (Greek for thirst) refers to this water. Medieval herbalists ascribed various magical properties to teasel water! The flowering stalks branch repeatedly, with a cylindrical flower head at the tip of each branch. The

---

1. Some botanists wonder if fuller's teasels are really a separate species from common teasels, and maintain that the difference between stiff curved spines and weak straight spines is a matter of where and how the plants are grown. An old wives' tale claims that if a crop of fuller's teasels is neglected, abandoned, or grown on poor soil, the plants will relapse into the wild form. After looking at many patches of teasel plants, I think that plants grown from fuller's teasel seeds bear curved spines, and plants grown from common teasel seeds bear straight spines. Growing conditions determine how big the plants get and how many teasels they produce, but not what kind of teasels they produce.

Fuller's teasel, *Dipsacus sativus*

flowers open from June to August in most regions, or earlier in very mild climates. The center head, first to mature, is the largest or "king" teasel, and may be four inches long and one and one-half inches thick. Secondary heads, smaller and later, are called "middlings"; the smallest are "buttons". Each head is an aggregate of hundreds of tiny lavender-petaled flowers, each with numerous chaffy bracts and a single curved spiny bract. As soon as the flowers have all dropped off, a teasel head is ready to harvest and dry. Wear gloves and use pruning shears to cut off the head and several inches of stem. Harvest repeatedly and tie the teasels in bunches to hang and dry. If left in the garden too long, the heads get discolored and the spines get brittle, but if harvested promptly, the heads darken from green to brown and gradually stiffen as they dry.

Like most biennials, teasels are difficult to place in the garden design. First they're small, then they're flat, then they're huge, and then they're dead – in just two growing seasons. It's worth finding a place for teasels, though, for their unique appearance and properties. I combine flowering annuals with teasels for the first summer, then let the teasels have the whole bed when they go to flower the second year. One or two teasel plants is enough to supply a dozen or so teasel heads. That will fill a hand-held teasel tool and raise the nap on many yards of woolen goods.

SUGGESTED READINGS

Textile Tools

The use of handspindles for spinning is described and illustrated in *Methods of Handspinning in Egypt and the Sudan* by Grace M. Crowfoot and H. Ling Roth (reprint of the 1931 edition; McMinnville, Oregon: Robin and Russ Handweavers, 1974), *Handspindles* by Bette Hochberg (Santa Cruz, California: Bette Hochberg, 1977), and *Reprints of Bette Hochberg's Textile Articles* by Bette Hochberg (Santa Cruz, California: Bette Hochberg, 1982).

For illustrations that trace the development of tools for spinning and weaving from ancient civilizations through the Industrial Revolution, study the engravings that accompany the informative text in "Spinning and Weaving" by R. Patterson, pp. 191-220 in Vol. 2 and 151-80 in Vol. 3 of *A History of Technology*, edited by Charles Singer (Oxford: Clarendon, 1956). A more specialized study is *The Wool Textile Industry in Great Britain* by J. Geraint Jenkins (London: Routledge and Kegan Paul, 1972).

A few reports remain from the days when teasels were raised as a crop; an example is "The Teasel and Its Cultivation" by Lorenzo Rouse, pp. 315-19 in *Part 2, Agriculture, of the Annual Report, Commissioner of Patents: 1850* (Washington: U.S. Patent Office, 1850). A description of the contemporary Ihana Brushing Mill is presented in "Tämä On Ihana" by Jean Scorgie (*Handwoven* 7, no. 1 [Jan.-Feb. 1986]: 45).

Fashioning simple tools from plants is the subject of *Plantcraft* by Richard Mabey (New York: Universe Books, 1978). Textile tools are included with many other topics in the appealing book *Home Life in Colonial Days* by Alice Morse Earle (reprint of the 1898 edition; Stockbridge, Massachusetts: Berkshire Traveller, 1974). See also the chapter on "Tools and Equipment" in *Keep Me Warm One Night* by Harold B. and Dorothy K. Burnham (Toronto: University of Toronto Press, 1972), and *The Textile Tools of Colonial Homes* by Marion Channing (Marion, Massachusetts: Channing Books, 1971). A particularly well-written and comprehensive survey of spinning is *Spinning Wheels, Spinners, and Spinning* by Patricia Baines (McMinnville, Oregon: Robin and Russ Handweavers, 1976). For a look at looms from around the world, find a copy of *The Book of Looms* by Eric Broudy (New York: Van Nostrand Reinhold, 1978).

CREATING A GARDEN

Sooner or later, after reading and reading about plants, you just have to go out and dig. Eager gardeners go forth in springtime with enthusiasm and optimism, ready to turn up sod, create new beds, sow seeds, and set out plants. According to surveys, gardening is America's most popular hobby — people of all ages find great satisfaction in watching plants grow. Whether you have a small patio or courtyard in town or acreage in the country to work with, you can create a garden and enjoy learning about and using different kinds of plants. If you already have experience in growing vegetables or flowers, you'll find it easy to branch out into something new and try some of the plants described in this book.

Different regions of the United States have vastly different climates and soils, and require different schedules and methods of gardening. There are several ways to learn more about gardening in your area. Information on average temperatures and rainfall, soil properties and requirements, pest and disease control, and other subjects is readily available from state extension agents. Check bookstores and libraries for books written particularly for your area, and look through the garden pages of regional magazines such as *Sunset* and *Southern Living.* Many community colleges and adult education programs offer workshops and short courses in horticulture; these are usually tailored to the local situation. Enrolling in a class is a good way to meet other gardeners. Joining a gardening club is another opportunity to find people who share your interests. For further study, several books that provide general information on gardening techniques, landscape design, and plant care are listed in the references for this chapter.

PLANNING AND PREPARATION

Site and Climate

In general, garden plants need six to eight hours of sunlight a day, so a garden site should be away from the shade of trees or buildings. Plants in gardens surrounded by trees also suffer from underground competition, as the trees' roots take up most of the available water and nutrients. Gardens located too close to buildings may be dry if they are sheltered from natural precipitation, or they may be splashed or flooded by runoff from the roof. An open site is best, but it's nice to have a water source and toolshed nearby. I think a garden should be convenient to your home so you can monitor and enjoy it daily during the growing season. You may need fencing to protect the garden from predators or trespassers. A surfaced path will make it easier to get to the garden in wet weather.

Several aspects of climate affect plant growth. More than any other factor, the annual temperature range determines which plants will do well in your garden. Data on the average temperatures for your area will give you a general idea of what plants you can expect to grow. Plant hardiness zones are based on wintertime low temperatures, and perennial plants are rated as more or less hardy depending on how much cold they tolerate. For annual plants, however, a more important consideration is the length of the frost-free season during which tender plants can be grown outside without protection. In cold climates, you can raise tender perennials in containers, setting them out in the summer and then bringing them inside for the winter. Also, you can extend the growing season by several weeks in both spring and fall by using cold frames, tent-like plastic greenhouses, mulches, and other plant protectors. In addition to temperature, precipitation also varies with climate. Both the total amount and the seasonal distribution of precipitation are important factors influencing plant growth. Some plants don't do well in areas with extremely high rainfall and humidity, although planting in raised beds and spacing the plants to allow good air circulation will help control mildew and fungus problems. In dry areas, irrigating and mulching can provide all the moisture plants need, within limits set by the supply and cost of the water and mulch. Finally, too much wind can cause problems in a garden, drying out the soil and the plant foliage, and breaking stems and branches. Hedges or fences used as windbreaks will reduce the damage. Different regions, and different seasons, all present their own challenges to overcome, but each year enthusiastic home gardeners produce vegetables and flowers in every part of the country. They have demonstrated that it's possible to grow a good garden in any kind of climate and to make the best of any site.

Soil Improvement

Few gardeners are lucky enough to start out with fertile loamy soil, but fortunately, any soil, no matter how poor it seems, can be improved. Plants are anchored and supported by their roots, and they absorb water and mineral nutrients from the soil. The important properties of soil are texture and particle size, organic matter content, pH and fertility. The texture of soil affects aeration, drainage, cultivation and root growth. Clay soils are made up of extremely fine mineral particles that pack into a dense heavy mass. Clay soil is hard to till. When wet, it sticks to your tools and boots; when dry, it hardens into brick-like clods. Clay holds water and nutrients well but isn't porous enough for air to penetrate down to the roots. (To grow and function well, roots require oxygen.) In sandy soils, the mineral particles are much larger, so the soil is light and loose. Water drains right through, leaving air to fill the spaces between the particles. Digging in sandy soil is as easy as playing at the beach, but sand dries out quickly and doesn't hold nutrients well. The ideal soil, loam, contains particles of different sizes. Loam holds moisture, has air spaces, and is loose enough to cultivate easily.

Most garden soils are improved by adding generous quantities of organic matter, such as compost, leaves, grass clippings, straw or hay, rotted sawdust, manure, or peat moss. In areas where topsoil has been lost through poor farming practices and erosion, adding organic matter to the soil in a garden will produce dramatic increases in plant vigor and productivity. Organic matter lightens up the soil and makes it so soft that roots grow easily. It acts like a sponge to hold moisture, and it supports a population of microorganisms that recycle minerals and supply a steady source of nutrients for plant growth. Returning quantities of plant matter to the soil is a natural way to balance out the loss of nutrients when a crop is harvested. It's almost impossible to add too much. I spread organic mulch at least four to eight inches deep during the growing season, let it decay during the summer, then till it into the soil in the fall or spring.

Kits are available for home testing of soil pH and fertility, but it is easier and more reliable to send a soil sample to your state soil testing laboratory. Get instructions from your extension agent on how to collect and submit a sample. Several commercial testing labs also provide this service and include a list of recommendations with their analysis. The pH value is a measure of soil acidity or alkalinity. Most plants mentioned in this book grow best in soil with a pH between 6.5 and 7.0 (neutral), but some will tolerate pH values as low as 5.5 (acidic) or as high as 8.5 (alkaline). It is common to alter the pH of soil with chemical treatments: Lime is used to raise the pH of acid soils and aluminum sulfate is used to lower the pH of alkaline soils. Soil pH is important in itself, and also important because pH affects the availability of nutrients that are dissolved in the soil water. Plants require nitrogen, phosphorus, potassium, calcium, magnesium, iron, sulfur, and several other elements for good growth. Soil fertility is determined by the supply of these nutrients. Nutrients can be added to a garden in the form of chemical fertilizers, which are simple salts that dissolve quickly, or as natural compounds, such as manure, blood, bonemeal, or compost, which are complex substances that break down more slowly. I use diluted solutions of soluble fertilizers to boost seedlings and transplants, and generous applications of organic fertilizers to release nutrients into the soil throughout the growing season.

Garden Design

Many gardeners get plenty of satisfaction just from choosing different kinds of interesting and attractive plants and watching them grow. For these gardeners, the focus is on the individual plants, not the garden as a whole. Other gardeners like to plan and design their gardens, and then step back to see the overall effects of combinations and groups of plants. These individuals design gardens that express their personalities, from formal and sophisticated to spontaneous and casual. On a larger scale, very distinctive garden styles are associated with different cultures and different periods in history; for example, compare British cottage gardens, Japanese temple gardens, or early American plantation gardens.

Designing a garden to meet horticultural, practical, and artistic concerns is quite a challenge. Horticultural concerns include choosing and combining specific kinds of plants; trying to position particular plants where they will get the most appropriate soil, drainage and exposure; providing enough space for plants to grow without competition; rotating crops of annual plants to minimize carryover of pests and diseases; and providing winter protection for perennial plants. Practical concerns include keeping the initial costs of materials for paths, borders and fences to a minimum; laying out beds that make it easy to cultivate, maintain and harvest your plants; avoiding plants that grow too large for the setting and have to be pruned continually or replaced; and using edgings or retainers to restrict the root growth of aggressive perennials. Artistic concerns include arranging plants by height and shape, combining different colors and textures of flowers and foliage, providing a sequence of attractive features over the entire growing season, and creating an effect or style appropriate to the owner and the setting.

My advice on garden design is to decide first which plants will be grown in large quantities and harvested as crops and which will be grown in small quantities. If you would like to grow enough ramie or cotton to yield a pound or more of fibers, or enough indigo or woad to dye a pound of yarn, set the plants out in rows or beds in the garden just as you would crops of corn or beans. Nice straight rows or beds look tidy and are easy to maintain, and evenly spaced plants grow uniformly to produce maximum yield. If you would like to grow just a few cotton or woad plants to see what they look like, try combining them with a few fragrant herbs, a soapwort, and perhaps a fuller's teasel in a specially designed display garden.

To combine different kinds of plants in a single bed, keep these principles in mind: Space individual plants far enough apart so that they don't have to compete with each other for soil, water and light; put tall plants in the back or center of the bed, and shorter plants up front or around the edge. As simple as these rules sound, it's very difficult to follow them! Little plants and seeds all seem so small on the warm spring day when you're setting them out — it's very tempting to set them too close together in the bed. And when they're still little, it's hard to judge which will get tall, which will spread wide, and which will stay compact. Plan ahead to know how much space to allow and where to position different kinds of plants. It is very useful to follow a planting diagram. Use a yardstick to be sure that your spacing is adequate.

It's nice to dream about having a big, beautiful garden, but don't despair if you have only a small city lot, a bare patch of hard-packed dirt and sod, or the rubble and mud left after the construction of a new house. Start small, working up a few square feet at a time, improving the soil as you go. It's much more satisfying to have a tiny garden with a few healthy plants in good order than to have a big unkempt patch of straggly plants and weeds. Don't try to do too much all at once. Enlarge and refine your garden over the years. Most important, take time to enjoy your work and to take pleasure in the plants. Experiment with different kinds of plants and learn about them. Use the plants you grow to make special products. Share your interest with other gardeners, and take the time to visit their gardens too.

Garden Plans

The four garden plans presented here are based on my experience and my measurements of how much room different plants require. I hope they will help you get started. After a few seasons, you will be ready to draw your own garden design.

A rectangular garden 4′ by 15′

1. Madder
2. Yucca
3. Flax
4. Woad
5. Weld
6. Camphor basil
7. Teasels
8. Coreopsis
9. Pennyroyal
10. Cotton
11. Tansy
12. Southernwood
13. Ramie
14. Lavender
15. Soapwort

Garden Plan #1 is for a rectangular bed or border four feet wide by fifteen feet long. It could be open on both sides or backed with a fence or wall. This plan is a good one to start with and demonstrates some of the most important sources of each product used by weavers. It features plants that are relatively easy to obtain and grow. Yucca, madder, tansy, soapwort, lavender, and southernwood are all durable perennials that require only periodic pruning and division. With a thick mulch for winter protection, ramie and pennyroyal can be grown as perennials in many regions. The biennials (woad, teasels and weld) will die back after flowering; they can be allowed to self-seed or you can raise new plants to set out as replacements. Pennyroyal, woad and weld can also be raised as annuals and harvested for use the first year. Flax and cotton can be sown in place: a square yard of closely spaced flax and a triangle of three cotton plants set eighteen inches apart. A plant of fragrant camphor basil and two or three colorful coreopsis or cosmos complete the garden.

A container garden for a patio 6′ by 10′

1. Cotton
2. Soapbark
3. Patchouli
4. Vetiver
5. Lavender
6. Bamboo
7. Eucalyptus
8. Dyer's knotwed
9. New Zealand flax
10. Cosmos
11. Annatto
12. Ramie
13. Indigo

Garden Plan #2 is for a container garden: all of these plants can be grown in pots. The L-shape extends approximately six by ten feet. The plants could sit around the edge of a patio all year in a very mild climate, or spend summers on the patio and winters inside the house in a cool or cold climate. For best growth, these plants require four to six hours a day of direct sun. New Zealand flax, confined to a large pot or tub, will make an attractive foliage plant for years. Wrinkly-leaved ramie should be cut back and divided every year or two to encourage steady production of new shoots. The cotton can be left to grow into a woody shrub, but it is more attractive as a young plant, so it's best to start one anew from seed each year. Annatto will grow from seed into an attractive small shrub in a few years. Cosmos, indigo and dyer's knotweed can be raised as annuals, harvested as they come into bloom, and discarded or replaced. French lavender and patchouli both appreciate a few months' rest in a cool, dry, but bright spot during the winter. Vetiver will quickly fill a container with spongy roots which can be trimmed off when it is divided and replanted. Lemon-scented or dwarf silver-dollar eucalyptus, soapbark, and dwarf bamboos can be kept in tubs for several years if they are pruned occasionally and not fertilized too much.

Garden Plan #3 is for a circular garden about twenty feet in diameter. It requires full sun and could be located in an open area surrounded by lawn. Tie one end of a ten-foot-long string to a stake in the center of the planned bed and hold the other end as you walk around marking the edge of the circle. Allow the intersecting paths to be three feet wide, and prepare the four wedge-shaped beds. One bed holds five cotton plants, a half-dozen dyer's knotweeds, and a single Indian tobacco. Another bed holds a half-dozen coreopsis plants, a small patch of flax, a single eucalyptus, one or two dye sunflowers, and a half-dozen plants of roselle. The plants in these two beds can all be grown as annuals, raised from seed sown directly in place or started in pots indoors. The other two beds are more permanent. One holds a supply of soapwort (which will spread, so contain it with edging!), a fragrant lavender plant, a biennial fuller's teasel (which will need replacement every other year), and a patch of madder. The last bed holds a clump of milkweed, a specimen of pokeweed, two or three pyrethrum daisies, a yucca, and a bushy patch of dyer's broom. Except for the teasel, the plants in these two beds should remain in place for years.

A round garden 20′ in diameter

1. Soapwort
2. Fuller's teasel
3. Madder
4. Lavender
5. Cotton
6. Indian tobacco
7. Dyer's knotweed
8. Roselle
9. Eucalyptus

10. Coreopsis
11. Hopi dye sunflower
12. Flax
13. Yucca
14. Pyrethrum daisies
15. Milkweed
16. Dyer's broom
17. Pokeweed

A low-maintenance border 7′ by 30′

1. Madder
2. Soapwort
3. Milkweed
4. Yucca
5. Reedgrass
6. Coreopsis
7. Fuller's teasels
8. Spindlebush
9. Tansy
10. Woad
11. Sumac
12. Wormwood
13. Pokeweed
14. Dyer's broom

Garden Plan #4 is a low-maintenance garden for a large sunny space—across the back of a lot, perhaps. It measures seven feet deep by thirty feet long. Use mulch between the plants to control weeds, and leave space to step in among the plants for harvesting. This large garden includes some plants that show up well from a distance and have interesting colors, textures and shapes. The shrubs sumac and spindle bush have bright fall foliage and attractive silhouettes all year. Pokeweed is also colorful in late summer and fall but dies to the ground over the winter. Reedgrass and teasels grow tall as a backdrop for a patch of free-flowering coreopsis. In this setting you could allow teasels to self-sow, and thin the seedlings to twelve inches apart. Yucca flowers are showy and fragrant in early summer, and both soapwort and milkweed blossoms give off a heavy sweet perfume on summer evenings. Madder will sprawl and fill in the corner area. Tansy, wormwood and broom will grow for years with little attention other than an annual clean-up and trimming. Watch the woad patch, removing extra seed stalks after flowering, and thin the seedlings to grow at least six inches apart. With minimum annual maintenance, this garden will provide a variety of products to harvest for years and years.

GETTING AND GROWING PLANTS

Sources

Finding seeds or plants of the different species in this book is a project in itself. Very few of these plants are available at your local nursery or garden center, but you can order them by mail or obtain them from other gardeners. Ordering seeds and plants by mail is very reliable these days. It's remarkable how many kinds of plants are available, and it's impressive to see how well little plants come through the packing and shipping process. I have listed several seed companies and nurseries that include various useful plants in their catalogs, but there is no single source that carries the majority of plants in this book. To get started, order several different catalogs. Once you get on some mailing lists and begin to place orders, catalogs will come to you! Check the advertisements at the back of gardening magazines to learn of new suppliers each year—perhaps they will have something you are looking for. Reading catalogs is both stimulating and confusing. You'll want to order dozens of kinds of plants, but you'll wonder if you can take care of them all. Remember, you can always wait until next year to try something new. Don't get overwhelmed. Most catalogs list a few new or different kinds of seeds each year, so keep looking for hard-to-find plants, and you may find a source sooner or later. Sometimes the plants are listed by common name, sometimes by scientific name, and sometimes by variation of the common or scientific name. Look carefully to find the plants or seeds under one or another listing. Some catalogs generously provide information on growing and maintaining the plants they sell; this is especially useful for learning how to get different kinds of seeds to germinate. Order seeds as soon as you decide what you want, because you'll get much prompter service before the spring rush begins. The sooner your seeds arrive, the sooner you can begin to grow them. Place orders for plants early also, because many nurseries have limited supplies and fill orders on a "first come, first served" basis. Your plants will be shipped to you at the best time to plant them outside.

In the past ten years or so, a grass roots movement has spread among gardeners nationwide: Saving seeds of special varieties of vegetables (particularly "heirloom" vegetable varieties that have been passed down through a family or a local community) and exchanging them with other gardeners. The Seed-Savers Exchange, at the forefront of the movement, began as a network of gardeners who wanted to preserve and share a wide variety of vegetable crops. The National Gardening Association, through a column in their monthly magazine, coordinates a seed swap program that includes flowers, herbs, and native plants, as well as vegetables. Other organizations have started up to promote saving and exchanging varieties of fruit trees, propagating and distributing wildflowers and trees, or locating and promoting regional plant specialties. I propose that gardeners and weavers organize an exchange network, sharing and distributing seeds and plants of fiber, dye, soap, scent and tool sources. Network members could list what they have available to distribute and what they are looking for, both sharing and gaining through the exchange. Members requesting seeds would pay for postage and handling. This would be an opportunity for gardeners to communicate directly with one another and to learn from each other's experience. It would serve to preserve and distribute plants that are special and useful to weavers which aren't included in commercial catalogs.

Propagation

Some plants are propagated from seed, and others from cuttings or division. With some practice and attention to detail, you can master different propagation techniques and produce your own supply of plants. You don't need a greenhouse or expensive equipment, but you do need to be watchful and solicitous of the little plants. When they are young and small, plants are much more vulnerable to damage caused by too much or too little water, too cold or too hot temperatures, and various fungal diseases. Follow these instructions to get started and read general gardening books for more information.

Some Plants to Raise from Seed. *Alkanet, camphor basil, coreopsis, cotton, dye sunflower, eucalyptus, flax, fuller's teasel, Indian tobacco, indigo, Japanese indigo, kenaf, lavender, milkweed, nettles, pennyroyal, pokeweed, pyrethrum, roselle, safflower, soap plant, soapwort, tansy, weld, woad, wormwood.*

Large seeds, seeds of plants that don't transplant well, and seeds of plants like flax that are sown by the thousands are all sown directly into the garden soil where they are to grow. Prepare for planting by cultivating the soil and raking the surface smooth. Sow seeds in rows or hills, or broadcast and mark their locations with stakes or labels. Cover seeds with fine soil to a depth of two to three times their thickness and gently pat the soil to settle it down against the seeds. To be sure that seeds sown outdoors will germinate and grow, pay close attention to the following factors. First, read the seed catalog or packet to learn the best soil temperature for starting each kind of seed. Some, such as lavender, require exposure to cold soil before they will sprout, but most seeds germinate best in warm soil. Second, check daily and never let the soil dry out after the seeds have been planted. Add water gently with a sprinkling can or spread cloth or paper over the soil to hold moisture in. Remove the covering when the sprouts appear above the soil. Third, be careful not to cover the seeds with too much soil; use a ruler, and don't plant small seeds more than one-quarter inch deep or pack the soil down too hard over them. Many kinds of seeds sprout in one to three weeks, but others take months to germinate. When seedlings are a few inches tall, thin to the appropriate spacing.

If seeds of many hardy annual, biennial, or perennial plants, such as woad, weld, milkweed and fuller's teasel, are allowed to mature on the plant, they will scatter on the soil and come up by themselves the next year. Some gardeners welcome this and tolerate or encourage self-sowing as an easy way to have new plants year after year. I don't find it all that easy, myself, because the plants that do come back are likely to come back in excess. All those extra seedlings are just more weeds I have to thin out. Often, I leave a few plants in the garden to produce seeds, but I prefer to pick off the mature fruits in the fall and harvest the seeds. Then I can save as many as I need to sow the following year and share or dispose of the rest. I think this is especially important if you are growing a plant like woad that is potentially quite weedy. Grow as much as you need, but be responsible about preventing its spread into agricultural fields or other people's gardens.

Small seeds, seeds of plants that need a long growing season, and rare or expensive seeds of unusual plants can be started indoors and later transplanted to the garden. Start sowing seeds six to eight weeks before the last frost date. Moisten a batch of sterile commercial potting soil and use it to fill individual plastic pots or trays. Then, sow one kind of seeds in each container and label containers with the plant names and the dates they were planted. Sow about twice as many seeds as you need plants to allow for losses, but don't waste seeds by sowing more than that. Try to space the seeds at least one-quarter to one-half inch apart, so the seedlings won't be too crowded, and cover them with a thin layer of soil. Most seeds sprout quickly in a warm place, with soil temperature between 65° and 80° F, but after germination, the seedlings grow better in air temperatures of 55° to 70° F. Check daily, and as soon as sprouts appear, transfer the pots to the bright light of a greenhouse, a south window, or a fluorescent plant light. Seedlings will get weak and spindly if the light isn't bright enough but will be compact and sturdy if it is. I raise hundreds of seedlings each spring on a simple rack that I made, with shelves to hold the trays of seedlings and inexpensive fluorescent shop light fixtures suspended over each shelf by adjustable chains.

After the seeds have sprouted, let the soil dry out a little between waterings, to encourage good root growth and to prevent a fungal disease called "damping-off" that often attacks seedlings growing in soggy soil. Instead of watering from above, which sometimes flattens the little plants against the soil, pour warm water into a tray and let the pots of seedlings soak up moisture from below. I feed seedlings each week with a solution of one-half teaspoon of 20-20-20 fertilizer in a gallon of water. After seedlings develop a few true leaves, transplant them to individual pots. Peat pots, Styrofoam cups, or recycled plastic six-packs (sterilize them by rinsing with household bleach) all work fine. Handle the plants gently by the leaves and fill fresh potting soil around the roots. Keep an identification label with each batch of plants. As the seedlings grow and the weather warms up, gradually harden them off for transplanting by setting them outdoors each day, in a sheltered location at first, then finally in full sun and wind. Water frequently, as the soil dries out quickly when the plants are large enough to set out. After frost danger is past, transplant them to the garden — during a spell of cloudy weather, if possible, to minimize wilting and stress.

Some Plants to Propagate by Cuttings or Division. *Abaca, agaves, alkanet, bamboos, bowstring hemp, camphor basil, Indian hemp, lavender, madder, milkweed, nettles, patchouli, pennyroyal, piña, pyrethrum, ramie, reeds, rosemary, soapbark, soapwort, southernwood, spindle tree, sweet flag, tansy, vetiver, wormwood, yuccas.*

To propagate plants from cuttings, choose firm shoots on healthy plants. Cut off tips or pieces of stem three to five inches long with several leaves on them. Cuttings root most easily during the long warm days of late spring and summer. Remove two or three of the lower leaves and dip the base of the stem in rooting hormone powder. Stick one or more cuttings into a pot of very porous soil mix, such as perlite or coarse sand, plus a fraction of peat moss. Put the pot into a large, clear plastic bag to retain humidity. Set it in a warm bright location, indoors or out, away from direct sun. Check after a few weeks to see if roots have formed by pulling gently on the stem. If there is resistance, the cutting is getting roots and can be hardened off for transplanting. Loosen the top of the plastic bag to let air circulate around the leaves for a few days, and then take it off altogether. Transplant rooted cuttings to individual pots filled with regular potting soil. When the roots fill the containers, set the plants out into the garden.

You can divide clumps of perennial plants in early spring, just as new growth appears. Use a sharp trowel or shovel to cut off a section of the parent plant and pull to separate the roots. Sometimes it's easier to dig up the whole clump and cut it apart with a big knife, leaving a few buds or stems on each section. Replant divisions promptly into fresh soil. Some plants, such as yuccas, produce distinct offsets or "pups" which can easily be separated and replanted. Others, such as vetiver and ramie, grow into a congested thicket of upright stems; you just have to decide where to slice the clump. Madder, sweet flag, Indian hemp, and other plants with spreading root systems will regrow from short sections of rhizome alone.

To grow tender perennial or woody plants in cold climates, there are two alternatives: Either keep the plants in containers year-round, or grow plants in the garden during the summer and make a rooted cutting or division to carry over the winter. When set out as small plants in the spring, ramie, vetiver and patchouli can grow so vigorously that they become too big to bring back inside after a summer's growth. How you handle these plants will depend on the length of your growing season and the facilities you have for storing plants over the winter. If you have a greenhouse, protected cold frame, or plenty of bright windowsills, then plan ahead and start your own new plants in midsummer to winter over for the next year's outdoor planting. Or, you can always take the winter off and get new plants from nurseries each spring.

Maintenance

Several of the plants in this book are so easy to grow that all you have to do is get them established, wait awhile, then harvest from them. In fact, they require so little maintenance that they grow quite well as roadside weeds; instead of raising them in a garden, you might prefer to drive around and find existing patches. Plants from every chapter — milkweeds and Indian hemp, woad and pokeberries, soapwort and yuccas, pennyroyal and tansy, reeds — are common weeds in many states, and it's usually a simple matter of asking permission to collect them.

Other plants are more demanding. Once you've gone to the trouble of getting seeds of cotton or indigo, or plants of ramie or vetiver, you'll want to tend them carefully. Routine maintenance is based on observing the plants frequently, watching them grow, and meeting their needs. I think that the best gardeners enjoy a daily tour of their garden, looking for signs of growth and progress, and fussing over individual plants. Prevent problems by watering plants before they dry out, pulling weeds before they get large, detecting insects before they cause much damage. Use a mulch to control weed growth, retain soil moisture, and add organic material to the soil. Keep plants tidy by cleaning away diseased or discolored leaves, and gathering debris together in a compost pile. Thin, prune and harvest plants during the growing season. In the fall or early winter, clean away dead stalks and leaves.

Even large gardens can be kept in good shape with a few hours' work each week. Watering, cultivating, mulching, controlling pests and diseases, staking and tying, pruning and thinning, and other jobs are not difficult if you keep up with them but are overwhelming if you get behind. Plants not only look better, but they grow better and yield more if they are tended to. Besides, when word gets around that you're growing some interesting and unusual plants in your garden, friends and neighbors will drop by for a tour, and you'll want to be ready for them!

Records

Although most gardeners prefer digging over doing paperwork, it helps to get in the habit of keeping a garden notebook. You can include several kinds of records in your notebook, and it will preserve useful bits of information that you would otherwise forget. My system has three components: plant records, with an entry for each species or variety I am growing; calendars, for the current season and from previous seasons; and maps and labels, to show the placement of plants and to mark their identity.

Begin with a list of plants you'd like to grow. As you look through seed and nursery catalogs, mark sources for these plants. Then keep track of the orders you send off and when you receive shipments. Make a note of the condition in which the plants or seeds arrive. File the invoice or shipping list away in case you need to correspond with the supplier. Although most mail-order nurseries provide top-quality plants, occasionally you may be disappointed, and you'll need a copy of your original paperwork if you have to ask for an adjustment or a replacement. During the growing season, record how the plants grow, how large they get, when they mature, how much they yield, and other observations. This information, based on your experiences in your own garden, will help you learn more about the different plants you grow and will supplement the background information found in reference books.

Many gardeners keep a special calendar each year and mark down the last frost in spring and the first frost in fall, extreme temperatures, major storms, dry spells, and other weather events. I also write down each time I apply fertilizers or sprays, when I till the ground, planting dates, flowering seasons, and harvest time. My calendar has these entries: "daffodils blooming—planted flax today", "first cotton boll open!", "used fresh woad leaves to dye wool", "picked lavender flowers to dry", and "frost killed indigo plants". Comparing a few years' calendars will reveal the basic weather patterns for your area and will provide a basis for deciding when to plant different crops and when to expect them to mature.

Even if you are following a diagram of a garden design, make a map of some kind to show where different plants are located in your garden. This can be a simple sketch on scrap paper, or a carefully measured scale drawing on graph paper; either way, the important thing is to mark down where you sow seeds or set out plants. Compare map and garden from time to time to be sure you have everything in the right place. A map is especially useful in the spring, when all kinds of mysterious green sprouts are eagerly popping up. Unless you're an experienced gardener or botanist, all those little plants look about the same. Referring to your garden map may help you decide whether a certain plant is woad or weld, ramie or milkweed, wormwood or tansy. In addition to a map, labels are helpful for identifying individual plants. Write in pencil or waterproof marker on plastic or wood labels and drive them firmly into the soil or fasten them to the plants. It will help you to learn the names of the plants, and to keep track of which is which. Labels are also appreciated by visitors to your garden and by family members who are curious about your plants and projects.

SUGGESTED READINGS
Gardening

For more information on growing particular plants or on specific aspects of gardening, go to a library and look for the old reliable *Cyclopedia of Horticulture* (in three volumes), by Liberty Hyde Bailey (New York: Macmillan, 1935), or the impressive new *The New York Botanic Garden Illustrated Encyclopedia of Horticulture* (in ten volumes) by Thomas H. Everett (New York: Garland, 1980). Also in the library's reference collection should be *North American Horticulture*, edited for the American Horticultural Society by Barbara Ellis (New York: Charles Scribner's Sons, 1982). It contains listings of plant societies, gardens to visit, educational programs, and suppliers.

To locate gardens for visiting, consult *Gardens of North America and Hawaii: A Traveller's Guide* by Irene and Walter Jacob (Portland: Timber, 1986). Or, to have the gardening world brought to your doorstep, make use of *Gardening by Mail: An Annotated Sourcebook* by Barbara J. Barton (San Francisco: Tusker, 1986).

For home reference use, look into *The Reader's Digest Illustrated Guide to Gardening*, edited by Carroll Calkins (Pleasantville, New York: Reader's Digest Association, 1978), *Taylor's Encyclopedia of Gardening*, edited by Norman Taylor (4th ed.; Boston: Houghton Mifflin, 1976), *The Complete Book of Gardening*, edited by Michael Wright (New York: Warner, 1978) and *The Complete Guide to Basic Gardening* edited by Michael MacCaskey (Tucson: HP Books, 1985).

The Principles of Gardening by Hugh Johnson (New York: Simon and Schuster, 1979) includes ideas about garden design, advice on planning and maintaining gardens, and plenty of inspiring illustrations. *Making Things Grow Outdoors* by Thalassa Cruso (New York: Alfred Knopf, 1974) is pleasant reading and gives good gardening advice. *American Gardens in the 18th Century* by Ann Leighton (Boston: Houghton Mifflin, 1976) reviews early American garden plants and practices. *The Principles of Gardening* by Hugh Johnson (New York: Simon and Schuster, 1978) is a good allaround book about gardening and garden design.

For inspiration and guidance on planning a garden or landscaping around your home, look through *Garden Design: History, Principles, Elements, and Practice*, edited by William Lake Douglas and other members of the American Society of Landscape Architects (New York: Simon and Schuster, 1984). Both formal and casual garden designs are included in the lovely book *Herb Garden Design*, by Faith H. Swanson and Virginia B. Rady (Hanover, New Hampshire: University Press of New England, 1984). *How to Plan and Plant Your Own Property* by Alice Recknagel Ireys (New York: William Morrow, 1975) is a useful guide, and there are plenty of ideas in wellillustrated books such as *Award-Winning Small Space Gardens* (San Francisco: Ortho Books, 1979), and *Container Gardening* by the editors of *Sunset* magazine (Menlo Park, California: Lane, 1984).

Gardening magazines abound: the major national publications include *Horticulture*, *American Horticulturist*, *Garden*, *National Gardening*, and *Flower and Garden*. There are also many regional magazines, such as *Pacific Horticulture*, *Southern Living*, and *Sunset*. Each issue of *Plants and Gardens*, published by the Brooklyn Botanic Garden, addresses a different aspect of gardening, and a collection of back issues is a valuable reference source. *The Avant Gardener* and *HortIdeas* emphasize new ideas, current research, and new sources.

RESOURCES

PUBLIC GARDENS TO VISIT

These botanical gardens and living history museums include examples of fiber, dye, soap, scent, and tool plants in their collections. Visiting a garden gives you an opportunity to see a wide variety of plants, and also gives you ideas for arranging and designing your own garden.

CALIFORNIA. The Arboretum of Los Angeles County, 301 North Baldwin Ave., Arcadia 91007
COLORADO. Denver Botanic Garden, 1005 York St., Denver 80206
DISTRICT OF COLUMBIA. National Herb Garden, US National Arboretum, 3501 New York Ave. NE, Washington 20002
GEORGIA. Callaway Gardens, P.O. Box 2000, Pine Mountain 31822
ILLINOIS. Chicago Botanic Garden, 1000 Lake Cook Rd., Glencoe 60022
MASSACHUSETTS. Hancock Shaker Village, P.O. Box 927, Pittsfield 01202
Old Sturbridge Village, Sturbridge 01566
MINNESOTA. University of Minnesota Landscape Arboretum, 3675 Arboretum Dr., Chanhassen 55317
MISSOURI. Missouri Botanical Gardens, 4344 Shaw Blvd., St. Louis 63110
NEW YORK. Cornell Plantations, One Plantations Road, Ithaca 14850
Genesee Country Village & Museum, P.O. Box 310, Mumford 14511
OHIO. Cleveland Botanical Garden, 11030 East Boulevard, Cleveland 44106
VIRGINIA. Colonial Williamsburg, P.O. Box 1776, Williamsburg 23187

SUPPLIERS OF HERBAL PRODUCTS

Many companies sell dried lavender and other herbs used in moth repellents, along with essential oils, herbal soaps, and other products. For current information, check the advertisements in *Herb Companion*, published bimonthly by Herb Companion Press, 201 East 4th St., Loveland, CO 80537, or other magazines.

SUPPLIERS OF SEEDS AND PLANTS

The plants described in this book are generally not available at local nurseries and garden centers, so you'll have to order them by mail. Each of the companies listed here offers several kinds of useful plants. Most businesses update their catalogs every year or two, and they may delete or add to their offerings with each revision, so be sure to write for a current catalog, then enjoy making your selections. Most companies charge a modest fee for the catalog, refundable with your first order.

Companion Plants, 7247 N. Coolville Ridge Rd., Athens, OH 45701
The Flowery Branch, P.O. Box 1330, Flowery Branch, GA 30542
Goodwin Creek Gardens, P.O. Box 83, Williams, OR 97544
The Herbfarm, 32804 Issaquah-Fall City Rd., Fall City, WA 98024
Hastings Seeds, P.O. Box 115535, Atlanta, GA 30310
J. L. Hudson, Seedsman, Star Route 2, Box 337, La Honda, CA 94020
Nichols Garden Nursery, 1190 N. Pacific Highway, Albany, OR 97321
Papa Geno's Herb Garden, 1951 S. 25th, Lincoln, NE 68502
Rasland Farm, Route 1, Box 65, Godwin, NC 28344
Richter's, P.O. Box 26, Goodwood, Ontario L0C 1A0, Canada
Sandy Mush Herb Nursery, 316 Surrett Cove Rd., Leicester, NC 28748
Shady Acres, 7815 Highway 212, Chaska, MN 55318
The Thyme Garden, 20546 Alsea Hwy., Alsea, OR 97324
Well-Sweep Herb Farm, 317 Mt. Bethel Rd., Port Murray, NJ 07865

SUPPLIERS OF FIBER, YARN, AND DYEING SUPPLIES

Many companies sell cotton, flax, and other natural plant fibers in ready-to-spin form or as yarn, and wool yarns that are excellent for dyeing with natural dyes. Other suppliers offer alum and other chemicals used in dyeing, related supplies and tools, and dried dye plants or dye extracts. For current information, check the advertisements in *SpinOff*, published quarterly by Interweave Press, 201 East 4th St., Loveland, CO 80537, or other fiber-craft magazines.

GLOSSARY

Acid. A sour-tasting substance that increases the concentration of hydrogen ions when dissolved in water; has a pH lower than 7.

Alkali. Any of a group of basic substances, often present in soil and water; has a pH higher than 7.

Alum. A white powdery substance used as a mordant in dyeing; usually aluminum potassium sulfate ($AlK(SO_4)_2 \cdot 12H_2O$).

Annual. A plant that lives through only one growing season.

Base. A bitter-tasting substance that increases the concentration of hydroxyl ions when dissolved in water and makes a caustic, slippery solution; has a pH higher than 7.

Bast fibers. Fibers obtained from the stems of plants such as flax, hemp, and ramie; stem fibers.

Biennial. A plant that completes its life cycle in two growing seasons, usually flowering and bearing fruit the second year.

Bracts. Leaf-like plant parts, usually small, that are located beneath a single flower or a flower cluster.

Brake. A tool for breaking the woody core of plant stems in order to free and clean the stem fibers.

Brushing. Raising a fuzzy nap on a fabric.

Bucking. Cleaning linen with lye obtained from wood ashes.

Calyx. The outer parts of a flower, consisting of the leaf-like sepals (usually green).

Cards, carders. Brush-like tools with short stiff wires set close together on a wooden frame, used to prepare wool, cotton and other short fibers for spinning.

Cellulose. An inert carbohydrate $(C_6H_{12}O_5)_n$ which is the main constituent of plant fibers.

Cold frame. A low structure with a glass or plastic top, used to protect plants from the weather.

Compost. A mixture of decayed organic substances, such as plant clippings and manure, used to improve soil texture and fertility.

Cordage. A general term for twines and ropes.

Crown. The part of a plant where the root and stem meet.

Deciduous. Falling off at the end of a growing season; not evergreen.

Degum. To remove the yellowish coating of silk-glue from the surface of raw silk fibers.

Detergent. A chemical product that has cleansing power.

Dicot or dicotyledon. A member of the group of flowering plants that characteristically has two cotyledons or food storage organs in the seed; a net-like pattern of leaf veins; and xylem and phloem tissue arranged concentrically in the stem, forming the "rings" of woody plants (cf. *monocot*).

Disk flowers. The tiny flowers packed into the center of the flower head of plants in the daisy family (cf. *ray flowers*).

Distaff. A stick or frame for holding fibers prepared for spinning.

Dormancy. A period of rest and suspended growth of seeds, buds or plants; usually during cold or dry weather.

Dyebath. The water and dye mixture in which fibers are placed for dyeing.

Epidermis. The outer layer or "skin" of a plant.

Essential oils. Highly volatile oils that are concentrated by distilling fragrant plant parts.

Extract. A solution made by soaking or boiling plant parts in water.

Family. A major subdivision in the classification of plants or animals, usually consisting of several genera.

Fast. A dye that resists fading in air, light, or soapy water.

Fixative. An ingredient added to mixtures of dried herbs to assist in retaining the scent.

Fugitive. A dye that fades quickly in air, light, or water.

Fulling. Washing woven goods (usually woolen) to shrink and thicken the fabric.

Genus. A subdivision in the classification of organisms; the first word of a two-part Latin name.

Germination. The sprouting of seeds.

Ginning. Separating cotton fibers from the embedded seeds.

Hackling. Combing bundles of stem fibers to clean and straighten them.

Hank. A bundle of combed fibers or a skein of yarn.

Hard fibers. Fibers obtained from the leaves of plants such as sisal or abacá; leaf fibers.

Herbaceous. Having a stem that remains soft, not woody.

Hue. Any color such as red, orange, yellow, etc.

Hybrid. A cross between two species or varieties.

Intensity. The degree of saturation of a color, ranging from pale to dark.

Ions. Electrically charged atoms.

Isomers. Chemical compounds that are composed of the same kinds and numbers of atoms, but differ in structure or arrangement.

Keratin. The kind of protein that is found in wool, fur and hair.

Lignins. A group of complex compounds that give strength and rigidity to plant stems and wood.

Linen. Fabrics for clothing and household use. Now linen usually refers to fabric woven from flax, but formerly fabric woven from hemp, cotton, ramie, nettles or other plant fibers was sometimes called linen.

Loom. A tool for holding a warp in tension so that fabric can be woven.

Lye. A caustic liquid obtained by leaching wood ashes; potassium hydroxide (KOH); or sodium hydroxide (NaOH). All are alkaline substances.

Mercerization. A process of treating cotton or other plant fiber products in a concentrated alkaline solution to make the fibers smoother, stronger, shinier, and more receptive to dyes.

Micelles. Clusters of molecules that form when soaps or other surfactants combine with oily substances in the washing process.

Monocot or monocotyledon. A member of the group of flowering plants that characteristically has one cotyledon or food storage organ in the seed; leaf veins in parallel arrangement; and bundles of phloem and xylem tissue scattered throughout the stem, not arranged in concentric rings (cf. *dicot*).

Mordant. A chemical compound, usually a mineral salt, that is applied to fibers to increase the intensity and fastness of dyes.

Mulch. A layer of straw, bark, paper, plastic, or other material spread over the soil to retain moisture, eliminate weeds, and stabilize soil temperatures.

Natron. Naturally occurring sodium carbonate ($Na_2CO_3 \cdot 10H_2O$), used as a cleansing product.

Oxidize. To react chemically by taking on oxygen or giving off hydrogen.

Pectins. Complex carbohydrates that fill the spaces between plant cell walls; in water, they make thick gels.

Perennial. A plant that lives two or more years.

pH. A measurement of the acidity or alkalinity of a solution, expressed on a scale from 1 (most acidic) through 7 (neutral) to 14 (most alkaline).

Phloem. The food-conducting tissue of vascular plants.

Photoperiod. The number of hours of daylight; important in regulating plant growth.

Pigment. A substance or compound that produces a characteristic color.

Pistil. The female organ of a flower, which receives the pollen and bears seeds.

Ply. A single strand of yarn; plies can be combined or twisted together to make two-ply, three-ply, etc., yarns.

Ray flowers. The "petal-like" flowers around the edge of the flower head of plants in the daisy family (cf. *disk flowers*).

Reducing agent. A substance that causes a chemical reaction in which hydrogen is added or oxygen is removed.

Reed. The part of a loom that separates and spaces the threads of the warp.

Retting. Soaking plant stems to separate the fibers from the other tissues.

Rhizome. A root-like horizontal stem that grows along or under the ground.

Rippling. The process of removing the seed capsules from bundles of flax stems.

Rosette. A flat and crowded cluster of leaves that radiates from a single stem.

Sachet. A small bag filled with fragrant dried herbs.

Saponins. Substances produced by plants that make sudsy solutions when mixed with water.

Scouring. Thoroughly cleaning raw wool to remove the dirt and grease.

Scutching. Scraping bundles of plant fibers with a dull blade to clean away debris and add luster.

Shuttle. A tool used in weaving to carry the weft thread back and forth between the warp threads.

Sizing or size. A preparation of glue, starch, or other substances used to add strength and smoothness to the warp threads for easier weaving.

Skein. A length of yarn wound into a loop.

Soap. A washing product made by mixing a fat and an alkali.

Solution. A homogeneous mixture of one substance and another; for example, a solution of salt dissolved in water.

Species. The basic category of biological classification, consisting of a group of individual organisms that resemble each other and are able to breed among themselves but not able to breed with members of another species. The second word in a two-part Latin name.

Spin. To make yarn or thread by drawing out a group of fibers and twisting them together.

Spindle. A slender stick used in spinning to help add twist and to hold the spun yarn.

Stamens. The pollen-bearing or male organs of a flower.

Substantive dye. A dye that reacts directly with the fibers and does not require a mordant.

Surfactants. Compounds which reduce the surface tension of water.

Tannins. Astringent compounds derived from plant parts, especially tree barks; used in tanning leather and as mordants.

Tex count. The weight in grams of one thousand meters of yarn.

Top dyeing. The process of dyeing yarn or fabric sequentially in two or more different dyebaths in order to combine colors.

Twist direction. The direction of the diagonal lines that appear on a twisted yarn, depending on how it was spun; corresponding to the crossbar in either "S" or "Z".

Variety. A subdivision of a biological species, distinguished by some difference such as color, size or form.

Vat dye. A dye that is deposited on the surface of the fibers.

Volatile. Quick to evaporate.

Warp. The set of parallel yarns stretched on the loom before weaving begins.

Washing soda. Sodium carbonate ($Na_2CO_3 \cdot 10H_2O$), used in washing and dyeing.

Weft. The set of threads which is inserted during the weaving process and goes across the fabric at right angles to the warp.

Whorl. A circular weight placed on a spindle to act as a flywheel.

Xylem. The water-conducting system of vascular plants.

PRONUNCIATION GUIDE

The accent falls on the syllable that appears in capital letters. Where "i" stands alone, it is short as in "hit". Where "o" stands alone, it is long as in "home".

Abutilon theophrasti — ah-BEWT-i-lon thee-o-FRAST-eye

Acacia catechu — ah-KAY-cee-ah CAT-eh-chew

Acorus calamus — ACK-o-rus KAL-ah-mus

Agave cantala — ah-GAH-vee can-TAH-lah

A. fourcroydes — a. for-CROY-dees

A. lecheguilla — a. lay-cheh-GEE-ah

A. sisalana — a. see-sah-LAY-nah

Alkanna tinctoria — al-KAN-ah tink-TOE-ree-ah

Ananas comosus — ah-NA-nas koe-MOE-sus

Anchusa tinctoria — an-KOO-sah tink-TOE-ree-ah

Anthemis tinctoria — AN-them-is tink-TOE-ree-ah

Anthoxanthum odoratum — an-thocks-AN-thum o-dor-AY-tum

Apocynum androsaemifolium — ah-POSS-i-num an-dro-se-me-FOE-lee-um

A. cannabinum — a. can-NAB-i-num

Artemisia abrotanum — ar-te-MEEZ-ee-ah ah-BRO-tay-num

A. absinthium — a. ab-SIN-thee-um

Arundinaria gigantea — ah-run-di-NAY-ree-ah jy-GAN-tee-ah

Arundo donax — ah-RUN-doe DOE-nax

Asclepias syriaca — as-KLEEP-ee-as sy-ry-AY-kah

Baptisia — bap-TIZ-ee-ah

Bixa orellana — BICK-sah or-el-AY-nah

Boehmeria nivea — bo-MEER-ee-ah NIV-ee-ah

Caesalpinia echinata — see-zal-PIN-ee-ah eck-in-AY-tah

C. sappan — c. SAP-pan

Calliopsis tinctorius — kal-ee-OP-sis tink-TOE-ree-ah-us

Cannabis sativa — KAN-na-bis sa-TY-vah

Carludovica palmata — kar-loo-DOE-vee-kah pal-MAY-tah

Carthamus tinctorius — KAR-tha-mus tink-TOE-ree-us

Ceiba pentandra — say-EE-bah pen-TAN-drah

Chlorogalum pomeridianum — klow-ROGUE-ah-lum po-mer-id-ee-AY-num

Chlorophora tinctoria — klow-ROFF-oh-rah tink-TOE-ree-ah

Chorisia speciosa — ko-RIS-ee-ah spec-see-OSE-ah

Chrysanthemum cinerariifolium — kris-AN-the-mum sy-nee-rare-ee-i-FOL-ee-um

C. coccineum — c. kok-SIN-ee-um

Cocos nucifera — KO-kos new-SI-fe-rah

Corchorus capsularis — KOR-ko-rus cap-sue-LARE-is

C. olitorius — c. oh-li-TORE-ee-us

Coreopsis — kor-ee-OP-sis

Cosmos sulphureus — KOZ-mose sul-FUR-ee-us

Cotinus coggygria — ko-TY-nus ko-JIG-ree-ah

C. obovatus — c. ob-o-VAY-tus

Crataegus monogyna — kra-TEE-gus mo-NOJ-i-nah

Crocus sativus — KRO-kus sa-TY-vus

Crotalaria juncea — kro-ta-LAY-ree-ah jun-SEE-ah

Dipsacus fullonum — DIP-sa-kus ful-LONE-um

D. sativus – d. sa-TY-vus
Eucalyptus cinerea – yew-ka-LIP-tus
  sy-NEER-ee-ah
E. citriodora – e. sit-ree-o-DOOR-ah
E. globulus – e. GLO-bu-lus
Euonymus europaea – yew-ON-imus
  yew-ro-PEE-ah
Galium – GAY-lee-um
Genista tinctoria – je-NISS-tah
  tink-TOE-ree-ah
Geranium maculatum – jer-AY-nee-um
  mack-yew-LAY-tum
Gossypium arboreum – gos-SIP-ee-um
  ar-BOR-ee-um
G. barbadense – g. bar-ba-DENSE-ee
G. herbaceum – g. her-bay-SEE-um
G. hirsutum – g. her-SUE-tum
Haematoxylum campechianum –
  hy-ma-TOCKS-i-lum
  kam-pee-chee-AY-num
Hedeoma pulegioides – hed-ee-OM-ah
  pu-leej-ee-OY-deez
Helianthus annuus – he-lee-AN-thus AN-nu-us
Heuchera americana – HEW-ker-ah
  ah-mer-i-KAY-nah
Hibiscus cannabinus – hy-BISS-kus
  kan-NAB-i-nus
H. sabdariffa – h. sab-da-REEF-fah
Hierachloe odorata – hy-er-ROCK-lo-ee
  oh-doe-RAY-tah
Indigofera suffruticosa – in-di-GO-fer-ah
  suf-frut-i-KOS-ah
I. tinctoria – i. tink-TOE-ree-ah
Isatis tinctoria – eye-SAY-tis tink-TOE-ree-ah
Juglans cinerea – JUG-lans sy-NEER-ee-ah
J. nigra – j. NY-grah
J. regia – j. REE-ji-ah
Juniperus scopulorum – jew-NIP-er-us
  skop-yew-LAR-um
J. virginiana – j. ver-jin-ee-AY-nah
Lavandula angustifolia – la-VAN-dew-lah
  an-gust-i-FOL-ee-ah
L. latifolia – l. lat-i-FO-lee-ah
L. stoechas – l. STEE-kas
Lawsonia inermis – law-SO-nee-ah in-ER-mis
Lindera benzoin – lin-DER-ah BEN-zoin
Linum usitatissimum – LY-num
  yew-si-ta-TISS-i-mum
Lonchocarpus cyanescens – lon-ko-KAR-pus
  sy-AN-es-cens
Maclura pomifera – ma-CLOOR-ah
  po-MI-fer-ah
Marsdenia tinctoria – mars-DEN-ee-ah
  tink-TOE-ree-ah
Melilotus officinalis – mel-i-LO-tus
  of-fi-si-NAY-lis
Mentha pulegium – MEN-tha pu-LE-jee-um
Morus tinctoria – MORE-us tink-TOE-ree-ah

Musa textilis – MEW-sah TECKS-till-is
Nicotiana rustica – ni-ko-she-AY-nah
  RUS-tik-ah
Ocimum kilimandscharicum – OSE-si-mum
  ki-li-mand-SHAR-i-kum
Pandanus odoratissimus – pan-DAY-nus
  oh-door-ah-TISS-i-mus
Peganum harmala – PEG-ah-num
  HARM-ah-lah
Phaseolus vulgaris – fay-see-OLE-us
  vul-GAR-is
Phormium tenax – FOR-mi-um TEN-ax
Phragmites australis – frag-MY-teez
  os-TRAY-lis
Phyllostachys aurea – fill-o-STACK-iss
  AW-ree-ah
P. bambusoides – p. bam-boo-SOY-deez
Phytolacca americana – fy-toe-LAK-kah
  ah-me-ri-KAY-nah
Pogostemon cablin – po-go-STEM-on KAB-lin
P. heyneanus – p. hey-nee-AY-nus
Polygonum tinctorium – po-LIG-o-num
  tink-TOE-ree-um
Pueraria lobata – poo-er-AY-ree-ah lo-BA-tah
Quercus velutina – QUER-kus vel-LOO-ti-nah
Quillaja saponaria – quill-AY-yah
  sa-po-NARE-ee-ah
Raphia – RAFE-ee-ah
Reseda luteola – re-ZEE-dah loo-tee-OH-lah
Rhus aromatica – ROOS ar-row-MAT-i-kah
R. copallina – r. ko-pa-LY-nah
R. typhina var. *laciniata* – r. ty-FY-nah *var.*
  la-cin-ee-AY-tah
Rosmarinus officinalis – rows-mare-EYE-nus
  of-fi-si-NAY-lis
Rubia tinctorum – ROO-bee-ya tink-TOE-rum
Salicornia – sa-li-CORN-ee-ah
Salsola kali – sal-SOE-lah KAL-lee
Sansevieria – san-se-VEER-ee-ah
Sapindus drummondii – sa-PIN-dus
  DRUM-mun-dye
S. saponaria – sa-PIN-dus sa-po-NARE-ee-ah
Saponaria ocymoides – sa-po-NARE-ee-ah
  oh-sim-MOY-deez
S. officinalis – s. of-fi-si-NAY-lis
Sesbania exaltata – sez-BANE-ee-ah
  ecks-all-TAY-tah
Spartium junceum – SPAR-tee-um jun-SEE-um
Tanacetum vulgare – tan-ah-SEE-tum
  vul-GAR-ee
Tillandsia usneoides – till-AND-zee-ah
  uz-nee-OY-deez
Toxicodendron – tock-si-ko-DEN-dron
Trilisa odoratissima – tri-LISS-ah
  oh-door-ah-TISS-i-mah
Umbellularia californica –
  um-bell-yew-LARE-i-ah
  cal-i-FORN – i-kah

Urena lobata — yew-REE-nah   lo-BAY-tah
Urtica dioica — UR-ti-kah   dy-OH-i-kah
Vetiveria zizanioides — vet-i-VEER-ee-ah
   zi-zay-nee-OY-deez
Washingtonia — wash-ing-TOE-nee-ah
Wrightia tinctoria — RITE-ee-ah
   tink-TOE-ree-ah
Yucca aloifolia — YUK-kah   al-oh-i-FOE-lee-ah
Y. baccata — y. ba-KAY-tah
Y. elata — y. ee-LAY-tah
Y. filamentosa — y. fill-a-men-TOE-sah
Y. flaccida — y. FLAK-si-dah
Y. glauca — y. GLAW-kah
Zea mays — ZEE-ah   MAZE

INDEX

Italicized numbers refer to illustrations.

A CATALOG OF SELECTED

DOVER BOOKS

IN ALL FIELDS OF INTEREST

A CATALOG OF SELECTED DOVER
BOOKS IN ALL FIELDS OF INTEREST

CONCERNING THE SPIRITUAL IN ART, Wassily Kandinsky. Pioneering work by father of abstract art. Thoughts on color theory, nature of art. Analysis of earlier masters. 12 illustrations. 80pp. of text. 5⅜ x 8½. 23411-8 Pa. $4.95

ANIMALS: 1,419 Copyright-Free Illustrations of Mammals, Birds, Fish, Insects, etc., Jim Harter (ed.). Clear wood engravings present, in extremely lifelike poses, over 1,000 species of animals. One of the most extensive pictorial sourcebooks of its kind. Captions. Index. 284pp. 9 x 12. 23766-4 Pa. $14.95

CELTIC ART: The Methods of Construction, George Bain. Simple geometric techniques for making Celtic interlacements, spirals, Kells-type initials, animals, humans, etc. Over 500 illustrations. 160pp. 9 x 12. (USO) 22923-8 Pa. $9.95

AN ATLAS OF ANATOMY FOR ARTISTS, Fritz Schider. Most thorough reference work on art anatomy in the world. Hundreds of illustrations, including selections from works by Vesalius, Leonardo, Goya, Ingres, Michelangelo, others. 593 illustrations. 192pp. 7⅛ x 10¼. 20241-0 Pa. $9.95

CELTIC HAND STROKE-BY-STROKE (Irish Half-Uncial from "The Book of Kells"): An Arthur Baker Calligraphy Manual, Arthur Baker. Complete guide to creating each letter of the alphabet in distinctive Celtic manner. Covers hand position, strokes, pens, inks, paper, more. Illustrated. 48pp. 8¼ x 11. 24336-2 Pa. $3.95

EASY ORIGAMI, John Montroll. Charming collection of 32 projects (hat, cup, pelican, piano, swan, many more) specially designed for the novice origami hobbyist. Clearly illustrated easy-to-follow instructions insure that even beginning papercrafters will achieve successful results. 48pp. 8¼ x 11. 27298-2 Pa. $3.50

THE COMPLETE BOOK OF BIRDHOUSE CONSTRUCTION FOR WOODWORKERS, Scott D. Campbell. Detailed instructions, illustrations, tables. Also data on bird habitat and instinct patterns. Bibliography. 3 tables. 63 illustrations in 15 figures. 48pp. 5¼ x 8½. 24407-5 Pa. $2.50

BLOOMINGDALE'S ILLUSTRATED 1886 CATALOG: Fashions, Dry Goods and Housewares, Bloomingdale Brothers. Famed merchants' extremely rare catalog depicting about 1,700 products: clothing, housewares, firearms, dry goods, jewelry, more. Invaluable for dating, identifying vintage items. Also, copyright-free graphics for artists, designers. Co-published with Henry Ford Museum & Greenfield Village. 160pp. 8¼ x 11. 25780-0 Pa. $10.95

HISTORIC COSTUME IN PICTURES, Braun & Schneider. Over 1,450 costumed figures in clearly detailed engravings–from dawn of civilization to end of 19th century. Captions. Many folk costumes. 256pp. 8⅜ x 11¾. 23150-X Pa. $12.95

THE INFLUENCE OF SEA POWER UPON HISTORY, 1660–1783, A. T. Mahan. Influential classic of naval history and tactics still used as text in war colleges. First paperback edition. 4 maps. 24 battle plans. 640pp. 5⅜ x 8½.   25509-3 Pa. $14.95

THE STORY OF THE TITANIC AS TOLD BY ITS SURVIVORS, Jack Winocour (ed.). What it was really like. Panic, despair, shocking inefficiency, and a little heroism. More thrilling than any fictional account. 26 illustrations. 320pp. 5⅜ x 8½.
20610-6 Pa. $8.95

FAIRY AND FOLK TALES OF THE IRISH PEASANTRY, William Butler Yeats (ed.). Treasury of 64 tales from the twilight world of Celtic myth and legend: "The Soul Cages," "The Kildare Pooka," "King O'Toole and his Goose," many more. Introduction and Notes by W. B. Yeats. 352pp. 5⅜ x 8½.   26941-8 Pa. $8.95

BUDDHIST MAHAYANA TEXTS, E. B. Cowell and Others (eds.). Superb, accurate translations of basic documents in Mahayana Buddhism, highly important in history of religions. The Buddha-karita of Asvaghosha, Larger Sukhavativyuha, more. 448pp. 5⅜ x 8½.   25552-2 Pa. $12.95

ONE TWO THREE . . . INFINITY: Facts and Speculations of Science, George Gamow. Great physicist's fascinating, readable overview of contemporary science: number theory, relativity, fourth dimension, entropy, genes, atomic structure, much more. 128 illustrations. Index. 352pp. 5⅜ x 8½.   25664-2 Pa. $8.95

ENGINEERING IN HISTORY, Richard Shelton Kirby, et al. Broad, nontechnical survey of history's major technological advances: birth of Greek science, industrial revolution, electricity and applied science, 20th-century automation, much more. 181 illustrations. ". . . excellent . . ."–*Isis.* Bibliography. vii + 530pp. 5⅜ x 8¼.
26412-2 Pa. $14.95

DALÍ ON MODERN ART: The Cuckolds of Antiquated Modern Art, Salvador Dalí. Influential painter skewers modern art and its practitioners. Outrageous evaluations of Picasso, Cézanne, Turner, more. 15 renderings of paintings discussed. 44 calligraphic decorations by Dalí. 96pp. 5⅜ x 8½. (USO)   29220-7 Pa. $4.95

ANTIQUE PLAYING CARDS: A Pictorial History, Henry René D'Allemagne. Over 900 elaborate, decorative images from rare playing cards (14th–20th centuries): Bacchus, death, dancing dogs, hunting scenes, royal coats of arms, players cheating, much more. 96pp. 9¼ x 12¼.   29265-7 Pa. $12.95

MAKING FURNITURE MASTERPIECES: 30 Projects with Measured Drawings, Franklin H. Gottshall. Step-by-step instructions, illustrations for constructing handsome, useful pieces, among them a Sheraton desk, Chippendale chair, Spanish desk, Queen Anne table and a William and Mary dressing mirror. 224pp. 8⅛ x 11¼.
29338-6 Pa. $13.95

THE FOSSIL BOOK: A Record of Prehistoric Life, Patricia V. Rich et al. Profusely illustrated definitive guide covers everything from single-celled organisms and dinosaurs to birds and mammals and the interplay between climate and man. Over 1,500 illustrations. 760pp. 7½ x 10⅛.   29371-8 Pa. $29.95

Prices subject to change without notice.

Available at your book dealer or write for free catalog to Dept. GI, Dover Publications, Inc., 31 East 2nd St., Mineola, N.Y. 11501. Dover publishes more than 500 books each year on science, elementary and advanced mathematics, biology, music, art, literary history, social sciences and other areas.